GOVERNMENT THAT WORKS

GOVERNMENT THAT WORKS

*Innovation in State
and Local Government*

by EDWARD T. WHEELER

McFarland & Company, Inc., Publishers
Jefferson, North Carolina, and London

British Library Cataloguing-in-Publication data are available

Library of Congress Cataloguing-in-Publication Data

Wheeler, Edward T., 1962–
    Government that works : innovation in state and local government /
by Edward T. Wheeler.
      p. cm.
    Includes bibliographical references and index.
    ISBN 0-89950-831-6 (lib. bdg. : 50# alk. paper) ∞
    1. Local government—United States.   2. State governments—United
States.   3. United States—Social policy.   4. United States—
Economic policy. I. Title.
JS341.W48   1993
350.007′2′0973—dc20   92-50948
                                              CIP

Manufactured in the United States of America

McFarland & Company, Inc., Publishers
  Box 611, Jefferson, North Carolina 28640

For Leslie B. Wheeler
and Samuel C. Wheeler

Table of Contents

Acknowledgments

Special thanks are in order for the staff of the Innovations in State and Local Government program of the A. Alfred Taubman Center for State and Local Government at Harvard University. In particular, I would like to acknowledge the assistance given to me by the program's director, Marc Zegans. His careful editing of the first draft of this book and his subsequent comments were extremely helpful and greatly appreciated.

In addition, I would like to thank the many program officials who took time to discuss their programs with me so that I could share their insights with others:

Dr. Mike Walters, superintendent, Tupelo Municipal Separate School District; Charles Owens, director of community affairs, New York City Housing Authority; Becci Bookner, director of the Extended School Program; Otis Baker, assistant commissioner, Division for Instruction, Missouri; Rayni Lambert, project assistant, the Community Mentors Partnership; Jacqueline Dault, coordinator, Health Care Access Project, Marquette County, Michigan; Sandy Lowe, director, Department of Community Action, Fairfax County, Virginia; Deborah Cordrey, program manager for maternity, Montgomery County, Maryland; Katherine Flaherty, director, Healthy Start Program; Karin Arnold, child protective services supervisor, Administration for Children, Youth, and Families; Tom Hearsey, coordinator of pollution prevention programs, and William Welisevich, environmental compliance specialist, Environmental Compliance Services; Thomas Donegan, engineering projects manager, Landfill Reclamation Project; Chris Luboff, senior planner, City of Seattle Recycling Program; Gene Rattan, environmental quality supervisor, Fort Worth, Texas; Richard Dent, executive director, Loxahatchee River District; Myles Pomeroy, senior planner, San Diego Planning Department; Kathy Beyerkehue, vice president for operations, Housing Vermont; Robert Jenkins, analyst, Massachusetts Housing Partnership Development; Berneta Walraven, fair housing specialist, Massachusetts Commission Against Discrimination; Don DeMarco, director, Community Services Department, Shaker Heights, Ohio; H. Michael Wehr, administrator, Export Service

Center; Joe Szocik, director, Attleboro Area Center for Training; and Jim Keogh, program manager, Washington State Employee Ownership Program.

I would also like to thank Prof. Donald Hambrick, Samuel Bronfman Professor of Democratic Business Enterprise at Columbia University Business School, for sharing his ideas about organizational congruence as presented in Chapter 7.

Although I have made every effort to confirm that the information presented in this book is correct, any errors that remain are my own and not those of the individuals listed above.

Chapter 1

The Case for Innovation

*The dogmas of the quiet past are inadequate to
the stormy present. As our case is new,
so we must think anew and act anew.
We must disenthrall ourselves, and then
we shall save our country.*
— Abraham Lincoln.

Although Abraham Lincoln spoke these words over a century ago, they
are as appropriate today as they were at the end of the Civil War. Times have
changed, and government must seek new, innovative approaches to the problems currently facing our nation. These problems include poverty, homelessness, pollution, and poor educational performance, among others.

In the wake of the federal budget crisis in Washington and the subsequent elimination or downsizing of many federal programs, much of the
burden for addressing contemporary issues will rest with state and local governments. They will be required to assume more responsibility for the
development and implementation of social programs.

Against this backdrop of increased responsibility and diminished financial resources, innovative programs at the state and local level are gaining increased public attention. They are gaining attention both because they are
successful and because they approach familiar problems in original ways.
These initiatives are making great strides toward meaningfully reforming
education, improving our health care system, preserving and revitalizing our
environment, providing low-cost housing, and fostering economic development in chronically depressed areas. Some of these programs are succeeding
without the benefit of tax dollars.

Many of these innovative efforts rely on close working relationships between the public and private sectors. Others cultivate nontraditional sources
of financing to pay for their services. Regardless of their sources of innovation,
the fact is that many state and local government programs are currently
meeting the needs of today's society, public perception aside.

1

Purpose of This Book

This book has three purposes: to profile exceptional, innovative programs sponsored by state and local governments which are successfully addressing today's major social issues; to identify the attributes which contribute to their individual success; and to extract from these programs lessons which can be applied more generally to the broad range of programs sponsored by state and local governments.

Although this book could have profiled programs which address any number of social issues, I have chosen to focus my efforts on programs that deal with educational reform, health care and drug abuse, environmental management, housing, and economic development. These policy areas were selected because they are primarily the responsibility of state and local governments and because there are many innovative programs in place which address these issues. Thus, there was a wide range of programs from which I could select a few to profile.

Each of the following five chapters begins with a brief overview of one of the five issues discussed in this book: education, health care and drug abuse, environmental management, housing, and economic development. Problems and key issues are identified, and programs profiled in each chapter are placed into their proper context.

For example, Chapter 2 begins with an outline of the major problems facing our educational system and briefly explains how the innovative programs profiled in the chapter address them.

Following the chapter overview are profiles of several specific programs that are directed toward the problems. I have briefly explained what each program does, how each works, and how each benefits its clients. In many cases, I have included information about a program's history or obstacles that were faced by officials during a program's early stages. To the extent possible, key ideas are presented in the voice of program staff and clients. Each profile identifies those attributes that contribute most to the program's success. General lessons are then extracted from these innovative ventures which can be applied more broadly to program management at the state and local government level.

The concluding chapter, Chapter 7, pulls together all of the key lessons from the entire book in summary form.

Who Should Read This Book?

This book was written for two distinct audiences: lay readers who want to know more about whether good government is possible and how it works and practitioners in specific policy areas who might want to adopt one or more of these programs or at least some of the basic principles which underlie them.

The first audience includes the vast majority of people who are "fed up" with government and are looking for fresh approaches to society's complex problems. The text will satisfy their needs by identifying programs that are as successful as they are unique. For this audience, the text will support the hypothesis that "good" (read effective) government exists, and that the public sector can be innovative, well-managed, and effective, even when it comes to solving particularly vexing problems.

The second audience includes officials in state and local governments who want to know what kinds of innovations are taking hold in their particular policy area and, in basic terms, how they work. This audience will benefit from the experiences and lessons of the program officials presented in the text. Readers will be brought up to date on the most innovative approaches to problems in their own policy fields.

How Programs Were Selected and Information Was Gathered

In keeping with the above-stated purposes of this book, I have profiled only a handful of innovative programs from the universe of all such programs. Although I have tried to select programs which are unique, effective, and illustrative of important points about the management of public programs, those profiled are not necessarily the most unique or the most effective. Some of the programs outlined in this book have been singled out for prestigious awards. Others, however, are too new to have been fully tested. Yet all of the programs profiled herein approach the problems they are supposed to solve in innovative ways which make them worthy of discussion.

The programs discussed in the following chapters were selected from among the several thousand programs which have applied for the Ford Foundation's Innovation Awards Program between 1986 and 1992. While they do not necessarily represent the best of the proposals submitted, I have tried to select a fair sampling of the kinds of programs that exist to address each of the five problem areas discussed in each of the following five chapters. For example, the next chapter identifies high dropout rates and distractions (such as drug abuse and teen pregnancy) which interfere with educational achievement as being major educational problems. Accordingly, I have profiled programs which address dropout rates and distractions to achievement.

Once I selected those programs which I wanted to profile, I reviewed the detailed applications submitted to the Innovations Award Program by the officials of the programs and then conducted follow-up interviews. Officials were asked a variety of questions about how their program was started, where the idea came from, and what were/are the major obstacles to their program's success. In each case, officials were asked to identify the main attributes which contribute to the success of their program.

Readers should be aware that what follows is not a scientific study. Consistent with the more modest purposes of this book, it is an account of the observations of those responsible for developing and managing unique programs (along with my own input). Financial and other data was provided by officials of the programs, themselves. No effort was made by me to verify the data other than to receive a verbal confirmation that the data is correct. Readers desiring a more rigorously academic approach to the subject of innovation in the public sector will be pleased to note that there are numerous articles and books available which would serve as useful complements to this book.

Major Themes

There are several major themes which will be elaborated on in much greater detail throughout the remainder of this book. The following serves as a useful, if general, outline of these themes:

- Despite public opinion which holds a contrary view, government is capable of tremendous innovation and effective management. State and local government programs are in place which are effectively addressing some of the most thorny issues of our time. While the programs profiled in this book are unique, the major principles upon which they were developed could be adapted throughout the public sector.

- The success of the programs profiled in this book is no accident. All of the programs were carefully planned, and in most cases, success was achieved by addressing persistent problems (such as poor academic achievement, homelessness, etc.) with innovative approaches.

- There are prerequisites for success. Program officials must make certain that these prerequisites are met prior to unveiling a new program.

- The content and management of a program are central to its success. There are a variety of ways of viewing these two variables, and the content and management of a program must be consistent with the goals and its available resources.

- The structure of a program is important. The organizational structure and human resources must be consistent with a program's objectives and strategy.

- The design of a program, the creation of alliances between organizations, the degree of autonomy enjoyed by a program's organization when it is sponsored by a larger organization, and how volunteers are used can all impact its effectiveness.

- Although program managers often spend a disproportionate amount of time worrying about getting a new program under way, an equally important issue is that of managing rapid growth.

• Many successful programs attract and meet the needs of clients by taking special care to be oriented toward "customer-service." They actively recruit clients who could benefit from the programs, conduct extensive outreach efforts, and encourage voluntary participation.

• Economic incentives are a powerful means of encouraging participation in a program and facilitating desired behavior.

• In the current environment of budget cutbacks, many successful programs emphasize unique sources of funding and cost-effectiveness.

With these broad themes as a guideline, we will now turn to the first substantive chapter which profiles state and local government programs that strive to improve the academic achievement of children.

Chapter 2

Education

A child educated only at school is an uneducated child.
— George Santayana.

Public education in America is in a pervasive state of decline. Many teachers, parents, public officials, and business professionals are convinced that schools are not adapting to meet the needs of today's changing society. A recent report by the Carnegie Foundation for the Advancement of Teaching indicated that nearly one-third of the nation's 21,000 high schools are "deficient" at meeting the needs of modern society. Clearly, the educational system that has been in place in the United States for the past 200 years has been rendered grossly inadequate by changes both at home and abroad.

Obtaining a high school diploma or its equivalent has become virtually mandatory for those wishing to secure meaningful employment in this increasingly technological age. Nonetheless, the dropout rate is at its all time high and students who do manage to graduate often do not have the skills they need to succeed. A September 1990 Education Department report noted that "only about half of our high school seniors may be graduating with the ability to use their minds to think through subject-related information in any depth."[1]

International comparisons of student achievement, against a backdrop of heightened global competition, set the stage for the raging debate currently taking place in educational circles. American students repeatedly rate at or near the bottom of most internationl comparisons of educational performance in science and mathematics.[2] The story is much the same for other disciplines. A National Assessment of Educational Progress (NAEP) study concluded that less than 40 percent of Americans aged 21 through 25 are able to read well enough to comprehend a newspaper article. The situation is far worse among minorities.[3] Other studies suggest that few high school students possess the writing skills necessary for either educational or vocational achievement.[4]

These statistics are cause for great concern, particularly because our democratic form of government requires an informed and well-educated populace. Many students are unaware of the important people and events that have shaped America's past and created our present. Over 40 percent of all 17-year-olds in a recent study could not place the time of World War I between 1900 and 1950. More than two-thirds did not know when the Civil War took place or who was the commander of the colonial forces during the Revolution.[5]

One of the most troubling educational indicators is the alarmingly high dropout rate. While dropout rates are high for the population as a whole, statistics suggest that American schools are especially ineffective in meeting the needs of the most disadvantaged students. While nearly one-quarter of all high school students fail to complete the requirements for a diploma, the high school dropout rate for blacks 18 to 19 years of age is 35 percent, and for Hispanic youths of the same age the dropout rate is a staggering 45 percent.[6] Although some of these dropouts will eventually obtain equivalency diplomas, many will be relegated to lives of poverty and dependence on public aid.

In order for the American educational system to get back on track it must address several challenges. First, schools will have to directly address the distractions that prevent students from achieving their full potential. These distractions, which can ultimately lead students to drop out, include drugs, teen pregnancy and low self-esteem. Second, schools will have to accommodate the needs of modern families. It is estimated that of 100 randomly selected children born in 1986, only 41 will live in "traditional" family units by the time they reach their 18th birthday.[7] The rest will live in families with only one adult present or in other non-traditional living arrangements. In addition, by the year 1995, 75 percent of all school-age children will have a mother who works outside of the home. The absence of parents will require schools to make a crucial decision: either take on many of the responsibilities of raising a child that were once a family's responsibility or find ways to work around the reality of today's family structure. The educational system must develop ways to retain and educate students who come from the most disadvantaged families since it is these students who are the most likely to leave school before they graduate.

This chapter profiles five innovative educational programs that are already meeting some of these educational challenges head-on. The Alternative High Schools in Public Housing Program and the Community Mentors Partnership Program demonstrate that government can make major positive contributions to the education of disadvantaged children. The Extended School Program has restructured the school day to accommodate the changing needs of parents and children of dual-income families. The Public/Private Partnerships in Education Program illustrates how a community's private and public sectors can work together to improve the quality of their schools. The Parents as Teachers Program shows how government can play an important role in preparing parents for their crucial role as the first teacher of their child.

While the programs profiled in this chapter do not provide a comprehensive outline of the unique educational programs currently in place in our nation's schools, they do offer convincing evidence that state and local governments are making measurable headway in restructuring America's educational system. Moreover, the lessons that these educational initiatives provide can be broadly applied to a range of management situations in the public-sector that extends far beyond education.

Meeting the Needs of At-Risk Students: The Alternative High Schools in Public Housing Program

Sarah Lee McWhite was fed up. During the six years that she had been a resident of Marlboro Houses, a Brooklyn public housing development, McWhite had watched a growing number of the neighborhood's children destroy themselves and their surroundings through vandalism, loitering and drug abuse.

As the supervisor of the development's Tenant Patrol, McWhite had demonstrated a strong commitment to her neighborhood. She had had enough of the stereotypes of project kids as a drain on the system and the negative impression that social service money "thrown at them" was wasted. McWhite decided that she was going to do something about the problems.

In February, 1985, McWhite created Marlboro Houses' first voluntary Youth Patrol, recruiting one member at a time. She spoke with young people she knew in the neighborhood and met with others at their hangouts. Most of her recruits were high school drop-outs. Within a few months, she was directing activities ranging from neighborhood beautification to assistance for the elderly. As residents who had a keen knowledge of crime in the neighborhood, the Marlboro Youth Patrol even worked with the police, checking out vacant apartments and keeping an eye on parks and playgrounds.

Although the accomplishments of the Youth Patrol pleased her, McWhite was frustrated by her inability to offer this group of high school drop-outs skills that would make them economically competitive in a city where finding a job is a challenge even for high school graduates. The individuals who made up the Youth Patrol were not stupid, and each, she contended, had a specific reason for leaving high school. Some left because of pregnancy. Others left to help support their families. More than a few had been involved with drugs and, prior to joining her patrol, spent most days loitering in and around the development grounds. McWhite began to evaluate the possibility of designing an educational program that would meet the needs of these youngsters. She wondered if it would be possible to educate these children at Marlboro Houses so that they could continue to be with their children and support their families.

McWhite's search for a solution to the drop-out problem eventually led her to the office of the principal of the board of education's Offsite Educational Services (OES), an operation whose programs are designed for students unable to attend regular schools. Although OES programs traditionally offered only the General Equivalency Diploma (GED) McWhite found that by creating cooperative agreements with local high schools to provide physical education and elective courses, she could expand the core of an alternative high school, enabling qualified students to earn a high school diploma.

In September of 1988, McWhite witnessed the realization of her dream when the New York City Housing Authority began operating a pilot alternative education program at Marlboro Houses.

One of the first students recruited by Sarah McWhite for the Alternative High Schools program was Rodney Peters, a 17-year-old drop-out, who spent his days languishing around the neighborhood with his friends. Sometimes he got into trouble, but mostly he just "hung out." Rodney had never fully adapted to the regular public high school programs in his area. He often felt that his time in school was wasted, and he was often bored. Although he never sold illicit drugs, he pointed out that he and his friends often used them, noting that drug use contributed to his educational problems. The Alternative High Schools program appealed to Rodney because he was able to learn in a familiar environment at his own pace. He received his high school diploma in 1990 and is attending a community college in New York state. Had McWhite not recruited him for the Alternative High Schools program, Rodney says he would still be "hanging out."

One year after the successful pilot education program was started at Marlboro Houses, a total of 14 alternative high schools had opened their doors to students. Today, there are over 30 sites, with more sites planned in the future. Students targeted by the Alternative High Schools program are dropouts from 16 to 21 years of age who live in and around New York City's 318 public housing projects. There are currently over 500 students enrolled in alternative high schools. Although it is difficult to assess the percentage of eligible candidates currently served by the program, the Board of Education believes that few of the students now enrolled would ever receive a high school degree without the Alternative High Schools program.

The alternative schools are operated jointly by the New York City Housing Authority (NYCHA) and the New York City Board of Education. According to Charles Owens, the Director of Community Affairs for the New York City Housing Authority, the Alternative High Schools program is "the right program at the right time" because it offers young drop-outs "a second chance at a quality education."

The Alternative High Schools in Public Housing Program

The Alternative High Schools in Public Housing (AHS) program is straightforward in both its intent and design. For every 20 drop-outs interested in the program, OES provides a full-time, licensed teacher and a paraprofessional educator, creating a "one room schoolhouse" in unused spaces in NYCHA facilities. The program offers students a great deal of individual attention and often provides them with individual assignments that address their particular needs.

The academic curriculum parallels that of a normal high school, not a remedial learning center. Specialists teaching music, art, the sciences and poetry circulate among the AHS sites each week for a few hours of instruction. The core subjects of English, social studies, cultural studies and mathematics, however, are the responsibility of the full-time classroom teacher. In response to the particular experiences and needs of the program's students, the curriculum also includes substance abuse prevention and parent care.

Since many AHS students have children, infants and young children of program participants are present in the classroom much of the day, looking on while mothers study, speak in class discussions and even while they take examinations. Increasingly, sites feature a separate facility where a volunteer from the housing development watches infants during class time.

For one student, the availability of this service was the primary reason she chose to attend AHS. A good student, she became pregnant during her senior year of high school. When she dropped out to take care of her baby, she was only one unit shy of a high school diploma. The program enabled her to finish her education and receive her diploma without worrying about leaving her baby unattended.

This creative innovation addresses New York City's enormous drop-out problem and increases the number of students enrolled in a sanctioned board of education degree curriculum. It also improves the self-respect of the housing development residents involved since active community participation is required to make the program a success.

Its most important objective is to rejuvenate aborted high school careers. Mere graduation is not classified as a value in and of itself by program administrators. The program does, however, celebrate re-entry into education by a group of youngsters that had given up on it. The program changes the mindset of students and the general public about young adults in public housing by directly combatting the feelings of hopelessness and inadequacy that confront the program's participants. For these students, a diploma can be the best competitive edge possible. For what may be the first time in their lives, the students become members of an upward group, an elite corps of young people who share a degree of self-respect and companionship generated by pride in their education.

Participants in the program point out that it fosters a sense of community that radiates to all corners of the housing development. Seemingly minor touches, like t-shirts with each school's name emblazoned over the housing authority logo or the blue sign that hangs over the door of each site issuing a welcome to the program, let residents know that a school is in session on the grounds. Importantly, this school serves the same young people who often spent much of their time and earned their livings in the parks and hallways of the same developments.

The strongest support for the program has come from the community, including tenant associations, tenant patrols, local politicians, and the local school boards, whose discharge lists now reflect revenue-producing transfers to other board of education programs instead of discharges. Says one school board official, "[AHS] creates a meaningful alternative for students who we would have lost in the past." According to Owens, mothers of children in the housing developments are the program's most vocal supporters.

As duly elected representatives of their neighbors, tenant association members' time and energy are instrumental in the planning stages of each site. Every site in the program is chosen based in large part on the strength of the project's tenant association and the enthusiasm that the group demonstrates for the program. Without the enthusiastic backing of the tenant groups, Alternative High School's impact in the communities would be negligible.

While they are among the program's most vocal supporters, tenant association members also serve as its watchdogs. They ensure that the professional staff treats students in the classroom with respect. Tenant association members often visit classes, take notes on the proceedings and report on their experiences to the other adults in the community. Suggestions are then presented directly to the Housing Authority.

The City University of New York has given the program potentially limitless support by guaranteeing a space in any of its two year colleges to all graduates of the Alternative High Schools program. Many of the sites proudly feature this unprecedented agreement on a bulletin board, and the opportunities presented by continuing education are mentioned in each classroom with regularity.

The tangible community support that AHS receives is above and beyond that which is available to other OES programs and cannot be overestimated when judging the success of Alternative High Schools in Public Housing.

Financing the Program

Since the schools are set up in vacant housing authority spaces, the program is reasonably inexpensive. The major expense (accounting for 81 percent of total outlays) is personnel, about $61,000 per site per year. This expense is assumed by the Board of Education. The housing authority covers the $8,000 annual salary of a community service aide with funds made available through the Department of Housing and Urban Development's Comprehensive Improvement and Assistance program. Furniture, textbooks and other instructional materials are provided by the Board of Education and a city-wide network of institutional volunteers and individual donors.

An important obstacle faced by the Alternative High Schools program is that school sites are not ready-made classrooms. To comply with board of education standards, careful planning is necessary to guarantee that students have access to bathroom facilities and to ensure that facilities are safe enough to permit infant children of students on the premises during the school day. Construction to meet sanitation and safety requirements could easily triple the annual budget of Alternative High Schools. The Housing Authority and the OES are constantly searching for adequate spaces at or near developments that meet both the budget limitations imposed by an increasingly cost-conscious Board of Education and the previously mentioned building standards.

Recruiting New Students

The program's success is largely dependent upon the number of students that can be recruited from the wide range of high school drop-outs at any housing development with an alternative high school. Experience has shown that year-round recruitment works to the program's advantage. It is the alternative high school teacher who makes initial contact with students who live near the school and whose names appear on the board of education's long-term absence list. The community service aide, a resident of the development, usually knows where the find these drop-outs, and may even know several of them personally. Negative peer pressure facing chronic high school drop-outs is fierce, but the community service aide, who is appointed by the NYCHA, tries to break down resistance and spark an interest in the program.

Often, a group of friends are recruited at the same time so that they can see each other through the program. One aide related the story of a young woman who was reluctant to enter any educational program while she was caring for her young daughter. "She really didn't think she could concentrate on school and her child at the same time," said the aide. But when the woman was introduced to a student who also had a small child to care for, she changed her mind. "Nothing I could have said would have been as persuasive," said the aide. "A peer facing the same situation who is making it in the program is the best pitch we have."

The community service aide is also instrumental in keeping students in the program once they are enrolled. If a student fails to show up by 9 A.M., the community service aide will knock on the student's door and find out why they are absent.

Program Results

Although it is a new program by the standards of educational reform, the Alternative High Schools program has already begun to make a difference in the lives of its participants. Since these young people have made a renewed commitment to education, other changes in their lives have followed. For example, participants in the program are able to find part-time jobs in the neighborhood, serve on their housing development's tenant patrol, and become positive influences and role models for younger teens.

The pilot school at Marlboro Houses graduated 13 students at the end of its first year. Two of these students went to college (Baruch College and Columbia University). Nearly all 100 members of the 1991 class went to college or have found employment in either the public or private sector in New York. Prospects should be equally good for future graduates.

Although the Alternative High Schools program is proud of any student who earns a degree, it constantly stresses that the degree is a ticket to a viable career. Its most important accomplishment is to equip graduates with the skills to be truly competitive in a job market, and an overall economic picture that did not always look so promising.

Program Organization

A unique feature of the Alternative High Schools program is that it is managed by two completely separate government agencies, one responsible for education, the other for public housing. As such, Alternative High Schools in Public Housing is monitored in two distinct ways.

The teaching staff, curriculum development, and completion of graduation requirements are governed by the OES under the direction of a principal. The community service aide, classroom maintenance, recruitment of students and managing community relations are monitored by the local housing manager. The housing manager, in turn, reports to the assistant director of the authority's Management Department for Tenant Relations. Despite their different missions and goals, these very different organizations have worked well together for the benefit of children in the housing developments.

Both agencies play a significant role in monitoring attendance and the academic progress of the students. The paraprofessional educator at each site reports to the Board of Education daily on attendance and monthly on discharges from the program. The community service aide makes a similar report to the Housing Authority each week. The aide also reports on the credit-earning progress of students as they pursue their diplomas.

A program-wide planning group meets monthly to discuss particular issues that develop at each school. These meetings include representatives from both the OES and the Housing Authority. At the individual site level, an advisory council meets monthly to encourage community support from the public schools in the area, local merchants, community colleges, and the tenant associations and tenant patrols.

This unique structure makes a meaningful educational atmosphere in public housing possible. While such arrangements are necessary and helpful (if well-managed) potential conflicts are possible and should be noted. For example, the Board of Education and the Housing Authority may not be equally well suited to judge academic performance. Any major disagreements over policy have thus far been dealt with during the monthly planning sessions.

The Future

New York City's sluggish economy suggests that there will be no drastic decrease in the number of high school drop-outs within the next five years. If anything, the drop-out rate is likely to increase, especially among the low and very low income families served by the Housing Authority. This population will be increasingly susceptible to the lure of drugs, especially if they do not have a high school diploma.

In recognition of the seriousness of New York's drop-out problem and the need for immediate action, the OES and the Housing Authority plan to expand the Alternative High Schools program to every public housing development in the city within five years. The sponsors of Alternative High Schools in Public Housing have an ambitious educational agenda as well. Both the OES and the Housing Authority plan to enhance the pre-college and pre-employment counseling available at each site by bringing in representatives from government, business and local colleges to speak with graduating seniors. The authority is also looking for ways to establish a scholarship fund for alternative high school graduates who intend to go to college.

As the curricular demands of a high school education change, alternative high schools will expand their core curriculum to embrace subjects of increasing importance to the twenty-first-century marketplace. Courses in computer science, word-processing, photography, video production, and accounting will improve the competitive edge that the Alternative High Schools program offers its clients.

Key Lessons from the Alternative High Schools Program

The Alternative High Schools in Public Housing Program suggests a number of important lessons about innovation in the public sector. First, the persistence of Sarah McWhite illustrates the critical role that "primary movers" can play in the development and acceptance of innovative programs. Second, the Alternative High Schools program offers an excellent example of the degree to which strong community support can enhance a program. Third, the unique relationship between the New York City Housing Authority and the New York City Board of Education provides an exemplary model for a strategic alliance between public-sector organizations. Finally, the Alternative High Schools program effectively demonstrates the importance of voluntary participation in community-based public programs.

PRIMARY MOVER. Several of the programs that will be discussed in this book were the product of one individual (or a small group of individuals) who demonstrated a "heroic commitment" to the program's development. Their commitment is heroic because they are willing to make hundreds of phone calls, talk to dozens of people, visit agency after agency, and spend sleepless nights on behalf of others in their community. Sarah McWhite is one such individual. These people are critical to the development of many programs because they succeed in bringing problems to the attention of civic leaders, and they champion unique solutions that bureaucracies may be reluctant to accept. Primary movers also serve as a focal point for information, publicity, and planning of the development of a new program. In the absence of such individuals, many innovative programs might never reach fruition. In the case of McWhite and AHS, her steadfast determination to change the condition of her housing development and the common perception of project kids as failures led to the innovative solution now in place.

COMMUNITY SUPPORT. Although it may seem elementary to note the importance of community support to the success of a program, the degree to which astute program managers develop such rapport and use it as a strategic tool is fascinating. The Alternative High Schools program cultivates public support to create the powerful impression that the entire community supports the efforts of drop-outs who wish to return to school. Important individuals and groups within the housing developments, including the community service aide, parents, and tenant organizations, take an active role in supporting the alternative high schools and the children who attend them. Recruiters point out to potential students that the AHS program is widely supported by the community, including their peers. This makes prospective students more comfortable with their decision to return to school.

STRATEGIC ALLIANCES. One of the most interesting aspects of the Alternative High Schools in Public Housing Program is the dual oversight responsibilities of the Housing and Education Departments. While scholars have long noted the propensity of public agencies to compete for jurisdiction over programs and resources,[8] exceptions do exist. The success of the Alternative High Schools program *requires* the full participation and support of both the housing and the educational authorities since both have a formal stake in the program. Either could independently squelch the program.

Increasingly, today's problems and their resulting broad programs require intra-agency alliances. These alliances are strategic because both agencies share common problems that neither can solve by itself. The following pages offer several other examples of strategic alliances between agencies. The Community Mentors Partnership program, described in this chapter, brings together the partnership and local community colleges to the advantage of both organizations.

VOLUNTARY PARTICIPATION. A final key lesson of the Alternative High Schools in Public Housing Program is the significance of voluntary participation by students. Although students are actively recruited by the program, they must make the decision to participate on their own and commit to the objectives and standards of the program. Since only dedicated students who want to be in the program are enrolled, the classroom environment is enriched for all of the participants. The Community Mentors Partnership Program, discussed later in this chapter, also benefits from a system of voluntary participation.

A Few Words about Transferability

Neither the problem of uneducated high school drop-outs nor the hard facts of economic survival are exclusive to New York City. Substance abuse among the program's target population became a national crisis with surprising swiftness. To implement a program like the Alternative High Schools in Public Housing, completely unrelated agencies (such as housing and education organizations) find it necessary to forge a close working alliance. Such alliances, although simple on paper, take careful planning and follow-up to be effective. Regular meetings between the OES and the Housing Authority serve this purpose. Supporters of the New York program state that the single most important requirement for success of an alternative education program is that all agencies involved understand the value of community. It will ultimately be the community that recruits students and determines whether the program succeeds or fails.

Meeting the Needs of Modern Families: The Extended School Program

Over the past two decades, the industrial environment in America has changed dramatically. Overseas competitors have multiplied, advanced technologies have proliferated, and increasingly families have found it necessary to have two wage earners rather than one. These rapid societal changes have necessitated a rethinking of our education system that is just beginning. Across the nation, many school districts have begun to define the needs of American society in the twenty-first century and to outline an education system that fills these needs.

Although there is much debate over what skills students must be given in order to produce the educated men and women who will be capable of conquering the challenges of the next century, there is a growing consensus that the structure of the school day itself needs to be modified in order to meet today's demands. Specifically, there is a growing awareness among parents and teachers that the six and one-half hour school day no longer fits the schedule of many dual-income families. The traditional school calendar means that many young children remain unattended for up to three hours a day during the school year and all day during the summer while their parents work. Since private day care is not affordable for many families, schools are increasingly being looked upon as an important part of the solution to the child care problem.

In late 1985, Dr. John H. Jones, superintendent of the Murfreesboro (Tennessee) City School System, recognized that the demand for professionally supervised before- and after-school programs for children in his area far exceeded the availability of services provided by the private sector. At the time, Dr. Jones found that over 60 percent of the mothers with school-aged children in Murfreesboro were employed outside of the home, yet there were professionally operated, licensed programs for less than 7 percent of the children in need of care. Many of the private programs were unaffordable to the mostly blue-collar families of Murfreesboro.

As superintendent, Dr. Jones saw in his school system the potential resources to meet the demand for child care and an extended school program. Believing that a meaningful, workable, and affordable experience could be developed for children right in their own schools, Dr. Jones championed the concept of an extended school day that would provide students with recreational and educational opportunities until their parents could pick them up after work.

Dr. Jones and other early supporters of the extended school concept, including members of the local school board, were moved to action by the plight of children like Shelly Charles. Then a fourth grader in Murfreesboro, Shelly was what educators referred to as a "latch-key kid" because both of her parents worked outside of the home until late in the evening. Shelly's parents often had to ask other parents (or sometimes teachers) to look after their daughter until they returned from work. While Shelly waited up to three hours after school for her parents, she often spent her time doing little more than sitting around.

Although Shelly's case might recently have been considered unusual, it is rapidly becoming the norm. By the year 1995, nearly three-fourths of all school age children will have a mother who works outside of the home.[9] The increased presence of women in the workforce, along with the increased prevalence of single-parent households, has placed significant demands on society to provide meaningful child care services.

The case of Shelly Charles highlights a unique initiative which has successfully met the demand for quality, professionally supervised, before- and after-school programs for children. The program is the Extended School Program (ESP) of the Murfreesboro City School System. Founded in 1986, the Extended School Program has exposed over 4,500 children to extensive educational and recreational activities while at the same time ensuring their safety and well-being.

The program is managed by Becci Bookner who worked closely with Dr. Jones to champion the extended school concept. According to Bookner, if programs like ESP were adapted on a national basis, nearly 50 percent of the child care problem in America could be eliminated without using tax dollars. She suggests that school systems will have to accept their role in addressing the child care problem. "The families and the need are right here," says Bookner. "If teachers can't address this problem, who can?"

The Extended School Program looks beyond the traditional roles of educators to solve the problems of latch-key children and to meet the needs of today's families. This program represents a truly grass roots, community effort to make schools a place where parents and children can gather to learn and grow on a full-time, year-round basis.

By forming working partnerships with the private sector, parents, and teachers, ESP provides an enriching atmosphere for children to develop confidence, self-esteem, and responsibility for themselves and their community.

The program combines several innovative features, including an extended school day (6 A.M. to 6 P.M.), mechanisms for parent participation, more efficient use of school facilities, and employment of young education majors from a nearby university to fill the ranks of program supervisors.

The Extended School Program is the only program of its kind in the nation that is totally funded by parents, is system wide, and is authorized and administered by the state Board of Education. The approach is also unique in that the program, unlike most education reforms, is not tacked on to an existing program.

Rather, ESP represents a major reconfiguration of the school schedule. The Murfreesboro school system is closed only six week days each year, meaning that it operates over 11,000 hours beyond the traditional 180-day school year.

After five years of intense scrutiny, the program continues to be fiscally solvent, educationally appropriate, and has attracted wide-spread attention in educational circles.

Beneficiaries of the Extended School Program

The Extended School Program targets children like Shelly Charles who may arrive home from school as much as three and one-half hours before their parents return from work. While some parents, particularly those of older school age children, do not see the early arrival of their children as a problem *per se,* many choose to enroll their children in the ESP to take advantage of the extended educational and enrichment opportunities.

The Extended School Program is broken down into two parts: a morning program and an afternoon program. Children can participate in one, both, or neither (the programs are optional). Programs are offered during the school year as well as during the summer, and offer flexible arrangements for children who only need to participate for short periods of time, e.g. one week while parents are away.

The morning program is designed to serve as a springboard into the school day for children who arrive early. Bookner characterizes the morning curriculum as "low-key."

Education aides visit with the children, go over homework assignments, and offer them breakfast. The program sets the tone for the rest of the school day by fostering within children a positive spirit toward the coming day. "It really reduces the apprehension many children feel about coming to school. Now they look forward to it," says Bookner.

The afternoon program is in marked contrast; it is characterized by much more activity. Students can participate in a wide range of educational and recreational activities, ranging from foreign language instruction (Spanish and French), music lessons, crafts, and athletics. Students are also encouraged to participate in an hour long homework period. This homework period gives students the benefit of doing homework in the presence of educators who can assist them and helps them develop good work habits. One parent of a child participating in the program said the following about the afternoon portion of ESP: "Its a win-win situation for both the kids and their parents. The kids are exposed to terrific new experiences, they develop disciplined work habits, and their parents are at ease knowing that they are in good hands."

A key component of the afternoon program is that its scope is largely determined by available teaching resources. The program relies heavily on retired teachers, professionals in the local community, and education students from a nearby college. The skills these teachers bring with them form the core of the ESP program. For example, one former teacher regularly offers students the opportunity to learn quilting, and the director of a local karate studio offers instruction in karate.

Program administrators are exceptionally resourceful when it comes to finding teachers. For example, cello and violin lessons are offered by two former members of the Rumanian Symphony Orchestra who defected after performing in the area. Since the pair spoke little English and lacked green cards, teaching with the program proved to be a worthwhile endeavor.

Some programs, such as violin lessons, are rotated throughout the system so that students are exposed to new areas of potential interest. This element of exploration is a central component of the ESP, according to Bookner. "It is intended to pique their interest and get them interested in the learning process." The former kindergarten teacher says that the program offers children activities that are "wonderful, exciting, and new."

Importantly, all children in the Murfreesboro City Schools are eligible to enroll in the Extended School Program. During the summer program, children and parents from outside of the school district are also invited to participate.

In line with its tradition of targeting at-risk children, ESP accepts referrals from principals and teachers on a cooperative basis. Children may be referred to the program on either an emergency or long-term basis. While there is a fee involved to cover the cost of referrals, the program attempts to deal with each referral on a case-by-case basis.

In the summer of 1989, the ESP began expanding its services to include classes for adults ranging from art to computer science. Plans are being made to increase the participation of adults by offering evening classes.

History of the Extended School Program

Contacts with those involved in the early stages of planning suggest that a critical component of the program's overall success was the cooperative working relationship that was formed between John Jones, the superintendent; Becci Bookner, the director of the Extended School Program; and the local school board which has supported the program from its inception.

Following six months of research and planning, and at great political risk, school administrators took a bold step in January of 1986 by setting up the core of the ESP at one local school, Hobgood Elementary. At that time, only four students were enrolled in the program.

The ESP was risky for several reasons. Teachers and school administrators saw ESP as a potentially serious threat because they were afraid that it would undermine their traditional authority in their own classrooms. Teachers not only resisted the ESP concept, but there was also resistance to the fundamentally new philosophy which gave birth to the idea of ESP: teachers, principals and school staffs were reluctant to have school facilities used for anything other than the traditional 8:30 A.M. to 3 P.M. school day. Moreover, teachers were hesitant to let others use their classrooms before or after hours. The issue of "my classroom, my territory" was a very real phenomenon. Many teachers felt that their areas of expertise were being threatened and challenged by the school board and the superintendent. In addition, many teachers were worried that their classrooms would be "messed up" after school. Finally, they were unclear about whether they would be required to work 6 A.M. to 6 P.M. days, a daunting prospect. It became clear to the program's founders that for ESP to work, teachers (who would ultimately implement the program) had to become an important part of the decision making process. They had to buy into the program and become an integral part of it.

Private providers of child care also expressed concern that ESP would force them out of business. Interestingly, since ESP began operating, three new private child care facilities have opened, an unlicensed child care business has closed because of competition from ESP. The ongoing viability of private facilities probably stems from the fact that ESP only serves school age children.

A major element of risk had to do with the solvency of ESP. Parents, employees, and even the local city council feared that ESP would become a white elephant dependent upon taxpayer support.

In order to overcome these concerns, the program's founders made a strategic decision to develop a test site to prove to skeptics that the program could work. Hobgood Elementary seemed like a particularly appropriate trial ground for the ESP since it was the school with the highest percentage of low-income families in the Murfreesboro school system. In the 1985–86 school year, 41 percent of students were eligible for free lunches, 33 percent of the families earned less than $10,000 annually, and nearly 60 percent of the families were headed by a single parent.

After several months of operating the ESP at Hobgood Elementary, it became clear that the ESP concept was accepted by teachers, that private care providers would remain in business, and that the ESP would be financially viable. Bookner quickly points out that "the kids were the best PR agents for the program. They really loved it." In many cases, children did not want to leave when their parents came to pick them up. Providing programs that the children wanted ensured that children would participate and bring their friends. The original fears of teachers were allayed by the decision to use public areas, and not classrooms, at first. Once the program gained acceptance among teachers, it was moved into classrooms, but only at the invitation of individual teachers. Thus, teachers were allowed to accept the program at their own pace. The decision to introduce the program classroom by classroom was key to overcoming a potentially serious obstacle to implementation.

The success of the demonstration site at Hobgood Elementary paved the way for school board support. In July 1986, the school board voted to expand the ESP to two additional sites. In April 1987, the program was extended to all seven elementary schools in the Murfreesboro City Schools system. In January of 1988, Governor Ned McWherter included a specific amendment to Tennessee law authorizing ESP as a part of his administrative program. This led to the authorization of school boards to establish day care centers in all public schools.

Today, there are 1,850 children enrolled in the ESP, representing 45 percent of the city's 4,150 school age children. This is a remarkable accomplishment considering the relative novelty of the program.

Cost-Effectiveness

Because the Murfreesboro School Board was adamant that the Extended School Program not be financed by additional tax revenues, cost effectiveness is continually stressed. The program achieves cost-effectiveness in two ways. First, each student is charged a small tuition ($10 to $20 per week, for morning or afternoon sessions only, respectively, and $26 per week for both programs) that helps pay for the cost of the program. Second, ESP provides for a more efficient use of school facilities. The increased cost of using school facilities for the ESP is minimal, but adds an extra 11,000 hours of school time each year beyond that provided by the traditional six and a half hour school day.

The fact that participants pay for ESP highlights its most serious shortcoming. The program is not yet able to support students whose families cannot afford the tuition. Consequently, it excludes many of the at-risk students which ESP most wants to reach. This problem is especially serious given the economic circumstances faced by many Murfreesboro residents. In order to overcome this potentially serious shortcoming, the administrators of the Extended School Program are diligently working to establish a scholarship fund and foundation that will enable the program to aggressively seek those children from families who cannot afford the tuition.

The ESP also achieves cost-effectiveness by using readily available teaching resources in the Murfreesboro area. The Murfreesboro City School System employs about 500 teachers, all of whom are able to work within the scope of the ESP. Nearly three-quarters of the program's instructors are education majors at nearby Middle Tennessee State University. Although some of these pre-teachers have as much as three years of teaching experience in a laboratory setting prior to their first teaching assignment, they receive a relatively modest wage of $4.25 per hour. Nonetheless, ESP is able to attract high caliber, extremely motivated teachers because of the excellent teaching opportunity provided by the ESP. Furthermore, many teachers welcome the supplemental pay that results from teaching ESP classes. There are few alternatives to the ESP in the area that enable education students to work under master teachers while at the same time offering the flexibility that their studies require.

Program Organization

Three policy-making entities are involved in administration of the Extended School Program — the school board, an advisory board, and the superintendent. The school board, however, has the ultimate decision-making authority. The board makes use of an appointed advisory committee composed of a cross-section of administrators, teachers, parents, school board members, and union representatives, along with the superintendent. Input from all of these sources helps to prevent strife and overcome any conflicts.

While ESP is part of the school system, it is a separate entity at the administrative level. The director is located at a central office to maximize interaction with the superintendent and the school board. Each of the seven schools in the Murfreesboro City Schools system has a site director who is responsible for overseeing the program at that school. Each school also has a ESP secretary and enough staff to ensure 10:1 student-to-staff ratio.

The Tennessee State Department of Education recently appointed a statewide ESP coordinator to oversee statewide expansion of the program.

Key Lessons from the Extended School Program

The Extended School Program is rife with widely applicable lessons. The most important lessons spring from three defining characteristics of the program. First, the program's founders carefully quantified the need for the program. Second, ESP operates with significant autonomy. Third, the program is cost-effective. Collectively, these three attributes broke down early resistance to the program, allowed it to operate effectively, and guaranteed that it would be financially viable. Let's examine each.

QUANTIFIED NEED. The Extended School Program was well served by careful analysis of the demand for ESP prior to setting up the program, on a limited basis, at Hobgood Elementary. The school board spent over six months researching the need for extended school hours. They asked parents if they would participate in the program if it was offered and measured the attitude of students and teachers toward the program. In addition, they attempted to determine which families would be most likely to participate in order to determine what types of services should be offered. Once the pilot program was started, a survey was conducted to determine the composition of families who actually enrolled children in the program.

The data collected prior to starting the pilot program gave program advocates solid ammunition to use during the debate over whether or not the ESP was appropriate for the area. Armed with quantifiable, measurable, and verifiable demand data, program supporters were able to make a strong case for the program. Given the original reluctance of many teachers and residents to support the ESP, imagine how things might have been different had program advocates relied instead on only a hunch.

DEGREE OF AUTONOMY. Most of the programs discussed in this book are operated under the jurisdiction of large agencies: education departments, port authorities, county health departments, and housing agencies, among others. Despite the oversight of these large bureaucracies, some of the most successful programs are afforded a relative degree of autonomy.

The Extended School Program benefits from autonomy in three ways. First, it is able to determine its own staffing needs and hire accordingly. Autonomy in this respect allows those who are closest to the needs of the program's clients to decide what types of activities and services should be offered to children.

Second, under the guidance of Becci Bookner, the ESP makes most of its own administrative decisions. Autonomy in administration gives the program added flexibility and separation from a bureaucracy which might otherwise slow down the administration process. Finally, the ESP enjoys some autonomy in the area of finance. Financial discretion has allowed program officials to allocate funds to the activities and services most in demand. Since program officials are closest to their clients, they are best suited to making these decisions.

Autonomy in staffing, administration, and finance does not mean that the ESP is removed from the educational bureaucracy in Murfreesboro. The director's office is in a central location near the superintendent and school board, and the three entities enjoy a close working relationship. The program benefits from the support and resources of the agency while still being able to make important decisions at the program level. Another program discussed in this book, the XPORT Port Authority Trading Company (Chapter 6), offers a parallel example of an organization that benefits from relative autonomy from its parent organization (NY Port Authority) while still reaping the benefits of affiliation.

COST-EFFECTIVENESS. In the first chapter of this book, I suggested that new programs will increasingly have to rely on sources of financing other than tax dollars. As a result, cost-effectiveness is rapidly replacing total cost as a performance measure. Throughout this book, we will see time and again that cost-effectiveness is a major concern of program managers in virtually every area of public management. It is worth noting that as new programs like ESP justify themselves using the cost-effectiveness criterion, pressure will grow for traditional programs to adopt cost-effectiveness as a performance measure.

The ESP demonstrates cost-effectiveness in two ways. First, the tuition charged to parents of students enrolled in the program is kept at a modest rate. Second, taxpayers are in no way burdened with the cost of administering the program. Becci Bookner noted that the ESP maintains cost-effectiveness primarily through using under utilized school resources including buildings, materials, and vacant spaces. In addition, as mentioned earlier, the program relies heavily on education students from a nearby college.

A Community Comes Together to Improve Education: The Public/Private Partnerships in Education Program

Tupelo, Mississippi, holds a prominent place in American folk lore as the birthplace of Elvis Presley. Each year, this town of twenty-five thousand offers its unique brand of southern hospitality to hundreds of the late entertainer's faithful fans. Alas, Elvis is not Tupelo's only claim to fame. Educators on their own crusade come from around the nation to witness one of the most interesting educational reforms of the last decade, the Public/Private Partnerships in Education Program of the Tupelo Municipal Separate School District.

The Partnerships program has forged a cooperative effort between the schools, local agencies involved in child development, and educational and business associations with the end result being increased achievement in the classroom. The Partnership program is a comprehensive effort to secure private funds to develop and implement quality educational and community service programs in Tupelo. The program not only seeks to finance innovations which improve basic learning skills, but it also attempts to minimize environmental distractions that can come between a promising student and academic success. These distractions include drug abuse, teen pregnancy, and poor health conditions, among others.

Setting a Precedent

The story of the Public/Private Partnerships in Education Program starts with a man named George McLean. McLean was the publisher of *The Daily Journal,* Tupelo's newspaper of record, until his death in 1983. During his tenure as publisher, McLean and his editorial staff extensively covered educational issues and strongly supported community service. After his death, the newspaper continued this style of coverage.

McLean himself was intimately involved in educational issues and often made personal financial contributions to educational innovations. For instance, he once contributed $1,000,000 for the installation of reading aides in every classroom in Tupelo. The reading aides assisted teachers in helping students to develop their reading skills. The program worked so well that the state legislature appropriated over $80 million to implement the program state wide. There is now a reading assistant in every elementary school classroom in the state.

McLean also founded a community foundation called CREATE which collects tax-exempt donations for educational projects. CREATE eventually became the primary funding vehicle for the Public/Private Partnerships in

Education Program. In an effort to ensure that CREATE would continue to be a self-perpetuating community foundation after his death, McLean willed *The Daily Journal* to the organization. Profits from the newspaper continue to support CREATE and the educational programs fostered by the Partnerships program.

The Public/Private Partnerships in Education Program

The Public/Private Partnerships in Education program is focused on a problem that threatens the education of at-risk children around the nation: lack of funds. As affluent citizens all but abandon the public school system for private alternatives, tax revenues that once went for classroom equipment, books, and teaching resources are increasingly scarce.

Civic leaders in Tupelo and elsewhere realize that this flight of funds from the public school system can have a serious, adverse long-term impact on a community. As a community's public school system declines, students are less able to compete for meaningful employment and are more prone to the conditions of poverty, including crime and drug abuse. Moreover, companies are less likely to locate in areas with poor public school systems, leading to high unemployment and a weak corporate tax base.

Faced with a school system that many thought to be inadequate, 15 couples of school-age children formed an informal alliance in late 1983 to begin rebuilding the Tupelo school system. Their goal was to marshal funds for local schools. These parents felt strongly that the critical shortage of funds facing the local schools system was depriving their children of an adequate education. They began to lobby local business organizations and private citizens for funds, and they encouraged educators to help them initiate new programs in the schools. The devoted efforts of these individuals laid the foundation for what would eventually become the Public/Private Partnerships in Education Program. Although the effort has received strong support throughout the local government and the school system, private citizens continue to take the lead in funding and developing projects and services that go beyond the scope of those traditionally funded by state and local governments. The Partnerships program puts the parents of school-aged children and other concerned citizens in a position to work directly with the school board and teachers to develop innovative policies and projects.

In addition to receiving a substantial amount of funds from McLean's CREATE (over $30,000 annually), the Partnerships program receives substantial financial support from a private association of parents and other concerned individuals. This private organization, the Association for Excellence in Education (AEE), raises over $100,000 each year for new programs and improved teaching techniques in the Tupelo school system. Innovations developed through the Partnerships program are funded without tax dollars.

The Public/Private Partnerships in Education Program has financed a surprisingly broad array of educational innovations. These include evening high school tutorial programs in math, science and writing skills; experiments with merit pay for outstanding teachers; and mini-grants for teachers who excel in advanced education courses. In the last case, teachers who take and excel in college-level courses that will directly improve their performance as teachers receive reimbursement for classroom materials in the amount of $200 if they receive an "A" grade and $100 if they receive a "B" grade. Thus, teachers have an economic incentive to both enhance their academic knowledge and perform well.

The Partnerships program also gives teachers financial incentive to come up with their own classroom innovations. Each year, the AEE awards up to $500 to teachers who develop innovative classroom programs and techniques that enrich the educational process. The initiatives are evaluated along several dimensions including estimated effectiveness, ease of implementation, and estimated demand for the program. The AEE has also provided private funds for the establishment of training programs for teachers, additional school personnel (including reading aides) which allows for smaller class sizes, and gifted programs for outstanding students. Funds are also used to sponsor teams for statewide academic competitions.

Although the focus of the Partnerships program is on the development of innovations for improving the academic environment, it also finances more basic, but equally important, efforts. For example, the fund raising efforts of the program have provided the Tupelo schools with basic equipment and supplies, including computers and textbooks. Prior to the establishment of the Partnerships program, severe budget restrictions made the procurement of even these most basic necessities difficult.

Attacking the Underlying Causes of Poor Academic Performance: A Broad Approach to Educational Reform

Several of the most successful programs in this book concentrate on attacking the root causes of the problems they are trying to address, rather than simply fixing the symptoms. The Public/Private Partnerships in Education program is an important case in point. While many educational reform programs seek to remedy poor academic performance through remedial efforts (i.e., after school make-up sessions), the Partnerships program goes beyond these efforts and directly addresses the environmental distractions that hinder performance in the classroom. As suggested earlier, these distractions can include poverty, drug-abuse, and teen pregnancy. In addition to providing remedial academic services, Partnerships also addresses the causes of poverty and academic underachievement.

The Partnerships program also attempts to preempt poor academic performance before it can take hold with an array of supplemental services to improve student performance. The Partnerships sponsors a comprehensive effort to identify at-risk children as early as the preschool level and provides services designed to address health, social, and employment problems that are directly related to later educational performance. Teachers identify students who could benefit from programs funded by the Partnerships and encourage them (and their parents) to participate.

In 1986, the Tupelo School System became a partner with the North Mississippi Medical Center and other civic and professional organizations to establish Project HOPE. This effort became the primary vehicle for addressing the environmental problems that affect the educational potential and performance of school-age children.

Project HOPE

Project HOPE has three main components. The first component, the Family Life Education Program, is based on the belief that a good education should start at birth. Accordingly, this element of Project HOPE deals primarily with the special needs of infants and preschool children. It includes efforts to reduce infant mortality rates by providing health education to preschoolers and their parents. Also funded by McLean's CREATE, these educational efforts are aimed at improving health habits among children and adults, alike. (The Family Life Education Program also provides basic health services to preschool children through the North Mississippi Medical Center.)

The second component of Project HOPE is the Dropout Prevention program. As the name suggests, this element of HOPE is aimed at older students who are struggling to stay afloat. In many cases, Tupelo educators have found that students who drop out of school are not necessarily the least gifted. Often, environmental factors wreak havoc on a talented child's ability to perform well in school. Accordingly, the Dropout Prevention program directly targets these environmental factors by offering counseling services, both in home and after school, for both students and their parents. In addition, the program offers after school tutoring and related academic services. "I was struggling like you wouldn't believe!" says one beneficiary of the counseling. "I probably would have dropped out—I really wanted to—but they [the counselors] convinced me that without a diploma I would have a tough time finding work. More importantly, they helped me put together a homework schedule and helped me stick to it so that I would keep up with the work. I really felt better about school once I knew I was caught up with everybody else."

The final component of Project HOPE is the Community Resource Committee (CRC). Established by concerned volunteers, the committee serves as a community-wide clearinghouse for volunteer work and community service. Problems addressed by CRC have included teen pregnancy, teen unemployment, and other social factors that come between students and their full academic potential. According to one student, "The program saved my schooling. The staff supported me and helped me make it through graduation."

Results of the Public/Private Partnerships Program

As with any comprehensive educational reform program, the success of the Public/Private Partnerships in Education program can be measured in a number of ways. In terms of educational performance, the American College Test (ACT) scores for Tupelo students have averaged about 20 percent higher than the Mississippi average and about 5 percent higher than the national average in recent years. Average ACT scores have increased about 15 percent in Tupelo since the Partnerships program was started. Program officials are quick to point out that these results have been realized in the context of a school system that has consistently had one of the lowest public expenditure rates (dollars per student) in the country.

Although educational performance is the most important measure of the Partnerships program's success, it is also worth noting the substantial resources that have been provided to the schools through the private funding mechanism. The Partnerships program has funded over half a million dollars in improvements and projects in the Tupelo school system.

A third way of evaluating the results of the Partnerships is to consider the impact that the program has had on the community's attitude toward education. Since the early days when the program was entirely operated by a handful of concerned parents, the Partnerships program has fostered widespread, direct involvement in the school system by Tupelo residents. In addition, the program's success has encouraged public officials to support other educational reforms in the Tupelo area. For example, the local Board of Aldermen recently allocated funds for a new program geared toward reducing class sizes in primary subject areas in an effort to give students more personal attention in the classroom.

The Community Spirit: A Consensus for Reform

Educators from outside of Mississippi (or outside of the Tupelo area, for that matter) are often surprised, even shocked, by educators' and the community's commitment to the program. The reason for their surprise is twofold. First, the Partnerships program has fostered and continues to encourage major changes in the way teachers do their jobs. Such innovations, even those that give teachers a larger role in managing their own classroom, are frequently opposed by teachers in other municipalities.[10] Second, visitors are often amazed by the degree to which the entire Tupelo community has involved itself in the education of its children. Indeed, the Partnerships program relies on the powerful bond which has been forged between disparate institutions, including the school board, educators, parents, and local businesses. A key point is that all parties to this initiative seem to share a common vision of an improved school system and are apparently willing to put aside issues of control and jurisdiction for the benefit of Tupelo's children. The school board and other government agencies do not behave as though they are threatened by the intrusion of private parties in the educational process, a process that has long been primarily the domain of public institutions.

Although the many programs that comprise the Partnerships program have, for the most part, been tried in other areas on an individual basis, no other jurisdiction has reported a level of support comparable to that reported in Tupelo. To understand why Tupelo has been able to implement such basic changes to its educational system one must begin with Tupelo's unique sense of community spirit.

Dr. Mike Walters, the current superintendent of the Tupelo School District, notes that Tupelo is "the most unusual community you have ever seen, spiritually and financially. The community is willing to work for improvement in education, and is willing to pay for it." With justifiable pride, public officials are quick to point out that the residents of Tupelo are not only committed to quality education, but they are also strongly supportive of community development (employment) efforts and improvements in the health care system.

The community-wide desire to work for the improvement of Tupelo has a long history. In part, according to Dr. Walters, it stems from poverty. Mississippi has long been a poor state, suffering from high unemployment, poor health conditions, and poor educational institutions. Furthermore, many parts of Mississippi, including Tupelo, lack a strong tax base. In the absence of public funds to combat the ills of poverty, cities and towns have had to rely on the generosity and ingenuity of private residents and corporations.

In Tupelo, according to Dr. Walters, organizations that develop and support promising social programs enjoy very high status. The highest levels of government and business work together to improve the community because they believe that they share the risk, responsibility, and credit for what is accomplished in the community.

Key Lessons from the Public/Private Partnerships Program

The Partnerships Program teaches two lessons. First, the public/private partnership form of organization contributes to its success by bringing together expertise from both the public and private sectors. Second, the program's holistic approach to problem solving effectively addresses root causes of educational under-achievement rather than simply focusing on the symptoms of poor academic performance.

PUBLIC/PRIVATE PARTNERSHIP ORGANIZATION. The degree to which residents of Tupelo can shape the educational system in their community is impressive. Tupelo residents share formal responsibility for financing and developing reforms in their schools with formal institutions. The use of private funding or reforms combined with formal links to the school board ensures that all parties with a stake in the educational process have a say in how it is reformed and to what degree. Public/private partnerships allow programs to benefit from the administrative expertise of the public sector and the managerial expertise and fund raising capacity of the private sector.

HOLISTIC APPROACH TO PROBLEM SOLVING. Environmental distractions, including poor health care, unemployment, and drug abuse can squelch academic success. Accordingly, the Public/Private Partnerships in Education program not only addresses existing academic short-comings, but it also addresses factors outside of the classroom that can contribute to underachievement by enabling child development and health care agencies to play a direct role in the education reform process.

We will see that public/private partnerships are the organizational vehicle used by a number of other programs in this book to address problems in areas other than education. For example, the Health Care Access Project (Chapter 3) uses a public/private partnership to bring together social service agencies and private health care providers to meet the health needs of a community. Similarly, a public/private partnership form of organization is used by a number of housing programs including the SRO Residential Hotel Program in San Diego (Chapter 5) to coordinate public housing authorities and private real estate developers.

An holistic approach to problem solving is also central to the Parents As Teachers Program, described in the following section, which addresses educational improvement by focusing on childhood development problems that hinder educational performance later in life. In a different context, the Massachusetts Commission Against Discrimination (Chapter 5) addresses underlying causes of discrimination in housing from a preventative posture rather than focusing solely on the results of discrimination.

Teaching the Teachers:
The Parents as Teachers Program

The raging debate over educational reform has often focused on the issue of who should have control over publicly financed educational initiatives.

Teachers, politicians, parents, and taxpayers all exercise legitimate claims to the policy process. Innovative programs in education rely on close cooperation between these disparate constituencies. Since the American educational system has traditionally deferred to the expertise of teachers and school administrators, these two groups have given up more of their authority than any other groups in the recent drive for educational reform. With this context in mind, it is refreshing to discuss an educational program that appears to be universally supported by teachers, parents, taxpayers, and government officials. The program is Parents as Teachers, operated by the state of Missouri.

Research has shown that the most rapid period of human development occurs during the first few years of life. At the same time, parents are forming and routinizing their approach to child-rearing. Although most parents want the best for their children, there is little support or systematic source of information available to them on the day-to-day nuances of shaping another human being. For parents like John and Tracy Moller, the program has been a godsend. "We were confused," says Tracy. "Having a child for the first time is overwhelming, emotionally and practically. We really didn't have time to worry about the educational needs of our one-year old, but we heard about the program, and knew we wanted to participate. The program's been a real help for us."

The Mollers and others were persuaded to participate in the program by officials who pointed out research which shows that a child's competency in intellectual, language, and social abilities at age six can be predicted with great accuracy at age three. The implication for public education is clear: empowering parents as the first teachers is the first logical step in educational improvement. Missouri educators were among the first to recognize that a child's education should commence at the onset of learning. They believed that the role of the school during these early years should be to assist parents with their teaching and nurturing responsibilities and to strengthen the family unit, not to replace parents as primary teachers and care givers.

The Parents as Teachers Program (PAT), which has now been replicated in 207 school districts across the country, is aimed at providing children with a solid start on their long road to reaching their academic potential. Parents like the Mollers welcome this program because it provides them with the guidance and support they need in their role as their child's first teacher. An effort is made to serve children and parents with special needs and problems through a delivery system that offers universal access to families with children under three years of age.

The Parents as Teachers Program differs markedly from other educational reforms that include early childhood and preschool initiatives. These other programs tend to focus primarily on the schooling of children between the ages of three and five who are considered at risk for academic underachievement. Such efforts are remedial, however, rather than preventative. Since these initiatives are usually conducted outside of the child's home, parents are often excluded from the process. In contrast, the Parents as Teachers Program begins assisting children while they are still in the womb. Women in their third trimester of pregnancy are eligible to participate in the program.

Families receive regular visits by trained educators who instruct parents about ways to encourage the language and thinking abilities of their children; how to make and choose toys that stimulate curiosity and creativity; how to foster social development; and how to discipline without punishing. Visits are scheduled to accommodate family needs, allowing for the active participation of fathers as well as mothers. Throughout the program, each child is carefully monitored by parents and educators to detect and treat any emerging problems which might interfere with learning. "It was a little awkward at first," says a parent who was still pregnant with her first child when she was visited by a PAT educator. "I thought I might be jumping the gun by participating before my child was even born. But once I found out just how important those first months and years are to a child's development, I became more determined to learn. My husband also got involved." This parent was also impressed by the degree to which educators accommodated her by coming to her home.

According to Otis Baker, the state's assistant commissioner for instruction, parent educators are largely drawn from the ranks of former primary and secondary school teachers. In other cases, parent educators are still actively teaching on a part-time basis. As such, they are uniquely qualified to understand the educational needs of children and to provide parents with useful advice on child development.

In addition to the private visits with parent educators, group meetings with other parents participating in the program provide opportunities to share concerns and successes in parenting. "Drop-in" and play times for parents and children are arranged through the program to promote networking among parents. Tracy Moller was particularly pleased by this aspect of the program. "It was great to meet with other mothers who were going through the same stage of parenthood that I was going through. It really helped. Not just in terms of giving me good advice, but also because I learned that I'm not the only one who has made mistakes. I'm not a bad mom."

The program begins with the premise that parents' need for guidance and support in their teaching role crosses all educational and socioeconomic boundaries. Rather than initiate early childhood education through programs that are exclusively for at-risk children, PAT offers access to any family with infants and toddlers, while providing additional help for families and children with special problems. At present, Baker estimates that over 30 percent of the state's eligible population, nearly 54,000 families, are participating in the program.

Baker also suggests that the Parents as Teachers concept has many incidental benefits for parents, children, schools, and society. Early detection and attention to potential learning problems reduces the need for remedial education later on.

Child care experts also suggest that an indirect benefit to parents is the support Parents as Teachers provides, thereby making parents lives less stressful and leading to a reduction in child abuse and neglect. Parents like the Mollers learn that the trials of raising a young child are not unique to them. They are not alone. The program also increases the links between the home and school leading to a positive partnership likely to continue throughout the child's formal schooling.

The Parents as Teachers Program

The Parents as Teachers Program provides information and educational guidance designed to help parents give their children a solid foundation for lifelong development. For children, the program seeks to enhance their intellectual, language, and social development. The program also identifies and ameliorates risk factors that interfere with a child's growth and learning. Such factors might include family stress or poor quality of parent-child interaction. For parents, the program strives to increase general knowledge of child development and increase confidence, competence, and pleasure in child-rearing. For schools, the goals are to reduce the need for costly remedial education programs and to build a positive relationship between schools and the students' homes.

By law, all families in Missouri with children under three years of age are eligible to participate in the PAT Program. Current state funding, however, provides service to only about one-third of the eligible parents and children. School districts must pick up the tab if they choose to serve additional families in their local area. The current annual cost of maintaining the program is about $9.5 million, most of which comes from state appropriations. The balance of the budget comes from federal funds, private donations, and local appropriations which increase the level of service above the 20 percent of eligible families.

Every effort is made to inform eligible families of the Parents as Teachers Program. A public service announcement has been made available to every major television station in the state. Additionally, radio and newspaper coverage has been extensive. Local advisory committees assist in recruiting and referring families to the program. Hospitals, health care professionals, social service organizations, churches, and community organizations have all been enlisted to help school districts disseminate information to families. Even local businesses have gotten into the act by including information about the program in their mailings to customers. John and Tracy Moller, for example, learned about the program from their pediatrician.

Since personal contact with prospective participants is extremely important, parent educators make monumental efforts to enroll families. This often
includes going door-to-door to inform people about the program with special
attention given to recruiting hard-to-reach and high-risk families, especially
families who are poor.

Administration of the PAT Program

The Parents as Teachers Program is under direct control of the Missouri
State Board of Education and the commissioner of education. The board has
constitutional authority for the general supervision of all educational programs in the state, including PAT.

The commissioner serves as the board's chief executive officer and is instrumental in statewide coordination. The board and the commissioner work
closely with the governor's office and legislative leaders to secure public appropriations for the PAT program. In addition, there is a 35-member Committee on Parents as Teachers whose members are appointed by the
commissioner.

The Committee on Parents as Teachers is the primary decision making
body for the program. Members of this statewide citizens committee represent
a wide variety of interests from business, medicine, the media, foundations,
social services, academia, volunteers, and public and private schools. Because
of its diversity, the committee has access to a wide variety of resources which
have enabled it to support quality PAT programs. (Note that many of the programs discussed in this book rely on diverse oversight committees to bring
together equally diverse resources on behalf of their programs.) One of the
Committee's most important functions is to keep state officials apprised of
early childhood education activities with special emphasis on the PAT
program.

The committee is also responsible for making sure that the program is
adequately funded. Funds raised by the committee have been used to train
more than 1,000 Missouri school district parent educators and administrators.
Funds are also raised to develop ongoing regional workshops and follow-up
programs for parent educators, on-site consultation, and technical assistance
for program personnel. Parents as Teachers Program training bases have also
been established in St. Louis and Kansas City in an effort to create regional
training centers.

Funds are solicited from a variety of sources other than tax revenues.
Tremendous emphasis is given to developing private/public partnerships in
support of the program. Contributions by private foundations and other
groups have provided much needed support for staff training and promotional
activities. Nonetheless, program officials have indicated a strong desire to increase the effectiveness of private fund raising efforts.

History of the Missouri PAT Program

Although the Missouri Parents as Teachers Program has received national acclaim only in recent years, the program's development literally spans decades. The State Department of Education's interest in early childhood education dates back to a 1972 position paper on the subject. Although the paper is now dated, it serves as a useful reminder of the sometimes slow pace of bureaucratic innovation. The paper, published by the Division for Instruction, made the case for early education efforts. At the time, there was no perceived value for universal early education programs such as PAT, but the paper got educators thinking about the value of educating parents.

The basic principles behind the 1972 position paper and Parents as Teachers are based on child development research dating from the 1950s and 1960s. This body of research emphasizes the importance of children's first years in terms of the development of their language, intelligence, and emotional well-being. This research also stresses the importance of parents' involvement in their children's early learning and development.

In light of this research, the Division for Instruction pushed for a Parents as Teachers pilot project which was eventually created in 1981. The pilot project was intended to demonstrate the value and practicality of helping parents to be effective first teachers of their own children from birth to three years of age. This four-year study was a cooperative effort between the Missouri Department of Education, the Danforth Foundation, and four local school districts. The school districts were chosen such that urban, suburban, and rural communities were all represented in the study.

The results of the pilot project were better than anticipated. An independent evaluation of the pilot PAT program conducted in 1985 found that three-year-old children participating in the project were significantly more advanced than their non-participating counterparts in language development. Likewise, they were more advanced in problem solving and other intellectual abilities, and they demonstrated more aspects of positive social development such as coping skills and positive relations with adults. Importantly, at-risk children (e.g. those with unusually young parents, single parents, or those who come from families with low income) derived as much benefit from the program as other children. Finally, participation in the project had a strong positive affect on parents' perceptions of themselves and the school district. Parent satisfaction was nearly 100 percent. (Preliminary results from a more recent study show similar results.)

In wake of the success of the pilot program and the survey supporting its success, several legislators and the governor acted to adopt the program statewide. In 1984, the Missouri State Legislature had passed the Early Childhood Development Act which authorized state funding for the development of PAT programs across the state. Since that time, the program has rapidly expanded to include as many eligible families as possible in every school district in the state.

Despite the rapid expansion of the Parents as Teachers Program and its early successes, the program's development faced serious challenges almost from the beginning. The first, and possibly most significant, challenge was to convince legislators, school officials, and taxpayers that early childhood education was a worthwhile undertaking. Many people viewed the parents as teachers concept as early schooling or babysitting. In short, says one former educator, "Most people I talked to were afraid that it was going to be a frill paid for courtesy of the taxpayers." To overcome this obstacle, the Committee on Parents as Teachers launched a major awareness campaign to explain the program and its potential benefits. The virtual absence of opposition to the program today indicates the effectiveness of this effort.

Competing for scarce funds was a second major challenge to the development of the PAT program. The legislature and the local boards of education had to be convinced that investing in early education was cost-effective and a legitimate expense for public schools. In an effort to overcome this obstacle, Governor Christopher Bond, who strongly and vocally supported the project, enlisted the cooperation of other state agencies including the Department of Corrections and the Department of Education to endorse funding of the PAT program. This concerted effort is repeated each year to ensure continued funding and support for the program.

Rapid expansion of the program has been a third challenge to program administrators. Increased publicity has led to overwhelming demand for new parent educators. For every family that participates in the program, there is another one that is still waiting to enlist. Given that the program is free to participants (beyond the taxes they pay) demand is especially strong. In order to meet this demand, new training programs have been established in cooperation with the state university system. In addition, regional training sites and model Parents as Teachers sites have been established to accommodate people in outlying areas who wish to become participants in the program. Efforts are being made to address the needs of special families, including those that are non–English speaking, functionally illiterate, or dysfunctional.

In the future, it is expected that the successes of Missouri's Parents as Teachers Program will be replicated nationwide. To this end, a national center for Parents as Teachers was recently established in cooperation with the University of St. Louis. A national advisory board has also been convened to provide guidance and direction on further program developments.

Key Lessons from the Parents as Teachers Program

The success of the Parents as Teachers Program suggests several courses of action for program administrators. As was the case with the Extended

School Program, supporters of the Parents as Teachers Program were able to overcome resistance to the program by undertaking several studies which quantified the demand for and the benefits of the program. Furthermore, the importance of community support, which was previously discussed in the context on the Public/Private Partnerships in Education and the Alternative High Schools in Public Housing programs, is underscored by the success of the Parents as Teachers Program. Community support has manifested itself in the form of quality parent teachers and financial support from taxpayers. Obviously, studies showing impressive results contribute to the high degree of community support which the program enjoys. Finally, the focus on root causes of poor educational performance rather than the symptoms, which was central to the success of Tupelo's Public/Private Partnerships in Education, is also central to the success of the Parents as Teachers Program. Instead of focusing on remedial education, the program starts targeting students at a very early age. In some cases, children who will be born into at-risk households (e.g. in poverty-stricken areas) are targeted before they are born. According to the program's administrators, children of parents who participate in the program are more likely to succeed in school than the children of parents who do not participate.

The Parents as Teachers Program also introduces us to some new lessons. First, the program has achieved success in recruiting families to participate in the program as a result of a carefully implemented public awareness campaign. Second, the program has generally been successful in accommodating rapid growth by using relatively simple means.

PUBLIC AWARENESS CAMPAIGNS. Officials close to the Parents as Teachers Program stress the importance of keeping the benefits and achievements of a program in the public eye. Public awareness campaigns are indispensable in terms of recruiting families to participate in the Parents as Teachers Program. Otis Baker indicated that public awareness is maintained through three means: formal advertising campaigns, free media, and extensive recruiting efforts.

Formal advertising campaigns consist of regular public service announcements on television, radio, and in newspapers. These announcements spell out the benefits of the program and indicate that anyone with a child under the age of three is eligible to participate in the program.

The free media is also a useful tool for increasing public awareness, but it has the drawback of being difficult to control. Administrators of the Parents as Teachers Program make an effort to maintain a good relationship with the media by inviting reporters to meetings and offering them well organized information about the program's goals and accomplishments.

Recruiting efforts along the lines of those used by the Alternative High Schools in Public Housing Program have also benefitted the Parents as

Teachers Program. The program has an active recruiting function that includes going door-to-door to inform parents about the program and making
special efforts to target hard to reach clients, such as those who do not own
telephones. The program also encourages referrals from hospitals, health care
clinics, social service organizations, churches, and community groups.

An ancillary benefit of public awareness campaigns is that they help
maintain community support for a program. When the benefits of a program
are reinforced through a strong public relations effort, legislative support is
likely to be stronger.

ACCOMMODATE RAPID GROWTH. Although program officials often
develop contingencies in the event that there is less demand for a program
than anticipated, far fewer consider the damage that can be caused to a program by demand that is *greater* than anticipated. A problem frequently faced
by organizations in both the private and the public sector is rapid growth. In
the private sector, rapid growth of demand may require new factories, increased
product output, enlarging the sales force, or increasing customer service functions. In the public sector, increased demand may require, in part, new services, increased facilities, more volunteers, and more funds. In both cases,
failure to meet the increased demand can lead to lost customers. However, increasing capacity without careful planning can lead to sloppy or uneven service
or outputs and, ultimately, increased dissatisfaction among users of the program or service.

The Parents as Teachers Program has faced rapidly increasing demand for
its services since the program started in 1981. At present, only about one-third
of the potential eligible population is being served by the program. Nonetheless, in addition to seeking increased sources of funding, directors of the program have taken specific steps to increase the service capacity of the program
and have developed more training programs in conjunction with local colleges
to qualify more teachers. Program officials have also created model sites which
can be used to train people who wish to develop new programs in areas not
currently being served.

Teaching by Example:
The Community Mentors Partnership

One usually thinks of innovations in education as being both urban-
oriented and complicated. Indeed, some of the most troubled schools in the
nation are located in blighted inner city areas with tax bases insufficient to support adequate educational systems. As such, complex solutions such as partnerships between private and public interests are needed in order to acquire
the resources necessary to make an educational system work.

Not all educational innovations are, however, urban-based. Small communities in economically depressed areas face many of the same challenges as their urban counterparts: high youth unemployment, high drop-out rates, teen pregnancy and drug abuse. Although it is less visible in many ways, the cycle of poverty in rural areas is just as vicious and just as difficult to break as it is in large metropolitan areas.

Similarly, not all educational reforms are complex. Some of the most brilliant innovations in educational administration are remarkably simple. Perhaps it is this simplicity that makes them so successful. Consider, for example, the Community Mentors Partnership of Douglas County, Oregon.

Douglas County is a rural county located in southern Oregon. Its economy is timber-based and susceptible to sharp downturns. In recent years, many local plywood plants have closed their doors due to increasing overseas competition and cost-cutting efforts by domestic plywood manufacturers. Plant closures have decreased demand for a variety of ancillary industries in the area as well. Most significantly, the logging industry has also faced severe labor cut-backs.

Life is hard in Douglas County, but it is even harder for those without a high school diploma. Luckily, schools, parents, and concerned citizens are working to keep the children of Douglas County in school through a program called the Community Mentors Partnership.

The Community Mentors Partnership extends a helping hand to young people destined to failure — as one program official put it "failure in school, failure in self, failure in relationships, and failure in life." Failure means that these young people will join their parents in an economically-depressed county in which one out of three adults do not possess a high school education and in which the current high school dropout rate is over 25 percent.

The Community Mentors Partnership pairs students who are at risk of doing poorly in school, or dropping-out, with adults who have similar vocational or recreational interests. These adults can relate to the needs of the children and offer them advice, encouragement, and friendship. Program officials related the story of one high school student who someday hopes to be in the U.S. Air Force. His mentor arranged for him to have lunch with an Air Force recruiter so that the student would understand what he would need to accomplish in order to be eligible to enlist. Says the mentor about his charge, "He knew that he wanted to be in the Air Force, but he hadn't developed disciplined work habits. I felt that hearing an enlisted officer explain the requirements might motivate him to work with me to develop a study schedule and stick to it." The meeting gave the student a clear set of academic goals which in turn gave him the focus he needed to finish school. "It woke me up," says the student. "Afterward, I had a clear idea of what was expected of me." The student's mentor then worked with the student to help him meet those expectations.

At present, the Partnership operates two slightly different Mentorship programs: one geared toward high school students, and one aimed exclusively at junior high students. The high school program, which has over 185 student participants, is more career-oriented. The experience of the student wishing to enlist in the Air Force is typical of this program. It seeks to entice students to finish high school by getting them excited about their possible career interests. Accordingly, students are paired with adult mentors based on their vocational interests. Often, however, students are paired with mentors based on similar hobbies or for other reasons. The program for junior high school students (sixth through eighth grade) is more academically focused. College-bound high school students are recruited as mentors for junior high participants. The mentors' efforts in this program are mostly tutorial in nature.

Students enrolled in the program are spread out among 11 schools in a county of over 500 square miles. This requires program administrators to rely heavily on local volunteers. The Partnerships staff includes only one paid coordinator and a part-time secretarial assistant. The Partnership, therefore, depends on the contributions of the 175 volunteer mentors from small businesses, civic organizations, churches, and the retired community. Over 20 volunteer community coordinators monitor student progress and recruit and oversee mentors at the local level.

In addition to helping at-risk students succeed in school, the Community Mentors Partnership has fostered an innovative method for business and industry to communicate with educators about what will make the students of today into the productive employees of tomorrow. To this end, speakers forums, job fairs, and work site visits help keep open a two-way channel of communication between schools and industry. Students say that the program is exciting because it gives them a first-hand opportunity to meet with people who have been down the road they are now traveling and have achieved the vocational goals to which they aspire. Thus, the program serves to inspire students as well as give them academic and emotional support.

The Community Mentors Partnership

Children who participate in the Partnership are identified as having problems in any one of a number of areas, including grades, attendance, discipline, self-esteem, social skills, and responsibility. The Partnership currently serves 250 students, an estimated 10 percent of the identified at-risk population in Douglas County. The Partnership hopes to double the participation rate. Approximately 5,500—or about 30 percent—of the 17,000 students (grades kindergarten through 12) in the district are considered at-risk.

Since intransigence on the part of any one of the participating students would jeopardize the success of the program for all participants, all students referred to the Partnership must voluntarily commit themselves to the program. Volunteer mentors must also formally commit themselves to build a relationship of mutual trust and understanding. An administrator explains the commitment in these terms: "It's a partnership between the student and the tutor. Both have expectations about what the relationship will accomplish. Both, therefore, have a responsibility for the outcome of the relationship."

Students and mentors agree to meet at least 10 times during a five month period, although many meet more frequently. These meetings typically entail once-a-month meetings in a group setting and once-a-month individually outside of school. The group meetings take place about once-a-month at the students' school. The group sessions provide both students and mentors with a valuable opportunity to share successes and discuss shortcomings of the program. The interaction afforded by these sessions also fosters a sense of community among the participants. This is especially important in largely rural areas like Douglas County. Topics addressed by mentors and students at the group meetings help build broad social skills necessary for personal success, including evaluating and building self-esteem, managing interpersonal relationships, developing career goals and expectations, improving communication skills, resolving conflict, and improving leadership and decision making abilities. In addition, students learn vocational skills, including interviewing techniques, résumé writing, and how to conduct a job search. A recent group session, for example, included a lively and informative discussion on time management skills. Students were given an opportunity to exchange ideas on the subject. Said one participant, a teenage mother, after the discussion, "I have so many things that I have to do each day besides school. It's really hard for me to concentrate on school. I have to shop and take care of the baby. But hearing the other guys talk about the same problems really gave me a lift. Hearing how *they* make it work helps. I know that I'm not the only one who is having a rough time. We're in the same boat."

During individual meetings, mentors strive to become trusted advisors to students on a variety of issues concerning school, personal growth, and career and educational goals. Often, the mentors build a trusting relationship by inviting students to baseball games, taking them shopping, or inviting them to their homes for a meal. In order to achieve the lofty goal of getting students to stay in school, mentors are trained in techniques which facilitate a close working relationship with students. Mentors spend a significant amount of time helping students understand the connection between classes taken and grades received in relation to future life in the work world. Students are encouraged to take personal responsibility for being successful both in school and in the future. An important part of the mentor's job is to reinforce the student's successes and increase the student's self-esteem. One mentor puts it this way, "I'm here for my student." Each year an awards banquet is held to honor mentors, students, and their families. Awards and scholarships are presented to outstanding student participants.

In addition to helping students achieve success in school, mentors have also been instrumental in helping students identify areas of career interest. A large number of local businesspeople, representing numerous occupations, have volunteered their time to speak to students on an informal basis. Visits and tours of local businesses have provided students with a first-hand look at the realities of participation in the workforce and have given them information they need to select an occupation. Emphasis is always given to directing students toward careers with high-growth potential.

Since many of the students in the Partnership go on to college, an alliance has been formed with local community colleges to recruit at-risk high school students to attend college. Regular visits are planned to these local community colleges so that students can sit in on classes, meet with professors, and explore the possibilities of post–secondary education. One high school student participating in the program stressed the impact of the college visit on his own academic performance: "I realized how much tougher college was than what I was used to. The professors expected more of the students than teachers do in high school. If I was going to go to college, I had to work a lot harder to prepare myself."

The Partnership program also tries to reach beyond the circle of people who are directly participating in the program. For example, parent support groups have been formed to help develop healthy family skills. Student support groups have also been organized through the schools to reinforce skills that foster success.

Although the Community Mentors Partnership offers so many services and benefits to participants, the annual budget for the program is less than $100,000. While this may seem like a substantial sum of money, it is not significant relative to the benefits accrued to society from educating hundreds of students who might otherwise live on public support for much of their lives in the absence of the program.

Organization of the Partnership

The Community Mentors Partnership is ultimately the responsibility of the director of career and vocational education for the Douglas Education Service District (ESD), which oversees public education for all of Douglas County. The director's primary role is to serve as a liaison between the superintendent of ESD and public education programs, such as the Partnership, which help students become viable contributors to the workforce. The director, in turn, oversees the director of the Community Mentors Partnership, who is responsible for the day to day operations of the program.

In order to ensure community involvement and awareness of the Partnership, three committees have been established to help guide the program. A steering committee has been established with representation from business, the community, students, counselors, and parents. This committee solicits input from all sectors of the community and develops new initiatives for the program.

A committee of professionals called STARS (Services Targeting At Risk Students) ensures that the program is using effective methods for reaching at-risk students. Members of this committee include curriculum specialists, special education experts, behavior specialists, alcohol and drug program experts, and career counselors. Every effort is made to help students improve their academic performance without making them feel like they are in any way inferior to other students.

The Chamber of Commerce Business-Education Committee explores the relationship between the Partnership and needs of the work force. This committee is composed of representatives from both the business and the education community.

All of these committees are responsible for determining what is successful for students and mentors and providing a menu of activities which will best enhance this success. The committees, STARS in particular, provide a necessary link with other services, such as alcohol and drug treatment, counseling, and family and student support groups. In this regard, the program relies on an holistic approach in much the same manner as the Public/Private Partnerships in Education and the Parents as Teachers programs.

Results of the Partnership

Although the Community Mentors Partnership is relatively new, it has already achieved measurable results, most notably its skyrocketing enrollment rate. There has been an overwhelming interest among young people who want to enroll in the Partnership. Although this is clearly a positive sign, it also creates problems because it has been difficult to sign up volunteer mentors quickly enough to meet the demand. (Recall that this was also a problem faced by the Parents as Teachers Program.) In the short term, this problem is being addressed by identifying mentors who are willing to work with more than one student. In the long run, efforts are aimed at attracting a broader array of mentors, including college-bound high school students who can serve as mentors to junior high students.

The Partnership's impact on students is constantly evaluated. In 1990, a survey was conducted to measure improvements in students' grades, attendance, self-confidence, social skills, personal responsibility, and discipline. Among students enrolled in the program, 85 percent reported improvement or maintenance of grades, 88 percent reported improvement in attendance, and an impressive 100 percent indicated a reduction in discipline problems. Similarly, 96 percent believed that their self-confidence had improved and the same percentage felt that they had improved their social skills. Additionally, ninety-two percent of the participants surveyed said that they were better equipped to take on more personal responsibility than before they had enrolled in the program. The results of this survey closely match the results of a survey taken one year earlier. A more detailed follow-up survey of former students indicated that the program made a substantial impact on students' motivation to make good grades and stay in school.

Interestingly, the program has also had an impact on those who serve as mentors. A survey of mentors showed that the partnership made them more aware of education-related issues and better able to relate to teenagers. This finding is consistent with the findings of surveys conducted on behalf of the Parents as Teachers Program. Parents who had participated in the program showed a greater interest in the educational system and the educational process of their child as a result of having participated in the program.

Plans for the Future

Already, plans have been drawn to enable the Community Mentors Partnership to meet the community's future needs. Specifically, a replication manual has been drafted for each school district to enable a rapid spread of the partnership concept. School district staff and parents of students are being enlisted to run in-school mentoring programs for all grades, not just for older students. This will enable educators to identify at-risk students at an earlier age, making their particular problems easier to solve. The Chamber of Commerce Education Committee has agreed to take a more active role in recruiting mentors from the business sector. This will help overcome the immediate shortage of mentors. Senior centers have also been enlisted to actively recruit mentors from among the ranks of the highly qualified senior community. Civic organizations have been approached to take on mentoring as a yearly service project for members. Finally, high school and college students are being trained to serve as mentors. With these strategies in place, the program should be able to expand for years to come.

Purpose, Mission, Goal, and Objectives

True to its nature of simplicity, the Community Mentors Partnership has a clearly articulated (and well-publicized) statement of purpose, mission, goals, and objectives. In general, committing this information to paper is an extremely worthwhile (and surprisingly challenging) undertaking. Doing so ensures that everyone who is responsible for implementing a particular program is working toward the same ends.

A quick glance at the Partnership's statement gives one a good overview of the program. The program's purpose is "to empower at-risk students to attain success both personally and academically."

The mission statement, which identifies the Partnership's clients, participants, and *modus operandi,* is "to create a climate, through mentoring, that allows at-risk students to progress to the best of their ability, including development of a healthy self-concept, motivation to set and achieve education and career goals, positive social relationships with peers and adults, personal responsibility, and achievement of academic success."

The primary goal of the Partnership is to improve student support systems, with an emphasis on at-risk students, in grades six through 12 on a countywide basis. In line with this goal, the Partnership identifies three broad program objectives. The first is to establish individual mentor/student partnerships countywide for up to 250 at risk students in grades nine through 12. The second objective is to expand the program to include more students in grades six through eight. The final objective is to expand the career outlook of at-risk students in grades six through 12 with an emphasis on career opportunities, both in state and nationwide.

Key Lessons from the Community Mentors Partnership Program

The Community Mentors Partnership Program suggests a few new lessons about program management worth discussing in more detail. The first of these lessons is the value of a clear statement of purpose, mission, goals, and objectives. The second lesson is the importance of getting participants to voluntarily commit themselves to the program. Finally, the Community Mentors Partnership Program illustrates the importance of constantly evaluating program results.

CLEAR STATEMENT OF PURPOSE, MISSION, GOALS, AND OBJECTIVES. The administrators of the Community Mentors Partnership Program have clearly stated the purpose, mission, goals, and objectives of their program and have committed them to paper. Doing so has ensured that everyone in the program is working toward the same ends. In addition, clearly stating the program's operating principles makes it easier to explain the program to others, including parents, students, and the press.

VOLUNTARY COMMITMENT TO THE PROGRAM. The second lesson of the Community Mentors Partnership Program is that getting participants to voluntarily commit themselves to the program will better serve the interests of all participants. Since group sessions are an important part of the Community Mentors Partnership Program, disruption on the part of any one participant could ruin the experience for all. As such, the Partnership only goes so far as to recruit and inform students of the potential benefits of the program, but leaves it up to the student to decide whether or not to participate. In this manner, a voluntary system of participation ensures that only students who want to make the program work will enroll. Once a student decides to participate, he or she is asked to commit themselves to the ideals and objectives of the program. In turn, mentors agree to meet with students on a regular basis.

CONSTANT EVALUATION OF PROGRAM RESULTS. The third lesson of the Community Mentors Partnership Program is that it is beneficial to constantly evaluate the program's results. By conducting regular surveys of program participants, program officials are able to determine ways in which the program can be improved. In addition, officials are able to determine if the program's goals are being met.

Chapter 3
Health Care and Drug Abuse

Health is the thing that makes you feel that
now is the best time of the year.
—Franklin Pierce Adams.

According to a recent report by the U.S. Senate Committee on Labor and Human Resources, America faces a health care "crisis of unprecedented dimensions."[11] Separately, the bipartisan Pepper Commission recently concluded that the American health care system is approaching a breaking point.[12] Both government committees conclude that the crisis is getting worse. Their reports single out the growing number of Americans who lack health insurance or whose insurance coverage is inadequate as the major component of the crisis. They also cite the rapidly rising cost of health care and the twin specter of drug abuse and AIDS as being too much for the current system to handle.

The lack of adequate insurance coverage combined with rising costs and the unprecedented epidemics of drug abuse and AIDS have created an environment where Americans are increasingly unable to afford services offered by hospitals, doctors, and clinics. While access to health care services is becoming more restricted for everyone, the extent to which the poor (especially poor children) are neglected by the health care system is especially troubling.

The national statistics on the state of the American health care system are disturbing. Over 37 million Americans are without health insurance. Another 60 million Americans have health insurance that is considered inadequate by the Department of Health and Human Services. This means that combined, there are nearly 100 million Americans, or more than one-third of the nation, that do not have adequate health insurance.[13] Most of these uninsured individuals are working Americans or dependents of workers who cannot get insurance at a reasonable price because their employers do not offer it.[14] Most of the uninsured are young. In 1987, nearly half were under 25 and nearly 30 percent were under 18 years of age.[15]

The inadequate insurance coverage of such a large portion of the American population means that many people who need medical care go without it. The Robert Wood Johnson Foundation found that nearly one million Americans seek health care each year but are turned away because they cannot pay. Another 14 million people do not even attempt to obtain health care because they know that they cannot afford it. Nearly two-thirds of the uninsured individuals with serious health problems such as persistent bleeding and loss of consciousness do not ever see a doctor.[16]

Sadly, it is children that shoulder a disproportionate share of the burden when it comes to inadequate health insurance. As such, they are denied access to health care at an early stage in their life when they are most in need. Almost 20 percent of all children have no health insurance coverage. This represents nearly 12 million children that are denied access to *regular* medical care. Almost 35 percent of children below the poverty line have no medical coverage because of gaps in Medicaid, the program that is supposed to care for the poorest Americans. More damaging still is the fact that most uninsured women do not seek prenatal care.[17] The result is that many poor children die before they reach their first birthday. At present, America ranks a deplorable nineteenth among developed countries in infant mortality rates. The end result of inadequate health care insurance (other than premature death) is that many of the untreated medical problems faced by children develop into chronic (and more costly) health problems later in life.

Combined with the growing number of inadequately insured Americans is the rapidly rising cost of medical care. The national bill for health care is a staggering $600 billion. This amount represents a near doubling of the amount spent on health care in 1980.[18] Health care spending now accounts for 12 percent of the gross national product (GNP) and is expected to account for nearly 15 percent by the year 2000.[19] To make matters worse, the cost of medical care is rising twice as fast as wages. These increasing health care costs make it very expensive for companies, especially small ones, to insure workers. Smaller businesses often pay up to 35 percent more than larger firms for the same coverage.

In addition to the problems of the lack of adequate health insurance for a large portion of the population and the rapidly increasing costs of medical care is the tremendous pressure placed on the American health care system by the proliferation of drug abuse and AIDS.

Drug abuse has become a major epidemic in such a short period of time that it has rendered the current treatment system wholly inadequate. Demand for treatment is so high that addicts are literally begging for admission to drug abuse treatment programs, yet many are turned away. A recent survey by the Therapeutic Communities of America showed waiting lists that average four months for admission to public treatment facilities.[20] The National Association of State Alcohol and Drug Abuse Directors estimated in 1989 that there were nearly 67,000 people on waiting lists for drug treatment programs.[21]

Increased infant mortality has been one of the unfortunate side effects of the drug epidemic. While the drug-addicted babies bear most of the burden of their addiction, society shoulders a huge burden as well. In California alone, hospitals are spending nearly $1 billion a year to care for babies born addicted to drugs.[22]

Intravenous drug abuse has led to a surge in the number of AIDS cases among addicts. Treating AIDS patients will place a major burden on an already strained health care system. The United States spent nearly $8 billion to care for AIDS patients in 1992. This represents an eight-fold increase in spending since 1986.

Increasing consensus on the need for reform has led to a number of proposals at the national level. These proposals range from insurance reform to radical restructuring of the health care delivery system. Unfortunately, there is no agreement on what health care reform should include, so progress to date has been limited.

Meanwhile, many state and local governments are sponsoring innovative programs that have begun to resuscitate our ailing health care system. This chapter will outline a few of these promising initiatives. The Medical Care For Children Project and Healthy Start represent unique efforts to foster early and ongoing medical care for children. The Health Care Access Project addresses the problem of insuring those who currently lack access to adequate health insurance. The Obstetrical Program for Indigent Women demonstrates how a community has begun to meet the health care needs of low income women. Finally, the Child Abuse Prevention Project outlines one program aimed at reducing the number of babies born addicted to drugs.

Providing for the Very Young: The Medical Care for Children Project

We are witnessing one of the most exciting periods in medical history. Impressive technological advances have allowed medical professionals to make great strides in diagnosing and treating many diseases that once wreaked havoc on the American public. Although improvements in treating catastrophic diseases such as polio and cancer have received most of the attention, the greatest advances have been made in providing basic health care. For most Americans, improved health care delivery has meant better health, an increased life expectancy, and a higher standard of living.

Unfortunately, not all Americans have benefitted from improvements in the health care system. For example, low income individuals are much less likely to have access to routine medical examinations, a significant development since many potentially debilitating health problems are identified and treated as a result of these routine examinations. Since many low income people do not have even minimum access to health professionals, low income people are disproportionately less healthy than their middle- and upper-class peers. Sadly, many of the people who lack access to basic health care are children. Nearly half of the uninsured are under the age of 25, and nearly 28 percent are under 18.[23]

Consider the case of Susan and Robert Hanlon.[24] A recently married, young couple, the Hanlons seemed to be living the American dream. They owned their own house in the suburbs and were financially independent. But when one of their children became ill and required hospitalization, the dream came to an end. The Hanlons, who were just starting out, could not afford private health insurance and Robert's employers did not provide him with insurance coverage. In desperation, he moved in with a relative and filed for a trial separation so that his child would qualify for Medicaid coverage.

One community, Fairfax, Virginia, was determined to address the issue of health care for children like those of the Hanlons. In 1986, the Department of Community Action (DCA), a public agency which oversees the needs of the poor in Fairfax County, conducted an in-depth survey of the local low income population in an effort to understand the nature and magnitude of the problem. The DCA officials were astounded to discover that over 78,000 individuals in the local community were without medical insurance of any kind. Many of these people were employed but had low incomes. For the most part, the uninsured in Fairfax County held low-paying, service-oriented jobs that did not provide them with health insurance coverage. Many of the adults who were offered insurance could not afford the extra cost of insurance for dependents. Some 50,000 of the uninsured were near or below the poverty line, and 19,000 were children.

At the time, neither the Fairfax health department nor any public or private organization had a program to provide primary, comprehensive, or acute care to these indigent children. As such, many children went without basic health care. Recognizing this serious gap between the health needs of the community's children and the services provided, the DCA went about the task of developing the Medical Care for Children Project (MCCP).

Support for the MCCP was widespread among organizations that wanted to help indigent children. The county's Department of Health, private physicians, hospitals, and other community organizations worked together to identify the health needs of indigent children so that the DCA could plan an effective program. Physicians, laboratories, pharmacies, and medical facilities were recruited to participate in the project.

After almost two years of intensive planning and discussions with the medical community, county agencies and community-based organizations, the DCA received authorization from the county Board of Supervisors to implement the MCCP.

The Medical Care for Children Project

The Medical Care for Children Project is remarkably simple in design. It serves its clients by capping health care costs for the low income population. The MCCP approaches group practices, Health Maintenance Organizations (HMOs), and individual physicians and asks them to serve indigent children at a predetermined, fixed rate. For example, the MCCP administrators approached eight well established group practices and asked if each would agree to serve 10 children for one year. In return, the MCCP agreed to pay the practices $150 per child. The children were then able to see a physician, in a group practice setting, as often as necessary. Sample medication and in-office lab work was offered free of charge. Several HMOs have also been recruited to offer medical services to the children. One HMO serves over 200 children. Another has agreed to serve 100 children.

A majority of children in the MCCP are served by individual physicians. These individual physicians agree to reduce their regular rate to $11 per office visit, and they also agree to accept a predetermined number of medically indigent children each month (usually 10). Typically, physicians agree to participate in the program for one year, at the end of which a new contract is signed. In return, a public/private partnership reimburses physicians for services rendered to the children.

It is important to note that the MCCP limits the demands placed on providers to a reasonable level so that they are not over-burdened. In order to ensure that some physicians are not more burdened than others, the children are evenly distributed among the physicians depending upon whether they have chronic conditions (such as diabetes or allergies) or acute illnesses (such as colds and chicken pox) which require less frequent visits. According to one administrator, "Distributing the cases in an equitable manner lessens the burden for individual physicians. It is essential that we do this in order to get physicians to agree to participate in the first place. Most would like to out of the goodness of their hearts, but physicians are under terrific pressures and time constraints in dealing with their own patients as it is."

Since most of the office visits are for minor problems, lab tests, or prescriptions, the office visit usually resolves the medical problem. If specialized care is required, the physician can refer the patient to a spectrum of specialized programs, clinics, or if necessary, a local hospital. This sets the program apart from the local health department which limits its services to preventative services such as immunizations and clinics for people with handicapping conditions.

The clients of the Medical Care for Children Project are indigent children, one month to 18 years of age. They must be from families that do not exceed the poverty level by more than 25 percent (e.g. a family of four must earn less than $15,125), they cannot be eligible for Medicaid, and they cannot have private health insurance or a private plan. These children often live in shelters, welfare motels, subsidized housing, trailers, and cars throughout the county. Although most of them have been identified through public assistance programs such as Head Start and the Department of Agriculture lunch programs, even illegal aliens have come forward with sick children, despite the obvious threat of deportation. Says one participating physician, "This program is of extreme importance to the families that participate. Without it [MCCP] most would have little, if any access to medical services."

In addition to providing participants with medical care, the MCCP also provides patients with case managers that give them a sense of continuity during their participation in the program. Case managers set the MCCP apart from the Medicaid program which offers no guarantee that anyone will follow individual cases. Each MCCP client is assigned to a case manager who makes certain that the client shows up for appointments and follows the doctors' orders. Case managers usually call clients the day before to remind them of their scheduled appointment. They also provide transportation to appointments, if necessary, and translation services for non–English speaking clients.

The case managers not only serve the needs of clients, but they also serve as an important liaison with the physicians. Case managers perform utilization rate reviews each month to ensure that the workload is spread equitably among the participating physicians, and they identify any possible problems with the program that need to be addressed.

The key to the MCCP is offering patients low-cost access to health care. Costs are kept at a minimum in four ways. First, as mentioned above, fees for services rendered at physicians' offices are prenegotiated. Setting the price per visit in advance ensures that the MCCP knows how many children it can afford to serve at any given point in time. Negotiating bulk contracts also helps reduce costs. Proposals are solicited and contracts are awarded to local agencies that wish to provide medical services to indigent children. Such contracts are awarded to pharmacies for the disbursement of prescriptions and health centers that specialize in the care of children. Third, costs are reduced by relying on volunteers to run the program. Finally, costs are minimized by restructuring existing medical services to meet the needs of indigent children rather than building a parallel health care system. Children participating in the program go to the same doctors, hospitals, and pharmacies as other children.

This last point is worth discussing in more detail. The MCCP administrators underscore the importance of mainstreaming the health care needs of the poor, rather than creating separate clinic style settings. The decentralized approach championed by the MCCP not only increases the convenience of the program for those using the service by reducing transportation obstacles, but it also preserves their dignity.

The decentralized nature of the MCCP organization makes it easier to duplicate the program in other parts of Fairfax County. It expands into new communities by using the resources available in the community. This has enabled the project to grow rapidly in the last few years.

Although the direct beneficiaries of the MCCP are the young patients, the medical community benefits as well. The MCCP reduces emergency room losses by eliminating unnecessary emergency room visits and reducing uncollectible fees which are ultimately passed on to other consumers in the form of higher rates.

Results of the Medical Care for Children Project

Without question, MCCP's most important achievement is that nearly 5,000 children have received medical attention during the past five years that they would not have otherwise received. In addition, the county was able to serve these individuals at a steep discount. Factoring in medical services provided at less than 50 percent of cost and grants received to provide medical services, it is estimated that Fairfax County has invested only $175,000 to obtain over $500,000 worth of medical services.

In addition to providing medical services to children in a cost-effective manner, the MCCP has long-term benefits that are difficult to measure. The medical problems that are inexpensively and routinely treated by MCCP might otherwise deteriorate into chronic conditions that would wreak havoc for these children later on.

Long-term savings will also accrue to the community. Since indigent children will be less likely to show up at hospital emergency rooms (the primary entry point for indigent children) these expensive and scarce facilities can be allocated toward more traumatic cases. Uncollectible fees are also drastically reduced.

In 1990, a survey was conducted to evaluate both physician and client satisfaction with the MCCP during the previous year. Physicians were asked about utilization rates, whether MCCP clients show up for appointments on time, and whether they were reimbursed promptly and accurately. Some 98 percent of the participating physicians were "very satisfied" with all aspects of the program. Overwhelmingly, their main suggestion was to expand the program to include more indigent children and to offer more services. Clients were asked how often they visited physicians, whether they were treated like other patients, and whether they were treated with dignity. Eighty-nine percent of the clients were satisfied or very satisfied with these aspects of the MCCP.

In recognition of its accomplishments, the MCCP has received awards from the National Association of Counties, the National Center for Public Productivity, and the Ford Foundation's Innovation Awards Program.

Obstacles to Implementing the MCCP

Although the Medical Care for Children Project has achieved impressive results, program administrators had to overcome quite a few obstacles before the program could be effective.

The first obstacle was to convince skeptical physicians to participate in the project. Since it was out of the ordinary, many physicians were not sure what they were getting themselves into. "When they approached me I thought 'Oh God, here we go again with someone asking physicians to do the impossible,'" related one participating physician. This initial reluctance was overcome by soliciting input from physicians during the initial planning of MCCP and working closely with health organizations to ensure that the needs of physicians were not overlooked. "When several of us got together and started hashing out ideas and plans, we really got excited about the possibilities. We thought 'hey, this just might work!'" said one physician.

The importance of getting input from individuals who will implement the program cannot be overemphasized. In the case of MCCP, potential resistance on the part of physicians was virtually eliminated by allowing them to contribute to the design of the program. Since they helped create it, they had a stake in seeing it prosper.

The second obstacle which had to be overcome was reaching legal agreements that were acceptable to all participants in the program. Since the MCCP relies heavily on the participation of many different organizations, reaching acceptable legal terms required extensive negotiations and compromise. The county attorney was instrumental in reaching terms that were agreeable to the county, the DCA, health care providers, and community agencies responsible for implementing MCCP.

While most of the major obstacles to the operation of MCCP have been overcome, there are several issues that continue to challenge MCCP administrators. Since the Medical Care for Children Project relies heavily on private contributions, ensuring ongoing private financial support is probably foremost among these issues. The DCA works in close partnership with a private, tax-exempt philanthropic organization, the Northern Virginia Community Foundation (NVCF), which also accepts funds on behalf of MCCP. The partnership with NVCF has been beneficial for several reasons, First, NVCF independently controls donations, relieving MCCP officials of the burden of control. Second, NVCF has 501(c)(3) status, so all contributions are tax-deductible. Finally, NVCF has contacts throughout the philanthropic community which expand the potential sources of funding for MCCP. A marketing plan is currently being developed which coordinates the solicitation efforts of DCA, community organizations, and NVCF. According to Sandy Lowe, director of the DCA, an important goal of the MCCP is to build an endowment large enough to allow the project to become self-supporting.

Another ongoing challenge has been accommodating non–English speaking residents of Fairfax County. In part, this problem has been addressed by printing outreach brochures in three languages (English, Spanish, and Vietnamese), but a few private and hospital-based practitioners, wary of the potential for malpractice suits, have been reluctant to diagnose and treat non–English speaking patients, even with an interpreter present. The DCA is currently working with malpractice health care insurance carriers to reach a solution to this problem.

The DCA has long been concerned about the status of individuals who become self-sufficient and are no longer eligible for MCCP. The DCA is working with private insurance carriers to develop a low-cost health care plan for individuals and families once their income is beyond MCCP eligibility guidelines. This will help guarantee access to medical care, even after they are no longer eligible to participate in MCCP.

Future Plans for the MCCP

Since the Medical Care for Children Project only reaches a relatively small percentage of the 19,000 indigent children in Fairfax County, a ten-year plan has been established to systematically reach all of them. The plan forecasts the number of clients to be enrolled in each of the next ten years and projects the amount of funding necessary to supplement county funding. To meet these ten annual goals, the DCA must: strengthen the outreach process to identify and enroll clients, encourage, support and maintain enthusiasm for economic development, and continue to enroll medical practitioners.

The DCA is also designing an education and treatment program that will target at-risk youth in the 12–15 year old range who face problems of adolescence. These problems include drug, alcohol and tobacco abuse, teen pregnancy, diet and nutrition, and sexually transmitted diseases.

Plans are being made to develop a curriculum, text, and video to help train other jurisdictions to implement the MCCP model. The DCA staff plans to make itself available to provide in-service training as necessary.

Replicating the MCCP

MCCP administrators insist that the program is replicable in almost any jurisdiction because it relies on resources that are already available in most communities. These resources are physicians, pharmacies, laboratories, and access to registration lists of families on public assistance.

Paramount to the success of any MCCP program, however, is the dedication of two or three people to plan, organize, recruit, and negotiate for the program. Any community that is willing to make the commitment to such a program will discover, as has Fairfax County, that a relatively small investment can go a long way toward addressing the health care needs of indigent children.

Key Lessons from the Medical Care for Children Project

The Medical Care for Children Project reinforces some of the lessons stated earlier. For example, like the Extended Schools Program, administrators within the DCA sought to gain a thorough understanding of the quantity and nature of demand for the MCCP concept prior to initiating the program. Doing so enabled officials to gain substantial community support for the program and helped them establish a program consistent with the clients' needs.

In addition, the MCCP has a concrete plan for accommodating rapid growth in a manner similar to that of the Parents as Teachers Program. Whereas the Parents as Teachers Program relies on model sites and comprehensive training programs to guarantee the program's expansion, the MCCP counts on its decentralized nature, such as the use of established doctors' offices and health facilities, to accommodate rapid growth. Since the MCCP uses medical facilities and physicians already in place, the program is easier to duplicate in new areas than it might be if the MCCP had to establish its own clinics. Also aiding the replication process are the standardized curriculum, text, and video tapes which are used to help other jurisdictions start similar programs.

Although the Extended Schools Program introduced us to one aspect of cost-effectiveness — namely use of available resources — the MCCP suggests three additional means of achieving cost-effectiveness: prenegotiated fees, bulk contracts, and reliance on volunteers. In addition, the MCCP introduces us to the role that client orientation can play in the success of a program.

COST-EFFECTIVENESS, REVISITED. The MCCP derives cost-effectiveness by encouraging physicians to serve clients in the context of their established practices rather than building a parallel health care system to serve DCA clients. Moreover, using existing practices makes it easier for DCA to expand the program and gives patients an opportunity to be served with dignity in the same type of medical setting as other patients.

The MCCP also derives cost-effectiveness by prenegotiating fees with providers. Since the DCA knows in advance how much providers are going to be paid for office visits, it is better able to budget financial resources and determine the number of clients it can serve. Moreover, since the cost of each visit is essentially capped, there is no risk to the DCA that some clients might run up exorbitant medical bills.

A slightly different take on the cost-effectiveness derived from prenegotiating fees is the negotiation of bulk contracts. Bulk contracts are most often negotiated with large group practices or managed care organizations (such as HMOs). Proposals are solicited and contracts are awarded to local agencies that wish to provide medical services to indigent children. Bulk contracts are also awarded to pharmacies for the disbursement of prescriptions and to health centers that specialize in the treatment of children. Such contracts often result in huge savings for MCCP in exchange for a steady flow of MCCP clients.

A final source of cost-effectiveness stems from the use of volunteers to help administer the MCCP program. Although volunteers often require more supervision than paid personnel, the cost savings are obvious. Recall that the Community Mentors Partnership Program was also able to derive huge savings by counting on volunteers to administer the program.

CLIENT ORIENTATION. The MCCP introduces us to the somewhat fuzzy notion of client orientation. Although the managers of various programs have slightly different ways of expressing the concept, all of them indicate the importance of treating people with dignity and respect. Just as program managers have different ways of expressing the notion of client orientation, their programs manifest client-orientation is different ways. For example, the MCCP strives to serve the needs of its clients by regularly asking them if they are satisfied with the services provided by the program and by soliciting their ideas about how the program could be improved. The MCCP demonstrates that customer orientation is more a philosophy that pervades a program's design and implementation than it is a formal function.

Caring for the Uninsured: The Health Care Access Project

Over the past decade, the cost of health care in the United States has nearly doubled. A one-day hospital stay can cost anywhere between $350 and $750. Not surprisingly, people are relying more on health insurance to cover these costs. Unfortunately, nearly 37 million Americans lack health insurance of any kind, and another 60–70 million lack adequate coverage.[25] As a result, many individuals and their families do not have adequate access to health care when they need it.

Health benefits, especially health insurance, have traditionally been provided either through the workplace, or in the case of the very poor, through Medicaid. Many businesses, especially small businesses, are finding it increasingly difficult to insure their employees. Consider the case of a catering company in Ohio. Although employees received health insurance as a condition of employment in the past, recent increases in the company's insurance premiums have imperiled the company's policy. Last spring, the company was notified by its insurance carrier that the premium would be raised twice-yearly in the future. At the present rate, the company's cost of providing basic health insurance to employees is $4.55 per employee, per hour. Says the owner of the small company, "I not only can't compete with costs like this, but I can't stay in business, either! I'll have to cut my employees health benefits entirely."

Many of those who lack insurance are employed but do not have the financial means to provide for health care coverage on their own. Many of these individuals are among the ranks of temporary workers or the self-employed. Michael Young, a 36 year-old, self-employed drywall worker was one of these individuals. On an income of $800 per month for himself and his wife, Young could not afford private health insurance. But his income, plus the fact that he is not physically disabled and does not have children, render him ineligible for government assistance. Tragically, when Mr. Young injured himself on the job he found himself with an unanticipated medical bill that he could not pay.[26]

Federal insurance programs for the poor are also inadequate. Low income individuals who leave welfare for low-wage employment often face a loss of medical benefits. In turn, these workers are forced to leave their jobs and return to welfare when they have medical problems. "I can't afford to work if I get sick," says a young woman caught in this paradox.

Medicaid does not reach more than a small fraction of the low income population. In fact, Medicaid covers only 42 percent of those below the official poverty line. Of those with incomes 25 percent below the poverty line, i.e. the destitute, one-fourth are not covered by Medicaid or any other program. Consequently, universal health insurance is increasingly regarded by many as a necessary part of the solution to the nation's goal of universal health care access. Progress on universal health care insurance has been slow in Congress, but it has met with some success at the state and county level.

Health officials in Genesee County and Marquette County, Michigan, decided to take action in response to the growing number of uninsured individuals in their jurisdictions. Their response was the formation of the Health Care Access Project (HCAP). The HCAP is representative of a grass-roots movement to increase access to health insurance in the absence of a federally-sponsored program.

The Health Care Access Project is one of the few demonstration projects around the country designed to address the issue of improving health care access to the uninsured. It is innovative because it provides a continuum of care for those on public assistance as they move from welfare to the workplace.

Like many of the other innovations discussed in this book, this project relies heavily on a partnership between public and private organizations. In the case of the HCAP, the government, health care providers, and businesses work closely together to assume responsibility for providing health insurance. In Genesee and Marquette counties, HCAP has succeeded in finding common ground for a usually contentious group of players.

The Health Care Access Project

The Health Care Access Project has two key components. The first, the one-third share plan, addresses the health insurance needs of employed individuals—like Michael Young—who do not currently have access to health care insurance. The one-third share plan offers a subsidy to businesses with 20 or fewer employees that do not offer health insurance to employees. In this manner, private insurance is made more affordable to small businesses, like the catering company, that otherwise cannot afford to offer employees insurance coverage. A sliding scale determines each employee's share of the premium. The employer must agree to pay one-third of the premium for all employees and their families. In an effort to make the program as attractive to employers as possible, they are able to choose from a wide range of comprehensive health insurance plans.

Originally, only businesses that hired a former welfare recipient were eligible for the subsidy, but the program was later expanded through open enrollment periods to include any business that had 20 or fewer employees.

The second major component of the Health Care Access Project, the Integrated General Assistance Medical program, provides comprehensive inpatient and outpatient coverage for persons on public assistance but ineligible for Medicaid. These individuals now receive a monthly identification card which entitles them to medical care offered by physicians who have agreed to participate in the program. The program also offers a four month extension of medical benefits to general assistance recipients who lose Medicaid when they become employed. This helps to ease the transition from public assistance to the work force and decreases the likelihood that people will return to public assistance solely to receive medical benefits. In an effort to strengthen the program, eligibility was recently expanded to persons who are financially, but not categorically, eligible for Medicaid.

Although the Health Care Access Project does not guarantee insurance for all employees, it does provide a new option not previously available to small business owners. The project also fills a gap in the Medicaid system that gave individuals strong economic incentive to remain on government assistance.

The Health Care Access Project is governed by an oversight committee comprised of six members representing a number of health organizations including the Michigan League for Human Services, the Michigan Primary Care Association, the Michigan Hospital Association, the Michigan State Medical Society, the Department of Social Services (DSS), and the Office of Health and Medical Affairs. The day to day operations of the HCAP are overseen by the director of the Bureau of Program Policy, a division of the DSS. Each county also has its own administrator and, of course, the support staff that actually implements the program.

History of the HCAP

Throughout the first half of the 1980s it became apparent to public officials that the problem of health insurance for the uninsured had to be addressed. The increasing number of uninsured workers and sky-rocketing insurance premiums moved the state legislature to action. The governor and several legislators held discussions on the topic. They eventually formed a task force to evaluate possible solutions to the growing problem.

In 1986, the concept of the HCAP began to take shape in the form of a grant application by the Robert Wood Johnson Foundation which had requested proposals for dealing with the uninsured. It was the Michigan League for Human Services that outlined the proposal for the HCAP and built a coalition in support of the effort.

The League applied for the 27-month grant to develop and administer the HCAP demonstration project. Vern Smith, a DSS official, was selected to be the first director of the project. Smith and members of the governor's staff worked overtime to build enthusiasm for the concept among health and human services agencies throughout the state. Initial support was strong because they recognized the need for reducing barriers to health care services.

Once funding was received for the pilot HCAP program, a newly-created oversight committee issued a request to all counties in the state for two demonstration locations for the HCAP program. In the name of fairness and intellectual curiosity, the oversight committee sought to award the program to one rural and one urban county.

In Genesee County, county health officers worked hard to organize a response to the request and build community support for the HCAP initiative. They wrote letters, lobbied politicians, and spent countless hours calling their professional peers to enlist their support. Meanwhile, local elected officials worked hard to bring the project to Genesee County.

At the same time, the Marquette County Board of Social Services and the Marquette Board of Commissioners were hard at work putting together their own application.

In May of 1987, both Genesee and Marquette counties were selected as sites for the trial HCAP program. Within one year, both the one-third share plan and the Integrated General Assistance program were enrolling participants. By January of 1990, the initial success of the program had convinced state officials to extend the HCAP program for a third year.

Considering the progress that has already been made in enrolling previously uninsured individuals in health care insurance programs, it is highly likely that the program will continue to receive vocal support from both the public and the private sectors. The question remains, however, whether or not this vocal support will be translated into continued financial support at the state level.

Funding HCAP

The HCAP is funded by state, county, and private foundation contributions. Funds are administered by the Michigan League for Human Services and the Michigan Department of Social Services. The DSS contracts with the Genesee County Health Department and the Marquette Department of Social Services for the administration and marketing of the project. All medical premiums are paid through the state DSS.

Since HCAP primarily benefits individuals with low incomes, it is primarily funded by the Michigan Department of Social Services. The total cost of operating the HCAP is approximately $9 million annually. Marquette County contributes about $100,000 per year, Genesee County contributes approximately $1.3 million and a local human services foundation contributes about $800,000 each year. The remainder is paid by DSS.

Challenges Along the Way

In both counties, getting initial support for the HCAP program was extremely challenging. Concern mounted that the project would result in a mountain of paperwork, adding to an already stressful workload at local human service agencies. Furthermore, providers wanted proof that they would receive speedy and appropriate compensation for their services. Rather than deny these concerns, each county's Health Department worked hard to develop a program that would minimize inconvenience to human services employees and ensure accurate compensation to providers. To this end, HCAP officials met with other agency officials and physicians to iron-out operational issues.

Another problem facing both counties was that the initial grant did not include funding for a marketing representative. Staff members had to work overtime to find sources of funds for the HCAP's initial marketing efforts. The marketing function was regarded as crucial to the success of the program because rapidly rising health premiums and a difficult economic environment made selling health insurance a particularly difficult task.

This difficulty was compounded by the initial decision to offer HCAP services only to businesses that hired welfare recipients. Many businesses assumed that the HCAP was only available to welfare recipients and not their co-workers. Additionally, welfare recipients were difficult to track, especially in Genesee County. Consequently, the program was broadened to apply to all businesses with 20 or fewer employees.

Although these initial obstacles were overcome, a major challenge continually faces the HCAP program. Since the general assistance portion of the HCAP is funded by the state, it must compete with other DSS programs for continued funding each year.

Preliminary Results of the Project

Considering that it has only been a little over two and one-half years since the first business enrolled in the Health Care Access Project's one-third share plan, and considering that the project has been largely viewed as a demonstration by its administrators, early results are encouraging. Over 200 businesses were enrolled in the one-third share plan by early 1991, resulting in health insurance coverage for over 1,000 employees and their families.

Efforts are being made on a daily basis to increase enrollment in the program. Each county has a full-time marketing representative who identifies eligible businesses and informs them of the services offered by the HCAP. Newspaper ads, direct mail and public service announcements have all been used to reach potential participants. HCAP is also trying to involve insurance agents in the recruiting process.

Approximately 10,000 general assistance recipients were receiving medical benefits through the HCAP by early 1991. This represents 100 percent of the eligible population, a commendable achievement for any social service program. More than 120 physicians are participating in a managed care network provided for HCAP's clients. Utilization for general assistance clients has increased by 50 percent for out patient care and by 100 percent for hospitalization so that it more closely matches state and national average utilization rates. Clearly HCAP has substantially reduced barriers to access.

In light of the early accomplishments of the HCAP, the program has received several awards including the American Public Welfare Association Successful Projects Initiative Award and an award from the Michigan Association of Public Health. Despite the successes of the HCAP, the future of the program is by no means guaranteed. A new governor with a mandate to scale back public assistance programs has targeted many state programs, including the HCAP, for possible cuts.

The Future Role of the HCAP

As the HCAP expands its services and client base over the next few years, administrators will gain insight into many of the unanswered questions surrounding health care insurance for the previously uninsured. These questions include the degree to which businesses will provide health care insurance if it is partially subsidized, the willingness of low-wage workers to pay a share of the premium, and the degree to which programs like the HCAP might be adopted on a nationwide basis.

Many of the national proposals addressing health care for the uninsured include a subsidy for small businesses that cannot afford to pay the full premium. The HCAP's experience fits well into these discussions and provides a model for how to market and administer a subsidy program to small businesses. The information gained through the HCAP demonstration will be invaluable to planners developing a national solution to spotty health care insurance coverage among low income families.

Key Lessons from the Health Care Access Project

The Health Care Access Project makes it clear that many of the lessons taken from the educational programs discussed earlier apply to the health care arena as well. For example, HCAP is organized as a public/private partnership. This organizational framework allows maximum interaction between all of the organizations that have a stake in the program. Government officials, physicians, insurance executives, and owners of small business are all represented on the HCAP oversight committee. Since the committee truly represents everyone with a stake in the program, problems can be ironed-out and disparate points of view can be considered prior to implementing new policy.

In addition, the HCAP was implemented only after formal studies were conducted to quantify the level of demand for the program. The studies were essential to the acceptance of the HCAP since it relies heavily on state funding.

The HCAP also relies on a deliberate marketing campaign to target likely users of the program (and physician providers) and increase public awareness of the benefits of the HCAP, the same purposes that drove the public awareness campaigns employed by the Extended School Program and Parents as Teachers.

The HCAP also illustrates the importance of including all parties with a stake in the program's implementation in the decision-making process. Although it is not a particularly new idea, HCAP's strategic use of demonstration sites is worth highlighting.

INCLUSION OF INTEREST GROUPS IN DECISION MAKING PROCESS. It is important to include all groups with a stake in the program in the dialogue prior to establishing a program. As is the case with the HCAP, these parties are often powerful, well-entrenched, local interests that can obstruct a program's development. Including these interest groups assures that their needs are taken into account and reduces the likelihood that they will oppose the program in the future. In the case of HCAP, the various parties with a stake in the local health insurance scene included insurance carriers who did not want undue regulation of their market, government officials who were being pressured to do something about decreasing access to insurance coverage, small businesses who were seeing the cost of providing insurance to employees sky-rocket, and physicians who were worried that they would not be adequately reimbursed for services rendered. All of these parties have been brought together on an advisory board that discusses differences of opinion and seeks to reach compromise positions. Since these differing interests are all party to the compromise solutions, they are all less likely to torpedo the HCAP concept.

DEMONSTRATION SITES. Even if overwhelming demand exists for a program, such as it did for the Health Care Access Project, it often makes sense to begin with a modest demonstration rather than unveiling the program on a large scale. The HCAP started with two demonstration sites before gaining support for a statewide program. According to officials, starting with demonstration sites had three major advantages over the alternative of a statewide push. First, the trial site proved the efficacy of the HCAP concept and broke down initial resistance to the program. The program was given a chance to prove itself to skeptics, including physicians, legislators, small business owners, and insurance company officials who might otherwise have nixed the idea. The limited demonstration was seen as less threatening than a major roll-out of a program that had not been tested and was not fully understood.

This leads us to the second major advantage of a demonstration: it gives people an opportunity to understand what the program is, and what it is not. The demonstration made it clear that despite popular perceptions to the contrary, the HCAP was aimed largely toward helping working people and their families. Furthermore, the demonstration allowed those whose cooperation would be necessary to make the program work better understand how the program works. The fears of physicians, who were worried that they would not be reimbursed for their services, were allayed by the success of the trial programs in Marquette and Genesee counties.

A third advantage is that they enable program officials to iron-out unforeseen problems and address them before the program is launched on a large scale. For example, the demonstrations revealed shortcomings in the program's physician reimbursement mechanism which were quickly remedied.

A County Insures Providers for a Good Cause: Meeting the Obstetrical Needs of Low Income Women

While many communities find it challenging to provide for the health care needs of low income people, the threat of malpractice suits make it even more difficult to meet the obstetrical needs of indigent women.

Montgomery County, Maryland, was one community faced with the prospect of losing all of its providers of low income obstetrical care. As in many other areas around the nation, Montgomery County hospitals faced soaring malpractice insurance premiums during the late 1970s and early 1980s. During an era when private hospitals were increasingly being forced to earn a reasonable financial return for their services, the increased insurance premiums forced many hospitals to close their delivery units. According to one hospital administrator, "We wanted to provide obstetrical services to all women who needed them . . . that was part of our mission as health care providers . . . but the insurance coverage for these services literally priced us out of the market. We couldn't possibly afford to continue to offer these services."

During the 1970s, there were five private hospitals in Montgomery County that provided obstetrical services for county health department clients. These clients were women who could not afford to pay for their own obstetrical needs. By 1984, two of these hospitals had ceased performing deliveries for county health department clients because of financial losses. A third hospital was too small to accommodate more than 50 indigent women per year. As a result, by the late 1980s, there were only two hospitals in the entire county providing obstetrical services for over 1,300 health department clients. County officials were certain that having only two hospitals providing obstetrical services left the community vulnerable to a health care crisis.

In the late fall of 1987, the county's worst fears were realized when one of the two remaining hospitals notified the local hospital board that it would no longer provide obstetrical services. The hospital, which had employed a small contractual obstetrical staff, found that it was no longer able to recruit additional contract obstetricians to provide delivery services. Liability insurance cost as much as $100,000 per year for each obstetrician for $1,000,000 in coverage. Combined with the relatively high risk of indigent patients having an adverse medical outcome, the barriers to providing care for women on Medicaid were too great. In addition, liability for deliveries covered individuals until they were 21 years of age, adding to the uncertainty surrounding the issue.

The county Health Department, desperate to find a solution to this unfolding crisis, was able to negotiate a contract which extended obstetrical services until October of 1988. This contract was to be replaced shortly thereafter by a long-term solution to this problem.

After months of planning and negotiations a solution was found in the form of the Montgomery County Obstetrical Program. Initiated by the county health director, the president of the Montgomery County Medical Society, and other county officials, it allows obstetricians to take advantage of the county's insurance mechanism rather than forcing them to provide for their own, costly malpractice coverage.

The obstetrical program was authorized in October of 1988 by Montgomery County officials. At that time, the program was viewed as a temporary solution to the problem of providing obstetrical care to low income women until the state could provide a statewide solution. Maryland, like many other states, has not developed a statewide approach to capping liability or providing immunity from malpractice. Instead, the state government has chosen to let each county address the problem as it chooses, thereby protecting the state from financial and liability exposure.

A legislative attempt to have the state take over the program or cap liability insurance failed in the 1989 session of the Maryland General Assembly. Another attempt was made that summer, but it also met with failure. Consequently, the obstetrical program has become an integral part of the continuum of care for indigent patients provided by the county Department of Health in combination with the obstetrical service providers participating in the program.

Potential Barriers to Success

Developing a workable solution to the obstetrical crisis facing Montgomery County was not a simple task. Three major challenges had to be overcome by the Department of Health before the program could become a reality. The first major challenge was concern surrounding liability insurance. The county agreed to provide insurance coverage for obstetricians who became part-time county employees for the period of delivery. While this removed them from the risk of lawsuits, they had to trust that the county and its legal mechanisms would adequately support them. In addition, an agreement was discussed with a major insurance company which would ensure that a doctor's activities as a program practitioner would not influence his or her future insurance premiums.

A second major challenge faced by program administrators was convincing hospitals to accept indigent patients with no payment from the county. Instead, hospitals would have to agree to rely on medical assistance reimbursements, arrange for patient fees, or accept charity cases. The hospitals agreed to participate on the condition that each hospital would share the burden proportionately according to the number of hospital births and county patients served in each hospital.

A final challenge was arranging for obstetricians to become county employees while they participated in the program. The county Personnel Office had to develop a special pay plan so that doctors would receive special pay for their employment. This required the approval of the county executive, the Merit System Protection Board, and the County Council. Additionally, the county would have to make a financial commitment to the program for salaries and insurance coverage for the obstetricians.

The Montgomery County Obstetrical Program

The Health Department now provides prenatal care to 1,300 indigent pregnant women in Montgomery County. Services are provided by full-time county physicians and nurse practitioners at five health clinics located throughout the county. Maternity patients receive a full array of community health programs offered by the department, including Women, Infants, and Children assistance (WIC), home visiting, and dental care. Services are rendered regardless of citizenship status or the ability to pay.

For the actual labor and delivery, clinic patients are assigned to one of four community hospitals in the county according to a predetermined equitable patient distribution plan agreed to by the hospital administrators. This distribution plan is based upon the percentages of total deliveries performed at each facility.

A county policy stipulates that the program covers only delivery and procedures associated with birth. Other procedures not directly associated with delivery, such as the provision of sonograms, would have to be decided upon by the patient and the obstetrician.

Private obstetricians serve as part-time health department employees during the period of labor and delivery. They are paid directly for their services and are protected from personal liability through the county's self-insurance program. By 1992, 92 obstetricians had become part-time county employees and more than 2,800 babies had been delivered.

Substantial efforts are made by health officials to inform women of the obstetrical programs offered by the county. Information about the maternity program is dispersed through brochures, a variety of public and private health organizations, public assistance agencies, and nurses in the local public schools. Most importantly, clients themselves make referrals. The campaign to inform potential patients has met with great success. Based on the estimates of potential clients in Montgomery County, the program is currently serving almost 90 percent of the eligible population. The racial composition of the women served by the program has remained fairly stable since its inception: 33.6 percent white; 31.5 percent black; 28.5 percent Hispanic; and 5.7 percent Asian.

The total obstetrical program cost for the fiscal year 1992 was approximately $976,000. The lion's share of this budget ($658,000) was allocated toward obstetrician salaries. About $318,000 went toward risk management charges. At present, 52 percent of the budget is funded by the county, and 46.8 percent is funded by Medicaid reimbursement and patient fees. Hospitals collect Medicaid for eligible patients or fees from patients, if possible. For those patients unable to pay, the hospitals render the services on a charitable basis.

The obstetricians receive reimbursement for their services at a rate of $720 per delivery. The county collects $895 per delivery from Medicaid. The difference between these two amounts helps to pay for services provided to indigent women who are not eligible for Medicaid, primarily undocumented immigrants.

Organization of the Obstetrical Program

Montgomery County's entire maternity and obstetrical program is administered by the health department's Division of Family Health Services Maternity Program. Four separate hospital boards provide policy guidance as it relates to their own hospital's participation in the program. The boards work closely with the Health Department to ensure that the needs of patients and obstetricians are being met.

The Medical Society provides the necessary leadership within the medical community to garner support for the obstetrical and related maternity programs. The Medical Society was instrumental in assisting the county to work with the obstetricians to determine what obstacles stood in the way of the program's development and finding solutions to overcome them.

There is one contractual relationship that is especially pertinent to the obstetrical program. In order for one group of obstetricians to participate in the program, the Health Department had to comply with the desire of their employer, Kaiser Permanente, to be paid directly for services rendered rather than the individual obstetricians who were their employees. A contractual agreement was reached between the county and Kaiser to clarify the arrangement.

Results of the Obstetrical Program

During its first three years of operation, the program has provided quality maternity services to all indigent women in the county who have needed them. *Not a single patient has been turned away.* Importantly, while litigation had been seen as the primary barrier to serving indigent pregnant women, there have been no lawsuits. In fact, there have been few complaints.

The number of women served has steadily increased over the short life of the program. In 1988, 850 women were provided with delivery services. In 1989, this number jumped to 1,270. At present, over 2,800 babies have been delivered.

Another indication of the program's success is the steadily increasing number of obstetricians participating in the program. At the program's inception, there were only 40 doctors signed up to participate. At present, about 92 obstetricians are participating in the program, nearly 75 percent of all obstetricians in the county.

The Future of the Obstetrical Program

It is anticipated that the number of patients eligible for the obstetrical program will increase dramatically over the next five years. Recent studies conducted by the county Health Department show that nearly 10 percent of county maternity patients use dangerous drugs at some point during their pregnancy, risking both their own health and the health of their babies. Not only will the number of pregnant women using drugs increase, but the number of babies born addicted to illegal substances will likely increase. Indigent women will increasingly find themselves facing complex social issues such as homelessness, dysfunctional family units, lack of income, and an inability to earn a living. All of these problems will guarantee their status as at-risk patients during pregnancy.

The obstetrical program is expected to respond to the increasing number of patients by expanding its services. The hospitals participating in the program have already accepted increased responsibility and have encouraged their obstetricians to participate in the program. Plans are underway to increase the number of doctors participating in a voluntary, on-call service.

The Health Department is working closely with the hospitals and other agencies to expand the range of services provided to health department clients. This is possible as a result of the close relationships which have developed between the Health Department and the hospitals as a result of the obstetrical program. Since women who use the obstetrical services often suffer from other problems, including drug abuse, the Health Department wants to offer women assistance in these other areas.

A new program to be offered teaches women how to take better care of their children once they are born. The focus of the program is accident prevention, since accidents are the leading cause of death among small children.

Key Lessons from the Obstetrical Program

The experiences of the Montgomery County Department of Health serve to underscore the value of public/private partnerships in solving today's complex, multifaceted problems. The obstetrical program benefits from the close working relationship between the county Health Department, health care providers, and local hospitals. Not only does the public/private partnership form of organization maximize communiation between all of the key participants in the program, it ensures that the interests of each party are being taken into account.

In addition to emphasizing the value of partnerships, the obstetrical program also provides another example of how a program can benefit from visible public awareness efforts. Dispersing information about the program through brochures, public and private health organizations, public assistance agencies, and nurses in the local public schools has helped the obstetrical program reach nearly 100 percent of its target population.

Setting a Precedent:
The Healthy Start Program

In 1984, public health officials in Massachusetts were shocked to learn that the statewide infant mortality rate had increased for the first time in over a decade. This finding was cause for concern among health experts and politicians alike because infant mortality (which includes the death of all infants under one year of age) is widely recognized as an important and sensitive indicator of a population's health status and general well being.

Further examination of the mortality statistics revealed an even more troubling story: the death rate for black infants was twice that of white infants. Moreover, poor, minority, and undereducated populations accounted for the bulk of the sharp increase in infant deaths. Contributing to this trend was the finding that poor, minority, and teenage women were much less likely than other populations to receive adequate prenatal care.

In response to the increased mortality rates, a task force was convened to explain the sudden reversal in infant mortality rates. The task force identified several barriers to prenatal care for high risk groups such as minorities, teenagers, and low-income families. Prominent among these barriers was the relatively high cost of prenatal care which prevented many women in these groups from seeking early and continuous health care. Women and families that did not have regular access to health care were found to delay initiation of care, skip expensive but important laboratory tests, and miss appointments rather than face high out-of-pocket costs.

While Medicaid covered very poor women and private insurance covered higher income groups, many pregnant women were caught in the middle. Consider the case of Tracy Dixon. At 22, Ms. Dixon was a high school dropout working in a Boston fast-food restaurant. Because she only worked part-time, her employer did not offer her health insurance coverage. But on her salary of $5.25 per hour, Tracy could not afford private insurance. By the time she was seven months pregnant, Tracy had seen a doctor only once. "I wanted to go sooner," she says, "but no way could I pay for it."

In addition to women like Tracy who do not have work-related health insurance and cannot afford private insurance, many women are denied access to prenatal care because they are switching jobs or are employed on an intermittent basis.

The task force developed a comprehensive plan of action for improving maternity and infant care for people like Tracy. This plan called for state, local, and community leaders to work together to "close the gaps in health status" among the different populations of women and infants. A major recommendation of the task force was to urge that an entitlement program be developed for all pregnant women without insurance. This payor of the last resort program for uninsured women would cover prenatal, delivery, and postpartum care.

The Massachusetts Legislature acted quickly to implement the task force's recommendations by establishing the Healthy Start Program. This initiative greatly improved the means of financing and delivering maternity care for low income women. Along with additional funds for prenatal clinics and initiation of community coalitions in high risk areas, the new legislation established a new public health payment program for women without insurance. Staff in the Department of Public Health and the Department of Public Welfare assumed responsibility for rapidly developing and implementing this program.

Today, Healthy Start stands as a national model for improving the health care provided to uninsured women. Since Healthy Start's inception, several other states have begun to develop similar programs. The National Governor's Association, The Institute of Medicine, and the Children's Defense Fund have all looked to Healthy Start for policy direction in the area of prenatal care.

The Healthy Start Program

After five months of intensive planning, the Healthy Start Program opened its doors for applications in December of 1985. The purpose of the program is to improve birth outcomes by encouraging ongoing, comprehensive prenatal care. The cornerstone of the program is the philosophy that paying for services is only the first step in promoting healthy birth outcomes. Outreach, effective case management, client advocacy, meaningful community education, and a program entirely designed to be receptive to women in crisis make Healthy Start much more than a payment program. Instead, it elevates it to the status of a unique, comprehensive public health program.

Women can enroll in the Healthy Start program by calling a statewide, toll-free number or by mailing an application directly to the central office. All maternity hospitals, health centers, and many private physicians offer assistance to women in filling out the application form. Currently, about 3,000 health care providers submit claims to Healthy Start. The program has five regional offices which provide case management and follow-up services to clients. Often, clients are referred to other related health care programs that offer services not provided by Healthy Start. Staff members also work with health care providers to make certain that their needs are met and their questions are answered.

Healthy Start serves about 5,000 women per year, about 80 percent of all uninsured pregnant women in the state. Of the women who meet the program eligibility criteria, an estimatetd 90 percent eventually apply to Healthy Start. To be eligible for Healthy Start, women residing in Massachusetts must be ineligible for Medicaid, not have private insurance, and have a family income less than 200 percent of the federal poverty level.

The program pays for prenatal, delivery, and postpartum care. It also covers costs related to pharmacy, laboratory, and pregnancy-related ancillary services and guarantees payment of inpatient services. The program emphasizes case management and provides follow-up services through regionally based staff members. Intake workers also provide extensive information to new clients about the Healthy Start Program and make any necessary referrals to other health care programs throughout the state.

The Healthy Start Program is funded entirely by state appropriations. Although the program has been receiving $10 million each year, recent statewide budget cuts may force the program to operate on as little as half that amount in the near future. About 90 percent of Healthy Start's budget goes toward paying for services rendered to clients. The remaining 10 percent is allocated toward administrative costs, including salaries for about 40 full-time staff members. The current cost per client is about $1,700. The lion's share of this cost goes toward reimbursing physicians for their services to Healthy Start clients, and the remainder goes toward laboratory tests, pharmacies, and other ancillary services.

The health care objectives of Healthy Start are fulfilled by a regional, grass roots outreach system complimented by a media campaign to inform women about the program. Virtually all public assistance and all public health agencies refer women to the program. Initial publicity campaigns were so successful that in the first year of operation nearly 85 percent of all eligible women enrolled. Such participation rates are extremely rare for any new public sector program.

The most important achievement of the Healthy Start Program has been the direct improvement of birth outcomes for women who participate in the program. A recent evaluation of the Healthy Start Program indicated that the program had a positive impact on birth weight and premature birth rates. Healthy Start clients had a lower rate of low birth weight babies than women with private insurance. The evaluation also found that Healthy Start clients had fewer premature births than women on Medicaid or with private health insurance.

The Future of Similar Programs

Healthy Start was the first program in the nation to provide health care to pregnant women without insurance. Since it began operating in 1984, program staff members have assisted in the development of similar programs in other states, including New York, Rhode Island, and Maryland. Few states have programs that are as comprehensive as that in Massachusetts.

Healthy Start administrators believe that the entire program can be replicated in any state provided that there is a willingness to commit the necessary resources and funds.

In the future, programs like Healthy Start will need to continue to work closely with Medicaid authorities because such programs, by their very nature, must work in tandem with the Medicaid eligibility structure. It may be easier in some states than others to implement services like Healthy Start due to differences in malpractice costs and a shortage of rural physicians. Nonetheless, there are probably no obstacles short of a lack of commitment that would actually prevent a Healthy Start initiative from succeeding.

Key Lessons from the Healthy Start Program

The innovations behind the success of the program are its holistic approach to promoting healthy birth outcomes and its focus on the needs of the program's clients. In addition, Healthy Start was able to reach a high percentage (85 percent) of its target population during its first year of operation because of a sophisticated public awareness/client outreach campaign.

Recall that the Public/Private Partnerships in Education Program was holistic in that it focused on the causes of poverty and educational underachievement that led to poor academic performance, rather than just focusing on the symptoms. The Partnerships program achieved this broad focus by enlisting the services of child development agencies, social service organizations, as well as educators. In this manner, the program targeted the root causes of poor academic performance, often before the child ever entered a school. Similarly, the Healthy Start Program attempts to head off poor health outcomes in children by educating parents to seek early and regular health care during pregnancy. To accomplish this, the program takes on the form of a comprehensive health program and enlists the help of case managers and client advocates to educate pregnant women about the importance of regular health care.

Healthy Start uses similar means to attract the attention of potential clients. All maternity hospitals, health centers, and many private physicians have program applications, and most are willing to assist women in filling them out. Women can enroll in the program by calling a statewide, toll-free number or by mailing an application directly to the central office. The success of Healthy Start in reaching clients suggests that such relatively simple methods can be quite effective in getting the word out about a program.

An Inexpensive Approach to Drug Treatment: The Child Abuse Prevention Project

Increasingly, state and local governments are finding it necessary to allocate more resources toward the prevention and treatment of drug abuse.

A pervasive and particularly troubling element of the drug abuse problem is the increasing number of babies who are born addicted to drugs, often with fatal consequences. Babies that survive the trauma of low birth weight and addiction usually require extensive and costly medical treatment. In many cases, this treatment will last for years and the burden of payment will rest with taxpayers. Once they reach school age, children born drug dependent are often subject to learning disabilities and chronically poor health. Once again, the taxpayers foot the bill.

One of the most effective means of treating drug abusers is through residential facilities. Typically, residents spend anywhere from three weeks to three months in such facilities. They are, however, expensive to maintain and are beyond the financial capability of many communities. In addition, they can often accommodate only a limited number of residents. Accordingly, it is worthwhile to briefly outline an alternative to residential programs that has also been proven effective in the treatment and prevention of drug abuse.

The Child Abuse Prevention Project, operated by the state of Arizona, provides an excellent example of one such alternative. This initiative is geared toward the needs of chemically dependent women and infants. It is different from residential programs in that it gives families the information they need to steer themselves to treatment rather than providing the treatment directly through a residential facility. Although this program is also geared toward families with infants, the basic structure of the program would be effective for any category of drug abusers.

The Child Abuse Prevention Project

The purpose of the Child Abuse Prevention Project is to provide services to families where the infant or the mother have a positive drug screen at the time of the infant's birth. There are currently about 50 families being served by the project. Since its implementation in February of 1989, nearly 200 families have received assistance through the program.

The program identifies and selects its clients by receiving referrals from the Department of Child Protective Services. The hospitals make these referrals when they suspect substance abuse, when the mother admits to substance abuse, or when the mother or infant test positive for drugs or alcohol. Originally designed to reduce child abuse, a disheartening by-product of drug use, the program provides a wide variety of services geared toward fostering a healthy family environment.

Unlike residential treatment programs, the Child Abuse Prevention Project operates within the family's own home environment. The most important element of the program is its complement of professional parent aides who serve as advocates and counselors to the families participating in the program.

When making house calls, the parent aides offer one-on-one assistance which helps families obtain the basic necessities of life, including adequate and appropriate food, clothing, shelter, transportation, and assistance in obtaining medical care for the infants. The parent aides, who work for the Department of Child Protective Services on a contractual basis, also monitor the growth and weight of infants in an effort to detect any early warning signs of potential problems.

For the most part, the parent aides provide information by accessing a wide variety of community social service agencies that already exist. In this manner, the program takes full advantage of resources that are already in place.

The goal of the Child Abuse Prevention Project is to help families obtain the basic necessities of life and perform more effectively as parents. The program's administrators believe that when this happens the client's need for drugs will be reduced, and they will be more motivated to enter a drug treatment program. Consequently, a major part of the program is aimed at educating parents about the effects of substance abuse on the family and the variety of treatment alternatives that are available. Efforts are made by parent aides to connect clients with resources available in the community so that they will be better able to utilize them *before* a crisis arises.

The project tries to reduce the number of children removed from their homes and placed in foster care. In the view of the program's administrators, removing children creates a potentially huge burden for the state and provides the child with a less than ideal environment for personal growth and achievement. The project also seeks to prevent the need for further involvement by the Department of Child Protective Services by fostering a stable home environment for the parents and the child.

In addition to using existing services to meet the needs of families in crisis, the project is innovative because services are provided to infants and their families in a preventative mode rather than a reactive mode. By successfully heading off potential problems associated with parental drug abuse, the likelihood of the child being exposed to abuse or neglect is reduced.

Developing the Program

The Child Abuse Prevention Project was conceived and instituted in February of 1989. The initial planning committee consisted of staff members from the Department of Child Protective Services and agencies already providing in-home support services (parent aide, counseling, and parenting classes) to clients of the Department of Child Protective Services. Planning and design was accomplished by Child Protective Services and then presented to the provider agencies for revision and approval. The input of the provider agencies was critical in the development of the program because they provided the only direct client contact. Child Protective Services has direct contact with the clients only in the case that the client is referred back to the agency for more intensive involvement. This team approach, which utilizes Child Protective Services as the case manager and the contractual service agencies as the direct service providers, has created an environment of enhanced cooperation and sharing of information among state agencies.

The clients themselves made major contributions to the development of the program by offering their input and outlining their needs for program administrators. This input is still solicited and is viewed as very important to the future of the program since the program must continually adapt to the current environment.

Contracted agencies met with the Child Protective Services staff on a weekly basis to work through concerns and refine referral and service procedures. Formal project reviews were scheduled quarterly. The original case load was managed by one child protective services worker who managed up to 35 cases and carried up to ten court cases at one time. At present, there are approximately seven full-time case workers and seven agencies participating in the program on a contractual basis. These agencies include nurseries, family service agencies, parenting organizations, and institutions that focus on minority issues.

Aside from the staff of the Department of Child Protective Services, the strongest supporters of the project have been the community agencies providing the services and local hospitals. These agencies and hospitals have been supportive because they recognize the future implications of the drug abuse and child neglect problems and have allocated substantial resources toward solving them. Clients have also shown strong support for the program. They particularly like the fact that the project emphasizes positive support rather than punitive action.

Since this initiative is relatively new, there is a strong likelihood that it will undergo substantial changes. Program officials are currently considering ways to make the program more cost-effective, including awarding exclusive contracts to private agencies which would administer the program under the guidance of the Child Protective Services. Regardless of its final format, the program will continue to emphasize preventative measures.

Assessing the Results: Early Indicators

The single most important achievement of the Child Abuse Prevention Project, according to those who run it, has been the recognition that child abuse and neglect as a result of parental drug addiction is a major societal problem with unknown future implications. The partnership approach used by the Department of Child Protective Services and the participating agencies that provide the direct client services has increased the state's awareness of the problem. Furthermore, the project has taken important steps toward providing a well-organized, government-sponsored solution.

The most tangible means of evaluating the program's success is to examine recidivism rates of participating families to Child Protective Services and tracking the number of children placed in foster care who were previously referred to the project. A recent study of the first 105 families who participated in the program shows that 53 cases were closed, 31 cases are still being processed by the project, and only 21 cases required additional services form the Department of Child Protective Services.

A major shortcoming of the program, according to officials involved in the program, is that Child Protective Services has no authority to require families to participate in the program. This is due primarily to substance-exposed infants not being included in the state's child abuse statutes. Administrators believe that many of the families who are most in need of the services provided by the Child Abuse Prevention Project are not participating, and are thus more likely to be referred to Child Protective Services in the future under less fortunate circumstances.

Adapting the Project to Other Jurisdictions

The Child Abuse Prevention Project appears to be very well suited toward other jurisdictions. In fact, the state of Arizona began the program as a pilot project in one area and then adapted it to other areas. The program is generic in its scope and nature, and thus could be replicated easily, provided that child protective service agencies are willing to recognize the problem and have the capacity to investigate referrals. Moreover, it is necessary for community agencies to be willing to participate in the program on a case management basis.

Since drug abuse and substance-exposed infants represent a growing problem throughout the United States, it is likely that social service agencies at the state and local level will increasingly create programs to address these issues. The Child Abuse Prevention Project represents one viable and readily available solution.

Key Lessons from the Child Abuse Prevention Project

The Child Abuse Prevention Project utilizes some of the most important elements that we have identified in other successful programs. Specifically, the project reinforces the importance of using an holistic approach to problem solving and underscores the value of client-orientation. The project also provides a good example of a successful strategic alliance between Department of Child Protective Services and agencies already providing in-home support services.

COST-EFFECTIVENESS BY PREVENTION. Previous discussions of cost-effectiveness have suggested that it can be derived from a number of sources: use of existing resources, bulk purchasing, reliance on volunteer labor, and pre-negotiated fees. While the Child Abuse Prevention Project takes advantage of one of these means, namely use of existing resources through the use of agencies that already provide in-home counseling services, it also introduces us to an important new source of cost-effectiveness: Prevention.

By heading off potential problems associated with parental drug abuse, the likelihood of a child being exposed to abuse or neglect is reduced. By helping families before abuse begins, the project prevents future involvement of the Department of Child Protective Services by removing the possibility that the agency will have to take the children from their homes and place them in foster care after they have been abused. Not only is foster care expensive in terms of tax dollars, but it also places a mental cost on the child. The preemptive nature of the project seeks to eliminate both of these costs by eliminating the source of the problem before it has a chance to take hold.

Chapter 4

Environmental Management

We have forgotten how to be good guests,
how to walk lightly on the earth as other creatures do.
—1972 Only One Earth Conference.

The environmental problems facing the United States have received increased prominence in recent years. This heightened attention, which mani-
fests itself in the press, public debate, and political forums, has resulted from
increased knowledge about the dangers of mismanaging the environment.
Health concerns, costs associated with cleaning up the environment, and prospects for permanent damage to our fragile ecosystem have all helped to push
environmental concerns towards the top of the public policy agenda.

Disposing of solid waste, curbing pollution, and conserving scarce
resources have become important priorities in virtually every community.
Many state and local governments have spearheaded new and exciting approaches which offer important solutions to the problems, from technological
innovation to hands-on assistance with environmental issues.

The need for innovative approaches is mandated by the magnitude of the
task at hand. For example, many cities and towns are finding it difficult to
dispose of an increased amount of garbage, creating a major crisis for some
communities that have little or no space left in municipal landfills. Complicating matters further, there is vocal opposition to the construction of new
waste facilities in many of these communities. The prospects for relief in the
absence of innovative solutions are bleak: total garbage "thrown away" is projected to increase by 20 percent, to 216 tons, by the end of the decade.[27]

There is some good news. As disposal capacity has become swamped by
waste generation, many state and local governments have developed promising programs which address community needs. Many communities have turned
to new means of waste management to prolong the life of existing landfills.
Other communities faced with solid waste disposal problems rely on aggressive recycling programs in hope of reducing the amount of waste generated.
Despite the early successes of these innovative programs, much remains to be

done. It is estimated that nearly 90 percent of all solid waste material could be recycled to some degree.[28] At present, Americans recycle only about 24 percent of their garbage. This effort pales in comparison with European countries and Japan where nearly 40 percent of all solid waste is recycled.[29] Thus, it is important that communities across the country notice and appreciate the results of the innovative programs discussed in this chapter.

Despite its importance, solid waste disposal is only one of many environmental problems facing state and local governments. Pollution, for example, is also a persistent problem. Two decades after the passage of the Clean Air Act, nearly 100 urban areas are not yet in compliance with the original air pollutions standards mandated by the act.[30] Severe pollution of waterways is also a concern in many communities. Another issue facing some communities is the management of scarce resources. Even the most basic natural resources, such as drinking water, are in short supply in some areas. Thus, many communities are developing innovative schemes to conserve limited resources.

This chapter provides a close look at a sample of innovative programs which exist to counter the environmental problems. These programs are making measurable progress in the areas of environmental regulation, solid waste management, pollution control, and resource conservation.

The chapter begins with a description of the Environmental Compliance Service. While this program is not geared toward any one environmental problem, it does provide an excellent example of how local governments can help businesses meet mandated environmental standards by providing information and technical assistance.

The Landfill Reclamation Project illustrates how one jurisdiction has skillfully addressed the problem of solid waste disposal by extending the life of its existing landfills while at the same time making them more environmentally sound.

A description of the municipal recycling program in Seattle provides an inside look at one of the nation's most promising municipal efforts to recycle a variety of solid wastes which might have otherwise been sent to the local landfill. While it is a relatively comprehensive program, elements could be adapted in nearly any community.

The Water Pollution Control Program offers a unique solution to the problem of water pollution. This initiative offers a relatively inexpensive alternative to water quality testing and enforcement procedures, suggesting a model for virtually all municipalities, regardless of their budget.

Finally, a discussion of the IQ Water Program illustrates a cost-effective means of conserving a limited resource: potable water. This program demonstrates that innovative thinking can result in practical and cost-effective conservation methods.

All of the programs discussed in this chapter serve as effective models for jurisdictions seeking solutions to major environmental issues. At the very least, they serve as proof that answers to the nation's toughest environmental problems are being developed at the state and local level.

Helping Businesses Clean Up: The Environmental Compliance Service Program

A common perception among many policy makers is that tough environmental regulation is tantamount to ensuring environmentally sound business practices. All too often, however, businesses are not given the guidance they need to understand and comply with federal, state, and local environmental standards. Many business owners who would like to comply with the regulations are not even aware that they exist. Others lack the technical assistance to meet the standards. This is particularly the case among smaller businesses which are often overlooked by the regulatory process.

Consider the case of Boris Schnellmacher. An immigrant from Germany, Mr. Schnellmacher had established a successful dry cleaning outlet in New York. Over the course of several years, he had purchased several additional outlets. It eventually became a priority of Mr. Schnellmacher's to build his own dry cleaning factory rather than sending all of his cleaning to other plants. Among the many obstacles he faced was the issue of environmental compliance. "I was surprised how complex the [environmental] regulations were. Different agencies gave me different answers to the same questions about regulations. I was frustrated and confused," says Mr. Schnellmacher. "I did not know where to go for help."

After confiding in a friend who was also in the dry cleaning business, Mr. Schnellmacher was put in touch with the Environmental Compliance Service (ECS) program of Erie County, New York. According to Mr. Schnellmacher, "The service saved my plans to operate the plant."

The award-winning[31] ECS improves the quality of life in the Buffalo, New York, vicinity by helping local businesses, especially smaller ones, understand and achieve economical and effective compliance with environmental mandates. While the program helps business owners like Mr. Schnellmacher overcome regulatory obstacles, the ultimate goal of the program is to ensure that Erie County residents enjoy a cleaner and better living environment as a result of increased rates of environmental compliance among businesses. This environmental program both fosters a friendlier climate for businesses and helps to reduce the amount of pollution in the environment.

The Environmental Compliance Service Program

The ECS program attacks pollution from several fronts, including cleaning up hazardous waste disposal sites, reducing air pollution from solvent emissions, and reducing dust and odor nuisances near home sites. In all cases, results are achieved by a partnership between businesses and local public officials.

Program managers assist clients by identifying environmental issues which might have an impact on their businesses and informing them of the services provided by ECS. Once clients are enlisted, they are provided with technical assistance, clarification of regulations and permit requirements, and identification of the permits and approvals which are needed. In the latter case, ECS helps businesses obtain approval of applications for air, wastewater, and hazardous waste regulatory permits.

The most important means of reaching clients is through workshops, bulletins, and guidebooks. In 1991 nearly 1,400 organizations attended ECS-sponsored workshops, up from about 200 in 1985. The workshops cover topics such as bulk chemical storage and the environmental aspects of buying and selling properties. Workshops are held at easily accessible locations, such as nearby colleges, the local convention center, and other downtown facilities.

Environmental Compliance Service bulletins are mailed to targeted businesses and are designed to deal with specific topics in detail. For example, a bulletin explaining the process of removing underground petroleum storage tanks was sent to 3,000 tank owners. In addition, officials sent special mailings targeted toward dry cleaners, vehicle maintenance shops, metal manufacturers, printing companies, and educational and vocational institutions. The bulletins speak in the language of each industry, making it easier for businesses to understand potentially complex regulatory procedures. In 1991, ECS received about 300 requests for more assistance from businesses which had received bulletins. This represented a three-fold increase since 1985.

In addition to workshops and bulletins, ECS relies on guidebooks to reach its clients. Guidebooks provide a valuable reference on a full range of environmental topics, including hazardous waste regulations, environmental permit requirements, and environmental aspects of real property transfers. As is the case with the bulletins, the guidebooks are geared toward specific industries.

Although its focus is clearly on helping local businesses achieve regulatory compliance, the ECS also helps public agencies and community organizations obtain environmental permits, solve problems with pollution control equipment, and evaluate alternatives for waste disposal and recycling. The program's clients include an estimated 3,000 businesses, 25 county agencies, and 44 municipal governments. Economic development agencies, banks, attorneys, state and federal agencies, school districts, and private citizens also receive regular assistance.

Clients are identified in several ways. Many are referred to ECS through regulatory permit renewal notices or referrals from other public agencies. Others respond to ECS environmental bulletins, word of mouth, or referrals from other clients. The organization maintains a good working relationship with state and federal compliance agencies which often results in referrals. According to one Environmental Protection Agency official, "ECS activities directly dovetail with [federal] programs. We get lots of calls about potential polluters . . . more than we can handle . . . and ECS can help bring those offenders into compliance with the law."

Once clients are identified, they are prioritized based on the nature and scope of their problem. The ECS generally gives priority to cases with immediate problems, such as permit applications and need for clarification on rules and regulations. Clients with problems outside the scope of the ECS program are referred to other agencies or to private sector professionals.

The Environmental Compliance Service differs from other environmental regulation agencies because it emphasizes preventative actions rather than enforcement. The program complements state and local regulatory agencies by emphasizing cooperation, pollution prevention, and compliance promotion. The ECS administrators proudly refer to the service as a "how-to" rather than a "what-to-do" program because of its focus on guiding businesses toward compliance instead of just setting standards and leaving it to the businesses to comply with them. In its capacity as a how-to program, ECS assists clients in filling out permit applications, evaluating environmental problems, suggesting alternative solutions, and preparing and presenting data to regulatory agencies.

The ECS program is different from most university and government-sponsored technical assistance programs because it is not limited to a narrow range of assistance. A client who calls and asks for help with an air pollution problem, for example, may also be offered assistance with water and hazardous waste issues. Furthermore, the ECS staff has a large network of environmental and economic development contacts which broadens the spectrum of help which can be provided. These contacts include agencies which provide assistance with business, finance, regulatory, technical, and educational issues.

Supporters of ECS believe that it has a positive impact on local economic development. It supports Buffalo-area economic recovery efforts by helping existing companies solve environmental problems. It also helps new companies obtain regulatory permits and evaluate potential development sites. For example, ECS recently helped a small printing company find a location for its plant which would make it relatively easy to comply with chemical disposal requirements. Additionally, ECS helped the company's managers understand which permits were required to operate the plant.

Program officials believe that their assistance makes the Buffalo area a more attractive location for new businesses. Indeed, many of ECS's clients credit the program with easing the regulatory and start-up process. "ECS was instrumental in our decision to locate [the plant] on its current site" says one printing company official. "They saved us money in the long run . . . more importantly they saved us grief in the short run by clarifying the rules." The success of the public-private partnership fostered by the ECS program serves to demonstrate that a clean environment and economic prosperity are not mutually exclusive.

As with many innovative programs, ECS tries to be a proactive marketer, aggressively searching for clients. Officials conduct extensive outreach efforts to identify environmental issues and promote the program's services to potential clients. These efforts include direct mailings, telephone calls, and even occasional site visits by ECS personnel. Efforts are concentrated on those businesses and organizations which could benefit most from assistance.

The total budget for the ECS program is approximately $500,000, about 80 percent of which comes from local property taxes. It is the only business assistance program in the Buffalo-area supported primarily through property taxes. The remaining 20 percent of the budget is funded through state and community grants.

History of the Environmental Compliance Service

Although ECS was not formally founded until 1984, its history dates back nearly 20 years to the old Erie County Division of Environmental Control (a division of the Department of Environment and Planning). The staff of the Division of Environmental Control had long helped local businesses to translate the regulatory jargon of technical regulations into understandable language, but it offered little technical assistance. The technical assistance program took on its own identity as the result of a federal grant to support a three-year program aimed at reducing the amount of air pollution in Erie County. The three-year demonstration program was initiated by the federal government in eight major cities that suffered a severe economic decline in the late 1970s as a result of the Clean Air Act.

Of the eight programs originally funded, the Erie County effort was the only one adopted at the end of the demonstration period and funded by the local government. It was clearly demonstrated to the county government and to the business community that local government can play a key role in achieving clean air and economic prosperity. As a result, the Industrial Assistance Program (IAP) was established in 1982 to help companies understand an array of environmental regulations and to provide technical support.

By 1984, the Erie County Legislature decided that county government could best serve the local economic development needs and the environmental quality goals of the community with an extended IAP. This more comprehensive program included additional staff and expanded educational opportunities. In 1986, the program was renamed the Environmental Compliance Service (ECS) when most of the staff was assigned to technical assistance and education activities. In 1988, the county administration officially amended the county charter, eliminating the Division of Environmental Control and replacing it with the newly created Division of Environmental Compliance. This significant change is primarily attributed to the program's extremely dedicated staff and their demonstrated success in achieving community support and consensus for all ECS activities.

The rapid growth of the program since 1988 has not been without pitfalls. Immediately after the founding of ECS, the lack of initial funding and reluctance on the part of some businesses to take advantage of ECS services provided staff members with substantial challenges. The funding problem was quickly overcome by using state and federal grants to support the program until it was established. Nonetheless, lack of funds to expand the program and provide services to a larger portion of the community continues to be a challenge. The reluctance on the part of some business owners to use ECS services quickly waned once ECS had time to promote its benefits and services to potential clients. The county economic development coordinator provided the program direct contact with area businesses and acted as liaison with many companies that were skeptical of ECS in its early stages. This cooperative effort was instrumental in overcoming the hesitations of local business operators. The owner of a small dry-cleaning plant, for example, was originally skeptical about the role of ECS: "I had heard rumblings about a locally-based pollution program. Frankly, I was unimpressed. Based on past experience, I was certain that the program would only be for the big guns . . . not for little guys like me. One day I got a pamphlet from ECS specifically targeted toward my type of business. It really helped me understand the rules, especially when I found out I could talk to experts in person."

Such successful cases helped ECS establish a positive rapport with the entire business community. Cosponsorship of programs with trade organizations has also contributed to the current level of cooperation and trust.

ECS Reporting Relationships

The Environmental Compliance Service is one of four divisions within the Erie County Department of Environment and Planning (DEP). The three other divisions (Planning, Sewerage Management, and Economic Development) assist ECS in obtaining information and solving technical problems.

The principal goal of DEP is to ensure that the planning and implementation of development projects are consistent with county-wide objectives related to environmental protection, energy conservation, and economic development.

The Director of the Environmental Compliance Service reports directly to the Commissioner of DEP. The Commissioner approves annual budgets and program plans submitted by the ECS Director. The DEP budget, once finalized by the DEP Commissioner, is sent to the Erie County Legislature for final passage.

The ECS cosponsors many of its outreach and educational programs with other organizations. These organizations provide a great deal of input into the development of programs which they co-sponsor. Institutions providing input include professional associations, research centers, state agencies, local trade organizations, and the local Bar Association.

Future Plans for the ECS

Over the next five years environmental requirements will become more stringent. They will be imposed on more types of businesses, including small businesses. In addition, community-based environmental groups will put more pressure on the business community to strive for increased environmental awareness. Accordingly, the ECS approach to pollution prevention and compliance promotion will be expanded in Erie County and duplicated by local governments across the nation.

The Environmental Compliance Service Program responded by establishing the Erie County Environmental Education Institute, a non-profit organization dedicated to enhancing the services offered by ECS. The education institute will be jointly funded and directed by private and public interests. This type of partnership is an encouraging sign that communities are increasingly recognizing that a clean environment and economic prosperity are not mutually exclusive and that both the private and the public sectors have an important role to play in environmental management. The widespread interest in the ECS program serves to underscore the increasing awareness among communities that future economic development must not come at the expense of the environment. Communities will need programs like ECS to help businesses understand and comply with new environmental standards.

Information on ECS has been publicized and shared with several other local governments as a result of an award from the National Association of Counties and publicity in magazines and trade publications. Interest in the ECS approach is not, however, limited to domestic governments. The economic development director of Melbourne, Australia, has visited Erie County to investigate the feasibility of establishing a similar program in Australia.

Key Lessons from the Environmental Compliance Service

Officials of the ECS suggest that three lessons can be derived from the program's success: extensive outreach efforts help to identify environmental issues and promote the program's services to potential clients; the ECS's broad service enables it to deal with most environmental issues that are relevant to small and medium sized businesses; and the program's focus on preventative measures and solutions to complex problems yields better results than just focusing on violations and enforcement.

OUTREACH EFFORTS. The ECS publicly markets its programs and actively solicits clients rather than waiting for clients to come to them. Unlike some other programs, ECS uses direct mailings and workshops to inform potential clients of services rather than recruiting door-to-door or through related service agencies.

BROAD RANGE OF SERVICES. The ECS is a comprehensive operation which provides clients with services ranging from information to hands-on technical assistance. In this manner, the program is characterized by a coordinated service approach that is similar to many other programs.

FOCUS ON PROBLEM PREVENTION. The defining attribute of ECS, according to those who administer the program, is that it focuses on preventative actions rather than on after-the-fact enforcement. Officials believe that such a proactive approach to pollution control ultimately reduces the amount of pollutants in the local environment. Many businesses that might not otherwise be in compliance with environmental standards (or even aware that they exist) are brought into the program. Furthermore, enforcement is a costly and relatively ineffective means of ensuring environmental compliance unless substantial resources can be devoted to such efforts.

Extending the Usefulness of Landfills: The Landfill Reclamation Project

As an increasing number of landfills across the nation are reaching capacity and are being closed, new concerns are being raised about the hazards which they pose to the surrounding environment. In particular, many jurisdictions are discovering that their landfills, even those that are closed, are potentially harmful to underground water sources. Although the Superfund legislation enacted by Congress was supposed to clean up many of these sites, only a small fraction have actually been neutralized. Consequently, some local governments are taking the initiative and cleaning up or modernizing on their own.

In Florida, the Collier County Solid Waste Department has developed an innovative process of "landfill mining" to reclaim recyclable materials and eliminate potential hazards to underground water sources. This unique process takes place at a facility that serves 120,000 people, 88 percent of the county's population.

Mining the landfill has many benefits:

Mining provides the basic ingredient for an earthen soil material that is used as a cover material and a soil additive at the county's new landfill.

Removing solid waste from the existing, unlined landfill greatly reduces the need for costly water quality monitoring and closure procedures.

Substances recovered from the landfill through mining, including ferrous metals, aluminum, and plastics, can be recycled. It also includes combustible materials removed from the landfill which can be used as a fuel for energy generation.

By reusing existing landfills, the need to expand old landfills or open new ones is greatly reduced.

The mining process is simple, cost-effective, and uses readily available industrial mining equipment and the existing labor pool.

The Landfill Reclamation Project

The Landfill Reclamation Project resulted, in part, from the curiosity of several engineers working on behalf of Collier County's Solid Waste Department in the mid–1980s. Having read in trade journals about the combustible properties of some materials in landfills, the engineers began to wonder if these materials could be retrieved and used for the benefit of the community. The county landfill reclamation efforts were originally proposed in 1985 as a pilot study to determine if waste previously deposited in local landfills could be reclaimed and used as a supplemental source of fuel. The recovery of space in a landfill that was rapidly approaching capacity, resulting in an extension of the useful life of the site, was seen as an important secondary benefit. Much to the delight of county officials, initial tests concluded that reclaimed waste did, in fact, have combustible characteristics.

As a result of these encouraging test results, the state's Energy Department provided the Solid Waste Department with the financial backing to develop the tools necessary to recover the combustible materials from the landfills. Rather than developing entirely new equipment, county engineers decided to concentrate their efforts on modifying mining equipment.

The equipment and procedures used for landfill mining are common to most basic quarry operations. A front-end loader was purchased for $113,000 and slightly modified screening equipment was acquired for approximately $180,000. The material excavated by the loader is fed to a bar screen which removes large items from the soil. The remainder then passes over a vibrating screen that has two ½ inch openings to remove finer materials. The materials that pass over the screen fall onto a conveyor belt equipped with a large magnet. The magnet removes light ferrous materials which can be recycled. The fine soil that passes through the screen is used as cover material for the new landfill, and the ferrous material is stockpiled for sale to scrap processors.

An ironic twist to the reclamation story is that the program's original objective—to reclaim supplemental fuel—is no longer a primary focus of the project. Not long after landfill mining began, plans to construct a waste-to-energy plant in conjunction with landfill reclamation were cancelled due to lack of funding. Nonetheless, the program remains a success because of the reduced expenditures for landfill cover material. During the last fiscal year, Collier County spent approximately $275,000 for the purchase of cover material for its landfills, an average cost of $3.95 per ton. The Reclamation Project produced 50,000 tons of cover material at an average cost of $1.80 per ton, resulting in a net savings of about $100,000 for the county.

The sale of recovered aluminum, ferrous materials, plastics, and glass also provide revenues, although on a much smaller scale. Of course, the most significant benefit to the community remains the removal of hazardous wastes from the unlined landfill. The reclamation process used by Collier County is worth noting because the process is applicable in virtually any community which uses landfills for solid waste disposal.

Challenges Faced During Implementation

Advocates of the reclamation process faced several early obstacles. Foremost among these challenges was convincing the Collier County Commission and some officials within the Solid Waste Department that reclamation would have measurable economic and environmental benefits. This obstacle was overcome once engineers were able to show that the project was a practical, cost-effective, and environmentally sound solution to a politically polarizing issue. Eventually, the commissioners authorized funding for the project, and the state gave its tacit approval to the program by issuing a $20,000 grant in support of the Reclamation Project through the governor's Energy Office.

A second challenge to project planners within the Department of Solid Waste was obtaining the necessary regulatory approval for landfill reclamation. First, according to Thomas Donegan, a project engineer, the Solid Waste Department had to obtain a permit to mine the landfill from the Florida Department of Environmental Regulation. "The petition process required the Solid Waste Department to demonstrate that mining landfills would not create potential environmental hazards," says Donegan. "The necessary permits were granted once the department had shown that the project could have a positive impact on the environment, including removing potentially dangerous substances from contact with underground water sources." Although the permits were granted, the Solid Waste Department was required to implement testing and operating procedures mandated by the Department of Environmental Regulation and the federal Occupational Safety and Health Administration (OSHA).

A third, but substantially less problematic, obstacle to implementing the program was modifying standard quarry screening equipment to allow the processing of materials that might be found in a landfill. Says Donegan, "Although the modifications proved to be relatively minor, a great deal of planning went into the process."

The Solid Waste Department is still addressing several ongoing challenges, including increasing the productivity of the reclamation process. The utility would like to be able to reclaim even more recyclable material, since doing so would drive down the average cost of the project. Another ongoing project is assisting the Department of Environmental Regulation in its efforts to encourage widespread adoption of the reclamation process.

Results of the Landfill Reclamation Project

The Landfill Reclamation Project has resulted in a widely applicable, environmentally sound, and cost-effective process to reclaim solid waste disposal sites. This includes older sites that are unlined and stable as a result of organic degradation. After its third year of operation, the program had already proven itself to be beneficial.

As mentioned earlier, the reclamation process is extremely cost-effective. The process also has a very positive environmental impact. The Reclamation Project has removed over 65,000 tons of waste material from direct contact with ground water. Additionally, the reclamation process prolongs the life of landfills which could lead to a reduction in land allocated for landfill use. Mining recovered over 50,000 tons of recyclable material which would otherwise have been wasted. Completion of the excavation will also permit installation of modern lining material in the landfill and reuse of the area in conformance with existing Florida Department of Environmental Regulation requirements.

Reclamation Project Organization

Since landfill management has a waste component, a utility component, and an environmental component, it usually requires input from a variety of departments within a local government. The landfills operated by Collier County are no exception.

The Landfill Reclamation Project is the direct responsibility of the Collier County Solid Waste Department. It employs supervisors and crew leaders to oversee daily operations at the two landfills and three waste transfer stations. Several other agencies, however, take a direct interest in the program.

The Florida Department of Environmental Regulation is responsible for issuing permits and inspecting solid waste operations. The Solid Waste Department works closely with the Department of Environmental Regulation to ensure that environmentally sound practices are followed.

The South Florida Water Management District regulates the design and operation of landfill disposal sites. Accordingly, this department has taken a strong interest in the planning and results of the Landfill Reclamation Project.

Although many government outsiders might think that all of this external regulation would slow down the implementation process, Landfill Reclamation Project advocates take a different view. Officials believe that the constructive criticism of the Department of Environmental Regulation contributed to the successful implementation of the program.

In the public sector, there is often a lack of communication between different jurisdictions that hampers the adoption of innovative programs. Agencies like the Department of Environmental Regulation and the South Florida Water Management District can help overcome this problem because of their broad geographical scope. They can also serve as channels of information between the Collier County Landfill Reclamation Project and other jurisdictions that might be interested in implementing similar programs. In addition, the Collier County Board of Commissioners has committed to an agreement with the University of South Florida for research and further development of the process to establish future solid waste policies and procedures.

Plans for the Future

The Collier County Landfill Reclamation Project has demonstrated an inexpensive means to excavate, segregate, and recycle stabilized solid wastes from an unlined landfill. Over the next five years, the state of Florida plans to apply the technology to other landfill sites which are polluting the ground water. The Solid Waste Department plans to improve the system to make solid waste segregation and collection of recyclable materials more efficient. Of course, it is hoped that as landfills are reclaimed, they can be lined, updated to meet current environmental and safety standards, and then reused.

Participants in the planning of the Collier County Reclamation Project are confident that the program can be replicated at virtually any landfill site in the United States. They point out that similar projects are underway outside of Florida. Thompson, Connecticut, for example, is reclaiming its landfill, leading to substantial savings and the extension of the landfill's capacity. Other reclamation projects are being considered in New York, Louisiana, and Delaware.

In the future, the Collier County Solid Waste Department believes that newly lined sites will be used as processing facilities rather than disposal sites. Increased attention to hazardous materials disposal will enable the composted organic material to be safely recycled as a soil enhancement. In support of this goal, several universities in Florida are researching means to optimize and accelerate the organic degradation which stabilizes landfill waste. In February of 1990, the Board of Collier County Commissioners approved a major cooperative research contract with the Department of Civil Engineering and Mechanics at the University of South Florida. The successful accomplishment of the objectives of this agreement will contribute to the national search for a safe solid waste management program.

Mining will also allow for the more frequent inspection and repair of cell liners in the future. This will, of course, lead to a reduction in landfill closure costs and reduce the number of new landfills.

Implications of Landfill Reclamation

Current federal and state landfill regulations are designed to encapsulate and isolate solid waste from the surrounding environment. This policy limits the natural process of organic degradation that stabilizes the waste material over time. Many jurisdictions require multiple liners and leak detection systems to ensure that these containment requirements are met. Long-term maintenance and monitoring are also necessary to confirm that the integrity of the liner is maintained.

The Landfill Reclamation Project has demonstrated that stabilized wastes from an unlined landfill "cell" can be safely and cost-effectively reclaimed and recycled. This finding has important implications for modern landfills that are lined: Combining the reclamation capability with accelerated stabilization would, in effect, enable lined cells to be repeatedly used as gigantic composting vessels. After each cycle of stabilization and excavation the liner could be inspected and repaired or replaced to provide more environmental protection. Such a procedure could greatly extend the lives and environmental safety of increasingly scarce landfill sites.

Key Lessons from the Landfill Reclamation Project

The Landfill Reclamation Project provides an example of government innovation at its best. The project adopts familiar technologies and procedures (in this case mining technologies and procedures) to a new context (landfills). The program is both technically innovative and representative of the kind of cooperation that is required to combat today's complex problems.

ADAPTATION OF FAMILIAR TECHNOLOGIES AND PROCEDURES TO NEW CIRCUMSTANCES. When thinking of innovation, one usually imagines futuristic technologies. Often, however, innovation results from adapting existing technologies and procedures to new situations. In such cases, the innovation stems from someone's ability to recognize the adaptability of the technology or process to new circumstances. In the case of the Landfill Reclamation Project, the Solid Waste Department recognized both the potential benefits from mining local landfills and the utility of existing mining equipment and processes. The recognition that mining equipment could be readily adapted to landfill mining resulted from practical thinking: engineers wanted to first explore the capabilities of existing mining equipment before spending lots of money on developing new equipment from scratch. Adaptation of existing mining technologies (with minor modifications) and procedures to the Landfill Reclamation Project provided a much less costly alternative to designing new equipment for landfill operations.

STRATEGIC ALLIANCES, REVISITED. The Landfill Reclamation Project requires several agencies to work together in a cooperative manner. Since the county Solid Waste Department, the Florida Department of Environmental Regulation, and the South Florida Water Management District all have a stake in the Project, they must work closely together. Each agency provided valuable input during the development of the program, and according to officials, early input from each agency prevented conflict later on.

Reducing Solid Waste: The City of Seattle Recycling Program

By late 1987, the city of Seattle, Washington, was faced with a garbage disposal crisis. Since the last of the city's landfills had stopped accepting waste in December 1986, the city was forced to take its garbage to landfills outside of the city. The result was an overnight tripling of disposal fees. To make matters worse, both of Seattle's closed landfills were designated Superfund sites with closing costs estimated at more than $100 million. Although recycling was an effective alternative to landfills, only about 24 percent of the city's 700,000 tons of garbage was recycled.

The Seattle Solid Waste Utility initiated a long-term approach toward sound management of the city's garbage. This initiative has resulted in an ambitious curbside recycling program in which virtually every household in the city is able to participate. Residents may recycle a wide variety of items, ranging from bottles and cans to paint and yard waste. Moreover, the program relies on sophisticated management techniques, including marketing efforts aimed at informing residents of the program and economic incentives which encourage residents to recycle.

History of the Recycling Program

During the 1980s, the Seattle Solid Waste Utility was the focus of a heated public debate on the issue of solid waste disposal. Each of three plans proposed by the utility to deal with the disposal crisis called for the incineration of a significant portion of the city's garbage. When it came time to locate a site for the incineration plant, citizens and environmental groups protested. The city was forced to indefinitely postpone the incineration plant proposal.

Meanwhile, both of the city's landfills reached capacity and were forced to close. Environmental problems associated with the landfills (mostly escaping methane gas) resulted in closure costs of $100 million to be paid by ratepayers over a 20 year period. Lacking its own landfill, Seattle was forced to contract with a nearby landfill for disposal of its solid waste. Closure of Seattle's landfills and fee increases at the new landfill site resulted in a tripling of consumer disposal rates in less than a year.

With direction from Mayor Charles Royer and the City Council to gain control of the situation, the Solid Waste Utility developed an array of options ranging from the status quo (recycling at drop-boxes and buy-back centers, and landfilling the rest) to the balanced approach (recycling 40 percent of the waste, incinerating and landfilling the rest). Once citizens became aware of the options under consideration, they again raised concerns about incineration and questioned the level of commitment to recycling.

It was at this point that the utility began seriously studying recycling on a large scale as an alternative to incineration and as a means of reducing landfill disposal. The City Council directed the utility to conduct an in-depth study to find out how much diversion of garbage would result if the city spent as much on recycling as it had planned to spend on incineration. The result of this first-of-its-kind analysis was called the Recycling Potential Assessment (RPA). Using a variety of econometric techniques borrowed from electric utilities, the city concluded that between 42 percent and 78 percent of the waste stream could be recycled, depending upon which set of programs was implemented. At the same time, the utility staff renegotiated garbage contracts, redesigned the rate structure to encourage recycling, and implemented the first curbside yard waste and recycling programs.

As is typical with any public sector initiative as unique as the City of Seattle Recycling Program, a number of individuals and groups played important roles in initiating the original curbside recycling programs. Mayor Royer, with support of the City Council, directed that curbside recycling be initiated and also set a goal of late 1998 for the city to recycle 60 percent of its solid waste. The director of the Solid Waste Utility set the process in motion, assuring that adequate planning and financial resources were committed by the utility to meet its long-term objectives. Utility staff members were acknowledged as having played a major role in the development of the program. Individuals with expertise in areas as diverse as contract administration, rate setting, landfill closure, field operations, and program development all contributed significantly to the breadth and depth of the city's program. Private citizens played a key role in encouraging waste disposal officials to seek alternatives to incineration of garbage.

The Recycling Program

One of the most unique aspects of Seattle's recycling program is that this government-managed program uses a blend of effective private and public sector management principles. These principles include strategic planning, forecasting, and economic incentives to encourage residents to participate in the program. In addition, market research, unique product offerings, and frequent promotions are employed by program officials to guarantee customer satisfaction.

The rate structure used by the Solid Waste Utility is also unique. It provides strong economic incentives to reduce the amount of garbage each family produces and to increase the use of recycling. In effect, residents who throw out more trash pay more than people who recycle. The first container of garbage collected is priced at the actual cost of collection, and subsequent containers are priced at greater than the cost of service. Ratepayers in Seattle pay an additional $108 per year for the weekly pickup of even a second container of trash.

An unintended side-effect of Seattle's approach to recycling is the presence of peer pressure to encourage people to recycle. Volunteer block captains are recruited by the city to encourage their neighbors to recycle. Block captains go from door to door explaining what can and cannot be recycled. In many cases, the block captains have been known to be very persistent with individuals who have not signed up for the recycling program. Block captains also hold meetings with neighbors to help them understand how to go about recycling their garbage.

The Seattle recycling program is also unique because of its breadth and aggressive rate of expansion. The program spread across the entire city in about one year. This is impressive when one reflects on the number and variety of programs offered to customers. These programs include: curbside recycling of paper, glass, plastic and aluminum; drop points for and curbside pickup of yard waste for composting; recycling for apartments; distribution of backyard composting bins; and, as mentioned above, a system for billing based on the amount of garbage produced. Additionally, the program has an active customer relations, marketing, and advertising component to encourage recycling. Educational programs have also been planned for use in schools to get young people to think about recycling at an age when they are still developing their trash disposal habits.

In addition to offering a broad range of services, the Seattle recycling program has championed several technological innovations. For example, its curbside collection program was the first in the nation capable of accepting mixed waste paper and among the first to accept hard plastic bottles. Seattle's program also initiated several experimental services, including hazardous household waste drop-off sites and disposable diaper recycling.

A key aspect of Seattle's approach is that it strives for complete customer satisfaction. Extensive marketing research is conducted to identify customer needs and services are implemented with customer-friendly procedures. Aggressive promotions and public information campaigns are used to ensure that people are fully aware of all the options available to them.

The city of Seattle has devoted substantial planning and financial resources to support the program. A program development staff includes a wide variety of professional disciplines, including economists, strategic planners, public information specialists, market analysts, and customer service experts. The city will spend over $5 million on recycling programs in 1992. Since the Solid Waste Utility, which manages the program, operates as an independent utility, it must be self-supporting, with no subsidies from the city's general fund or property tax revenues.

Clients Served by the Recycling Program

Although the program's clients are generally considered to be the 500,000 residents of Seattle, administrators differentiate classes of clients based on the amount of waste material they can direct from the so-called waste stream. Since single family homes are considered most likely to support a recycling initiative, curbside yard waste collection for single family homes was among the first programs established in the city.

Although participation in the Seattle recycling program is voluntary, participation rates are surprisingly high. Nearly 80 percent of the 147,000 eligible households (single family through fourplex) are enrolled in the curbside recycling program. Almost nine out of 10 households have reduced their garbage to one container or less per week, resulting in a 30 percent decrease in landfill usage. About 65 percent of the 230,000 eligible households in the city are participating in the yard waste pick-up effort. A program was also recently started for the 83,000 multi-family units that have more than 5 residential units, making recycling available to the vast majority of Seattle's residents.

Challenges to Success

Several obstacles were faced by program administrators during the early stages of the program's implementation. The first obstacle was anxiety among staff and elected officials about the feasibility of building a solid waste system with such a heavy reliance on recycling. Although the benefits of recycling were beyond doubt, no municipality had attempted to build such a comprehensive system in such a short period of time. The early planning process, particularly the estimates of participation rates, helped to persuade city officials. Once the commitment was made to the program, elected officials made it a policy, staffing, and budget priority.

A second cause for concern among program planners was the degree to which the public would participate in a voluntary program. Original estimates called for a 35 percent participation rate at the end of the first year of the program. Fortunately, this concern was completely alleviated when, by the end of the first year, actual participation rates were an impressive sixty-three percent of eligible households. The rapid acceptance of this program is largely attributed to aggressive marketing efforts, price incentives, the program's convenience, and the citizen's innate desire to help the environment.

Not surprisingly, the needs of small private recyclers needed to be addressed as well, since approximately 25 percent of curbside material was previously diverted through these organizations. These small recyclers claimed that a government-sponsored recycling program would put them at a competitive disadvantage. The city partially addressed the concerns of independent operators by offering them a credit of $35 per ton for the collection of recyclable materials from apartments.

Although the rapid implementation of the program was largely a success, it did lead to a number of operational and customer service problems, centered on confusion over pick-up schedules and the like. Increased experience has eliminated most of these problems. Making sure that customers receive regular pick-up and understand all program options is a continual challenge. The staff regularly evaluates ways to reduce missed pick-ups and enhance the convenience of the program.

Results of the Program

The results of the City of Seattle Recycling Program have been surprisingly positive. The residents of Seattle are recycling 38 percent of the total waste stream, compared with just 24 percent in 1987. A residual benefit is that tonnage disposed in the landfill dropped nearly 25 percent between 1988 and 1989.

Not only have residents recycled more, but they have also produced less garbage. Nine years ago, the average Seattle resident produced three and one-half 30 gallon containers of garbage per week. Now, residents average less than one container per week. Program administrators attribute the success of the program to peer pressures. If you are one of the few on your block who are *not* recycling, everyone knows.

By the end of its second year, 78 percent of eligible residents had signed up for the curbside recycling program. Today, that figure has peaked at 85 percent. Already, the curbside program is 75 percent of the way toward its 1998 goal. Residents recycle an average of 63 pounds per month per resident, most of which is newspaper, waste paper, and glass.

Not only has this program achieved tremendous results in terms of participation and waste reduction, it is also cost-effective. Currently, all of the services provided through the City of Seattle Recycling Program are projected to cost less in the long run than taking the same material to a landfill.

These results demonstrate that local governments can have a major impact on individual behavior in a very short period of time through voluntary means, provided that the program is well planned and directly addresses the needs of its customers.

Administrators of the City of Seattle Recycling Program believe that most, if not all, of the features of its recycling efforts can be duplicated in many areas across the country. The primary condition for success is spending the time to develop a program that meets the test of avoided disposal costs. This means that over the long run, these programs must save the ratepayers money. The program has proven, thus far, that this is an achievable objective.

Key Lessons from the City of Seattle Recycling Program

The City of Seattle Recycling Program is one of the most ambitious programs discussed in this book. It has a substantial budget, targets a large client base, and offers a wide variety of services. It should come as no surprise that this program is based on sophisticated management principles not unlike those used by private-sector corporations. Managers of the Seattle recycling program credit the early success of the initiative to sound business practices, the program's aggressive customer orientation, the use of economic incentives to encourage residents to participate in the program, and the program's cost-effectiveness.

USE OF SOUND MANAGEMENT PRINCIPLES. Considering the budget and the scope of the Seattle recycling program, it should come as no surprise that officials credit much of the program's success to sound management principles. These principles include careful planning, development of new services, and attention to the needs of customers. What may come as a surprise to many readers is the level of sophistication used by program managers in accordance with these principles. First, managers thoroughly research new proposals before they offer new services. They use quantitative forecasting techniques (such as those adapted from the electric utility industry) to estimate demand for new services and determine whether the service is economically feasible. Once officials decide to offer a new service, they carefully plan the delivery of the service before it is offered to the public. Paramount to the planning process is setting the price of the service such that costs are covered.

Customer satisfaction is often at the center of the research. Program officials go to great lengths to identify the needs of Seattle residents. Many of the services offered by the recycling program (including yard-waste recycling and diaper recycling) were started as a result of customer suggestions.

In a broader sense, customer satisfaction is a major goal of the recycling program. To that end, the program maintains an aggressive customer service function which provides information on the wide variety of product offerings, solicits customer complaints and suggestions, and develops consumer promotions to encourage the recycling of selected materials.

ECONOMIC INCENTIVES. While peer pressure, the use of block captains, and ensuring customer satisfaction by providing a wide variety of relevant services have undoutedly contributed to the exceptional levels of community participation in the recycling program, economic incentives serve as the major boost to participation. As mentioned above, residents that throw out more trash pay more for their trash collection. The pricing is structured so that residents are financially rewarded for recycling.

COST-EFFECTIVENESS: RECYCLE NOW OR LANDFILL LATER. Cost-effectiveness has been mentioned several times in previous sections of this book as an important component of successful programs. Cost-effectiveness helps stretch limited funds, increases support for programs among taxpayers, and allows programs to charge lower prices for services rendered. The City of Seattle Recycling Program was able to overcome initial opposition by quantitatively demonstrating that recycling now would be less expensive than shipping solid waste to out-of-town landfills in the future.

Pollution Control Made Simple: The Water Pollution Control Program

In one of the most devastating ecological disasters in the history of Fort Worth, Texas, tens of thousands of fish were found floating dead in the Trinity River on August 7, 1986. According to federal environmental officials, the fish were either dead or floating near the river's surface "gasping for oxygen." It was determined that the fish had been killed by a combination of pollutants in the water. Sadly, this was not the first time that huge numbers of fish had died in the river near Fort Worth. Only one year earlier, an estimated 184,000 fish were found dead under similar circumstances.

It was widely hypothesized that urban storm drainage was a major contributing factor to the death of the fish. However, it was not until people working on a mosquito patrol noticed chemical and sewage discharges from storm drains into open waterways that real action was taken to address the problem. The Fort Worth Health Department developed a practical, low-cost program to test and treat drainage water throughout the city. A key aspect of this program is that it uses simplified and innovative variations of expensive, highly sophisticated, and time consuming techniques traditionally used to monitor the quality of water in drainage systems.

What is Runoff?

Urban runoff comes from storm drainage systems made up of natural and manmade conduits that collect storm water from curb drains, ditches, and the surrounding landscape. These conduits convey the storm water to larger waterways such as rivers and lakes. Unfortunately, these systems also collect toxic substances that are washed into the drainage, including oil from roadways, chemicals, and even sewage. In many instances, toxic substances are poured untreated into waterways via the drainage systems as a result of illegal or improper connections to the drainage system. The result can be contamination of drinking water reservoirs and recreational waterways. Local governments are often reluctant to treat these sources of pollution because underground drainage systems are numerous and complex, and the quality and quantity of water is extremely variable. As such, it is difficult to assess drainage water quality and to locate and control specific sources of contamination. Conventional raw water evaluation techniques have been ineffective in most cases because the equipment, methodology, and levels of expertise required to conduct large-scale, drainage-water, pollution-control programs are too expensive.

The Fort Worth Program: How It Works

Consistent with the overall philosophy of the program, the goals of the Water Pollution Control Program are straightforward. The ultimate goal is to maintain clean water throughout the city of Fort Worth. To attain this goal, program officials have established five short term objectives:
1. the prevention of future municipal water contamination
2. the correction and removal of existing water contamination sources
3. the detection of drainage water contamination
4. the investigation of the nature and source of water contamination
5. the determination of existing water quality within the City and the development of reference standards (i.e. profiles) to assess both subtle and obvious changes in water quality over time.

In an effort to systematically achieve these objectives, the Water Pollution Control Program focuses on four areas: problem detection, problem investigation, problem correction, and problem prevention. According to Gene Rattan, an environmental quality supervisor for the city of Fort Worth, equal emphasis is given to each area. "Ignoring any one of these functions would undercut the entire program," says Rattan. "The point is to fight pollution along key fronts."

Problem detection and investigation require the use of several innovative applications of simple technologies and procedures to test for and control contamination in storm drains. Rattan notes that simplified chemical tests of water samples to detect contaminated discharge and routine testing of drainage water for heavy metals and pesticides are among the methods used. Program officials have also trained a storm drain tunnel entry team that investigates sources of pollution. "Their ability to investigate and pinpoint pollution sources firsthand makes a big difference," according to Rattan. Finally, the program relies heavily on citizen complaints, a patrol of city employees to detect drainage water contamination, and even occasional helicopter surveillance. "An effort is made to use all of the resources that are readily available to us," adds Rattan.

Preventative measures ensure that businesses are aware of local water quality standards. Blanket letters are sent to target industries to inform them of the standards. New businesses are provided with detailed water quality guidelines and the roving patrol makes spot checks to ensure that they are complied with.

The targeted population for the Water Pollution Control Program is divided into two groups—those who are investigated by it and those who benefit from it. Those who are investigated by the program include a variety of entities who knowingly or unknowingly discharge contaminants into the storm drains. These entities include industry, residents, and even the city of Fort Worth.

The entire community benefits from the increased protection of its water source. People who live near the waterways also benefit from the elimination of sewage discharge since they will not be exposed to the increased mosquito populations associated with such conditions. Approximately 25 percent of the city's population lives near waterways that are regularly tested by the program.

The Water Pollution Control Program is an example of a program which tackles a persistent policy problem by seeing it in a new light. The attitude of program officials is that there may or may not be pollutants in the drainage, but every effort should be made to at least remove obvious pollutants such as oil and sewage. It is not as important for them to know the amount and content of the pollutants, since this information requires much more costly and precise techniques. Nonetheless, there is effort made to test for six specific heavy metals and pesticides in drainage sediment.

There is nothing revolutionary about any one of the techniques used by the program. The high-tech protective gear and breathing apparatus used by the storm drain tunnel entry teams is the same as that used by firefighters and storage tank maintenance workers. Likewise, helicopter surveillance is nothing new. Enlisting the help of citizens in reporting problems is commonplace. As a bundle of techniques, however, the program stands as a shining example of how using a simplified approach can pay off. Previously, it was thought that only espensive, sophisticated testing programs would suffice. Indeed, at the time that Fort Worth was developing this program, it was rumored that a nearby community was spending over $250,000 per year on water testing that would provide precise information on the chemical components of the pollution.

A fascinating aspect of the Water Pollution Control Program is that while the program, and thus water quality, is the responsibility of the Fort Worth Health Department, responsibility for the physical infrastructure (especially the sewers and storm drains) is the responsibility of two other departments: Water and Public Works. One might reasonably expect such an arrangement to lead to turf battles among the city's brass, especially since the Health Department's investigations occasionally find that the city itself is a polluter. People close to the program insist that the director of the Water Department supports the program because he views the Health Department's investigations as an impartial check on the performance of his own team.

The Water Pollution Control Program: Is It Too Simple?

The driving force behind the success of Fort Worth's water pollution control effort is an almost fanatical devotion to simplicity and cost control. One inexpensive method used to test storm drains consists of placing a live fish in a perforated two-liter soft drink bottle attached to a block of styrofoam and tethered to a brick. The whole setup is left near the outflow of a storm drain for one or two days. If the fish lives, officials can be relatively certain that the water is safe enough to support fish. If the fish dies, then there is cause for further investigation, perhaps even sending in the storm drain patrol to identify potential sources of pollution. Other techniques include dry weather field screening which relies on visual inspections of waterways for oil sheen or discoloration.

Some people scoff at the techniques used by the Health Department. The fish (specifically, minnows) in the soft drink bottle and other techniques used by the department are often ridiculed by water pollution specialists, particularly those who prefer expensive, exact scientific techniques. What these people ignore, however, is that the simple and inexpensive techniques serve the needs of the department well. They allow the testing efforts to focus on the most likely problem sites. Health Department officials do not believe that detailed chemical analysis is necessary to determine if there are unacceptable levels of pollution in the drainage systems. Rather, the use of minnows allows testers to determine whether there are unacceptable levels of toxicity in the runoff over time.

People who have witnessed the activities of the Health Department suggest that the program's simplicity is one of its major advantages. In particular, the simplicity of the techniques suggests a possible role in pollution contorl for the ordinary citizen. Indeed, the Health Department encourages people to report possible sources of water pollution by calling a special phone number. In addition, the simple nature of the program makes it easy to replicate in other jurisdictions. The entire program has been outlined in a procedures manual which details inspection and observation methods as well as statistical means used to evaluate test results. The manual, which is offered to other jurisdictions interested in starting similar programs, also explains how to establish a tunnel entry team and ensure safety during confined space entries.

Accomplishments of the Water Pollution Control Program

The most important accomplishment of the Water Pollution Control Program has been the identification and cessation of discharges of sewage and chemicals from several office buildings and industrial sites. In its first year of operation, a ten-story office building was found to be unknowingly discharging huge quantities of waste directly into storm drains. Officials have also developed a series of sophisticated statistical water quality measures which help to find and prevent inappropriate discharges into water systems.

Indirect accomplishments include demonstrating that effective, low-cost, low-manpower water pollution control programs can be successfully implemented in large cities. The complex nature of drainage systems, both on the surface and underground, need not be a prohibitive factor in cities developing their own pollution control programs. Instead, cities can tackle the problem of water pollution through the innovative use of resources already at hand. Use of these resources allows cities to forgo the conventional "shotgun" and "putting out fires" approaches to pollution control in favor of a consistent and effective program.

The most significant shortcoming of the program, according to local officials, is the inability to use the entry team on more than a sporadic basis. At present, the team is only used if pollution is suspected and the source needs to be located. The primary reason for the spotty use of the entry team is that all of the team members have other full-time commitments in city agencies. It is difficult to schedule times when all four members of the team are available.

Effect of the Clean Water Act

Since the Environmental Protection Agency mandated the use of systems like Fort Worth's for all cities with populations of 100,000 or more as of April 1990, the city has been working with the EPA to develop a field screen methodology to be used nationwide. The EPA mandate requires cities to obtain permits to operate storm drainage systems, making Fort Worth's low-cost pollution control methods attractive.

The program has received substantial publicity, especially since the director of the U.S. Fish and Wildlife Agency named it one of the ten most outstanding environmental programs in the country. The program was also awarded the Innovation Award by the Ford Foundation, which resulted in a grant which has been used to help teach other jurisdictions how to develop similar water pollution control programs.

Key Lessons from the Water Pollution Control Program

The Water Pollution Control Program provides another example of a program which benefits from a strategic alliance between agencies. In this case, the alliance is between the Health Department (which wants to reduce contaminants in the water supply), the Water Department (which is also concerned about water quality), and the Public Works Department (which is responsible for the drainage system). The input of the Public Works Department is important in terms of identifying the sources of run-off. The Water Department views Health Department investigations as an important check on its own performance. Once again, these relationships may be regarded as strategic because they further the goals of each of the departments.

The Water Pollution Control Program also benefits from adapting existing technologies and procedures to pollution control. The high-tech protective gear and breathing apparatus used by the tunnel entry teams is the same as that used by firefighters and storage tank workers. Similarly, helicopter patrols are common for police work, but are easily adapted for pollution control duties. The bottom line with respect to adapting technologies and procedures is to think in simple terms. Ask the question: Are we already applying technologies elsewhere that would work in other situations? Many programs find that the answer to this question is a definitive "yes."

Officials of the program cite simplicity as being the key to the program's success. Simplicity makes the program easy to administer and replicate, and it suggests a role for the public in the abatement of water pollution.

SIMPLICITY. Programs can exhibit simplicity of design and simplicity of approach. The Water Pollution Control Program provides an excellent example of both. The design of the program is relatively straightforward—people inform the community about water pollution standards and then use relatively simple procedures to identify violations. In this case, simplicity has four advantages: (1) the program is relatively easy to administer; (2) costs are contained; (3) the program is easy to replicate; and (4) the public can play an active role in the pollution control process that has traditionally been technically complicated.

Aside from shortages of labor for tunnel entry teams, the Water Pollution Control Program relies on relatively simple procedures that are easy to undertake. The minnow in the soft drink bottle is easy to set up and doesn't take a great deal of resources to administer. Fort Worth is apparently saving thousands of dollars by using this simple testing procedure rather than using chemical tests. Such cost efficiencies suggest that many jurisdictions that cannot afford more complex testing procedures now have an affordable alternative to test for water pollution.

Since the testing techniques used by the program (other than the entry teams) are easy to replicate using household items, the program is easy to replicate in other jurisdictions. There is no need for setting up expensive laboratories with highly trained technicians. Instead, a booklet detailing how to set up the minnow contraption suffices. This simplicity suggests an obvious role for the average citizen in testing for water pollution. With this in mind, the program has set up a hotline which citizens can call to report possible sources of water pollution.

One final clarification: The virtue of simplicity as it is discussed in the context of the Water Pollution Control Program should not be confused with the vice of being simplistic. Although the program has been designed with simplicity in mind, the techniques employed are sophisticated to the extent that they help the Health Department achieve pollution control standards in a straightforward, cost-effective, and easy-to-understand manner. This stands in sharp contrast to simplistic programs which might not lead to meaningful pollution control because either their approaches or techniques (or both) are ill suited to the task at hand.

A Cost-Effective Way
to Save a Limited Resource:
The I.Q. Water Program

Jerry Reid had reason to be concerned. The greens keeper at a popular Florida golf course, he knew that news of a prolonged drought could only mean that irrigation of the 18-hole golf course would have to be curtailed. While most people probably wouldn't think twice about the condition of a golf course when water is in short supply, Mr. Reid knew that his community's tourism trade, and thus its economic well-being, depended largely on its reputation for having well-maintained golf courses. Thus, cutting back on irrigation of the greens could lead to a sharp decline in business if the quality of his and other courses suffered.

A few miles away, treated wastewater was pouring from a large pipe into a tributary of the Loxahatchee River. As the drought situation worsened, officials of the local water control authority began to wonder whether the wastewater could be used to ease the concerns of people like Jerry Reid. Local officials began to consider ways in which wastewater, which was usually "thrown away," could safely be used for irrigation and other purposes in times of water shortages. The result was the I.Q. (Irrigation Quality) Water Program of the Loxahatchee River Environmental Control District, near Jupiter, Florida.

The handling of wastewater once it has been treated at water treatment plants is a problem facing nearly every community in our nation. In the past, disposing of improperly treated wastewater has often resulted in undesirable environmental consequences. Such has been the case when wastewater is dumped into lakes and rivers after only cursory treatment.

Today, increased shortages of potable water have created powerful economic incentives for communities to re-evaluate the disposition of waste-water. Practices such as watering lawns with water that might otherwise be used for drinking or bathing has been called into question. Additionally, the practice of throwing away treated water that might be used as an alternative to potable water in many applications (including watering lawns) has been reconsidered. The Loxahatchee River District has found that conserving its limited water resources through effective reuse of treated wastewater is as effective as it is unique. Reusing treated wastewater not only allows a scarce resource to be conserved, but it also minimizes the environmental damage which used to result from dumping wastewater into clean waterways.

The I.Q. Water Program

The Loxahatchee River basin's drinking water comes from groundwater aquifers, or wells, which are replenished solely from rainfall. Water shortages, therefore, are quite frequent during prolonged dry spells. Diminishing sup-plies of quality groundwater, in combination with the demands of a growing population, have increased the need for water conservation measures in the area.

Charged with the responsibility of managing the area's water resources, the Loxahatchee River Environmental Control District developed a program to encourage the conservation of potable water and provide an environmen-tally sound wastewater disposal method which is easily understood and ac-cepted by local residents.

The I.Q. Water Program is fulfilling the area's conservation needs by treating wastewater to very high levels and selling it to the area's numerous golf courses for irrigation. This reclaimed wastewater replaces the pure groundwater which was previously used to irrigate golf courses. The program saves nearly 500,000 gallons each day from each golf course. The conserved groundwater reserves can then be used in a manner more beneficial to society, including drinking, cooking, and bathing.

Serving a population of nearly 50,000 residents, the district's governing board recognizes that water conservation requires extensive public awareness. To that end, the district keeps its constituents informed of the program's progress and accomplishments through a carefully planned public relations campaign. The program now enjoys public recognition and local acclaim.

The business-like approach to conservation employed by the I.Q. Water Program is creative because of its emphasis on reusing wastewater while conserving good water at the same time. Nonetheless, the idea of recycling wastewater is not entirely new. Plans for recycling wastewater were abandoned in the early 1980s when program officials were unable to convince golf courses to participate. A severe drought in the mid–1980s finally helped persuade course managers, including Jerry Reid, that the program was needed.

There are about 65,000 people within the Loxahatchee River Environmental Control District who have benefitted from expanded water resources as a result of the I.Q. Water Program. By the time the project reaches its full potential in the mid–1990s, nearly 85,000 people will benefit.

There are currently 12 major golf courses that have agreed to purchase irrigation water from the I.Q. Program. Contracts have been executed with each of the golf courses and scheduled commencement dates are set through 1994. Nine golf courses are already purchasing water. Combined, these courses reuse an estimated 4.2 million gallons of water *each day*. This volume represents nearly 70 percent of the original program objective of 6.2 million gallons per day.

Goals of the I.Q. Water Program

According to Richard Dent, executive director of the Loxahatchee River District, the I.Q. Water Program has four goals. Since its formation in 1971, the primary goal of the district has been to preserve the basin's environmental quality in a time of rapid urban growth. Since a significant by-product of urban growth is the creation of wastewater, the I.Q. Water Program helps solve the wastewater problem.

The second goal of the program is to conserve water. Dent indicates that this goal was established nearly 15 years ago when the district conducted studies and generated a water budget for the entire basin area. "The budget had projected that all of the water available from rainfall would be used by the beginning of the 1990s," says Dent. "This meant that alternative means of producing additional water supplies would have to be found and existing sources of fresh water would have to be conserved." The program fulfills this conservation goal by replacing the previously used natural water resource with treated water.

A third goal of the project is cost-effectiveness. It is expected that the entire project will eventually pay for itself through the fees paid by the golf courses. Thus, the program is paid for by those who benefit from it and will not burden water and sewer customers. At present, operating costs are fully covered by fees received from the sale of I.Q. water. The most recent operating budget for the I.Q. Water Program is $460,000, with $170,000 allocated for operating costs and the balance set aside to amortize the debt resulting from the initial capital outlay. The program is funded from the sale of I.Q. water to the golf courses at a contract rate of 20.5 cents per 1,000 gallons. Projected revenues will increase to $488,000 by 1994 as a result of signing up more golf course customers.

Program officials are pleased by the fact that no tax dollars have been used to augment the I.Q. Water Program. It thus serves as a striking example of how taxpayers can benefit from a government initiative without bearing any direct costs. Program officials also point out that the program seems to benefit from economies of scale. During a three year period, the cost per 1,000 gallons of water produced and sold decreased nearly 16 percent. Furthermore, the revenues generated by the program are predictable because the contract with each golf course specifies the amount of water that will be paid for whether they use it on a given day or not.

The fourth and final goal of the I.Q. Water Program is to gain public acceptance. Few government initiatives, whether they are innovative or old hat, can succeed without strong public awareness and support. Recognizing this, the district has taken great strides toward gaining and maintaining public enthusiasm for the program. Most importantly, the district wants to ensure that the public remains conservation-minded. Officials are continually informing the community of the benefits and accomplishments of the program. The editorial staff of the local community newspaper has been very supportive of the district's conservation efforts and has helped to keep the program before the public.

Challenges to the I.Q. Water Program

Although there was substantial interest in the I.Q. Water Program during its initial stages in 1984, the district found it very difficult to convince large users of water to enter into a contract at that time. Increased public awareness of the benefits of the program helped to overcome this challenge, but it was actually the severe shortage of water late in the year that convinced large golf courses to participate.

Another challenge to administrators of the I.Q. Water Program was resistance to change on the part of golf course managers. After decades of irrigating their greens in the same manner, they were reluctant to switch to a new, unproven source of water. Once again, it was sheer salesmanship on the part of district officials, combined with the threat of a severe water shortage, that helped convince course managers to participate.

Golf course managers were not the only individuals concerned about using new sources of water for irrigation purposes. The program also caught the attention of public health officials who were uncertain about the health consequences of using I.Q. water. Since some of the recycled wastewater used to irrigate the golf courses would inevitably find its way into drainage systems, there were obvious reasons for the health community to be concerned. Once purity standards were established, based on considerable research, the regulatory community accepted I.Q. water as a safe resource.

The economics of supplying I.Q. water also provided challenges to program officials. The actual value of wastewater was difficult to define and the 20.5 cents per thousand gallons price charged to golf courses was deemed by some to be excessive. For most golf courses, however, the possibility of having their current source of irrigation curtailed during severe water shortages made the price seem reasonable. In effect, many golf course owners viewed the use of I.Q. water as a kind of insurance against droughts that might endanger the beauty and quality of their greens.

Although treating the water and applying it to the golf courses provide few regulatory or operating problems, managing the stockpile of processed I.Q. water has been an on-going challenge. The reason that storing and transporting the water is complicated stems from the fact that demand for irrigation water fluctuates with both the time of year and the amount of rainfall in the immediate area. Supply of wastewater depends on the number of local residents, which can vary as much as 30 percent, depending upon the season. Unfortunately, the supply and demand curves for water are poorly matched. The greatest demand for I.Q. water is in the spring and summer when turf grasses are in their most productive growth stages. Supply of wastewater is at its lowest point at this time because winter residents of the area have already moved away. Consequently, advanced means are being implemented to store the treated wastewater until it can be used by the golf courses. Planners are also using computer simulation models to optimize the storage and delivery of the water in an effort to smooth out the variances between supply and demand.

I.Q. Water: Making a Difference

According to program officials, the I.Q. Water Program has achieved success along three different parameters: water quality standards, usage of I.Q. water, and public acceptance of the program. The I.Q. water must meet or exceed established water quality standards. It is regularly tested for turbidity and chlorine residue. Tests have consistently shown that the recycled wastewater substantially exceeds these levels, proving the effectiveness of the treatment process.

Officials consider it very important to keep track of how much water each golf course actually uses and track the usage against season, rainfall, and other parameters. In 1987, the golf courses used 404 million gallons; in 1988 the volume increased to 607 million gallons. In 1989 and 1990, the usage exceeded 900 million gallons. The increased usage of I.Q. water suggests that golf courses are becoming increasingly reliant on I.Q. water.

Without the I.Q. Water Program in place, the demand on the water supply would have been from two to four million gallons greater each day during 1989 and 1990. Substantial environmental damage and resource depletion could have occurred without the use of the recycled wastewater.

Finally, program administrators believe that it is very important to establish open channels of communication with the public and the professional community. The district receives regular requests for information about I.Q. water as a result of technical papers, meetings with civic groups, and information sessions and tours with engineers and environmental specialists. As long as the public supports the program, administrators believe that the demand for I.Q. water will continue.

Meeting the Needs of the Future

The Loxahatchee River basin has experienced three major droughts in a decade. Residents have been required to cut their water usage by 15 percent. For example, they are only allowed to water their lawns on prescribed days. The 12 million gallons per day of water that comes from the district's aquafiers is at a stress point, and salt water is threatening to intrude on certain supply wells. Against this backdrop, it is clear that initiatives like the I.Q. Water Program will be needed in the foreseeable future.

By 1995, the population of the district's service area will have grown by nearly 30 percent to 65,000 residents. While the I.Q. Water Program is projected to produce 6.2 million gallons of water per day by the mid–1990s, it will not, by itself, be enough to balance the area's water budget. As a result, officials are working feverishly to develop new technologies that will work in tandem with the I.Q. Water Program to conserve water resources.

In addition to increasing the scale of its efforts, program administrators are also planning to increase its scope. The district has already begun plans to provide recycled wastewater to clients other than golf courses, including tree nurseries, cemeteries, recreation areas, transportation corridors, and the lawns of condominium complexes and single family homes. These efforts would substantially reduce the current reliance on potable water for irrigation purposes.

Program officials are also working with resource managers in other parts of Florida to develop similar programs. Not surprisingly, the I.Q. Water Program has received widespread attention throughout the state. District officials are bullish about the chances of duplicating this program because many of the financing, public acceptance, and regulatory hurdles that were in place during the mid–1980s are now gone.

Key Lessons from the I.Q. Water Program

The I.Q. Water Program introduces us to yet another, and possibly the most important, manifestation of cost-effectiveness: The program pays for itself without the benefit of taxpayer dollars. Additionally, the program's success hinges on a comprehensive public awareness campaign. Finally, officials were able to reduce the initial resistance to the I.Q. Water Program by having a neutral, third-party conduct replicable and verifiable safety tests.

COST-EFFECTIVENESS. The I.Q. Water Program, like the Landfill Reclamation Project, achieves cost-effectiveness by selling its by-product. In this case, the by-product is water for irrigation. Unlike the Landfill Reclamation Project, however, the I.Q. Water Program strives to be totally self-supporting by charging rates which cover the costs of administering the program. Although the program has not yet achieved self-sufficiency, the promise to do so has gained the program widespread support, especially among taxpayers.

PUBLIC AWARENESS. Although many of the programs profiled in this book rely on public awareness programs to alleviate resistance to unconventional programs and to inform potential clients of available services, few programs have public awareness programs as comprehensive as the I.Q. Water Program. The main reason for the extensive public awareness efforts, according to program officials, is the controversial nature of the program. Environmentalists are worried about the quality of the I.Q. water and groundskeepers are worried about switching to a new, relatively untested, source of irrigation.

As described above, the I.Q. Water Program not only actively markets its water to golf courses in the local area, but it also conducts information sessions for golf course managers, environmentalists, civic groups, and the local media. In addition, special ties are forged with engineers and environmental specialists to educate them about the safety and reliability of I.Q. water.

When forging ties with engineers and environmentalists, officials stress that it is important to have both accurate facts and the ability to discuss them in the language of engineering and environmental management. Accordingly, experts involved with the I.Q. Water Program frequently write technical papers outlining the results of the program. These papers not only underscore the credibility of the program from a technical standpoint, but they also communicate the viability of the program to other jurisdictions which might benefit from it.

REDUCE RESISTANCE THROUGH THIRD-PARTY STUDIES. In the preceding sections, we have discussed ways to reduce resistance to a controversial program, especially the use of public awareness campaigns and recognizing the needs of (and soliciting the input of) entrenched players. The I.Q. Water Program reduced opposition by conducting verifiable studies which demonstrate the benefits of a given program. Officials hired a neutral, third-party to verify the safety of the I.Q. water for irrigation purposes. The data demonstrating the safety of the water is there for all to see and replicate or verify, if necessary. The existence of such a study lessened the impact of safety arguments which might be posed in opposition to the program.

Chapter 5

Housing

*The strength of a nation . . . is in the intelligent
and well-ordered homes of the people.*
—Lydia Sigourney.

Like the other subject areas discussed in this book, housing in America has become the subject of increased public debate. People have become more aware of the acute shortage of affordable housing. This increased awareness has resulted, in part, from the increasing numbers of homeless people who have flooded public streets. It is estimated that somewhere in the neighborhood of 600,000 Americans are homeless.[32] In some urban areas, the homeless problem is so severe that one cannot walk even a short distance without encountering a homeless individual. Regardless of one's attitude toward these unfortunate people, the problem of homelessness is increasingly everyone's problem.

Housing the poor has become an especially salient issue in the wake of lower real income growth and rising housing costs. At present, an estimated 6.1 million poverty-level households are spending more than one-half of their income on housing. Despite this, the poor do not necessarily live in adequate housing. In fact, more than one-third live in housing deemed inadequate.[33]

Although some people question whether it is the appropriate role of the government to assist in the provision of housing, for over five decades it has been the explicit policy of the federal government to ensure that Americans have access to affordable housing.[34] A dramatic retreat from this policy during the 1980s unquestionably contributed to the large numbers of homeless people we are seeing on the streets today. Since the beginning of the 1980s, federal support for subsidized housing has been reduced by nearly 60 percent. Federal support for new low income housing has virtually disappeared. The result has been a decline of nearly 2.5 million units in the aggregate supply of low income housing.[35] Another impact has been that state and local governments have been forced to take the lead in housing policy.

It would be unfair, however, to place all of the blame on the federal government. Communities have also exacerbated the problem by failing to preserve an adequate stock of low-cost housing. Many communities have witnessed the widespread destruction of low- and medium-income housing. Often, these housing units became so run down that they had to be condemned. In other instances, affordable housing was either destroyed to make room for urban renewal projects or was replaced by more expensive housing. During the last two decades, nearly one-half of the nation's low income, single room occupancy (SRO) housing has been lost to destruction, urban renewal, or conversion to more expensive forms of housing.[36]

This chapter identifies a few community programs that represent the range of alternatives currently in place to combat the declining stock of affordable housing units. The SRO Residential Hotel Program shows how one community has successfully preserved and rehabilitated its existing low-cost housing units. The program also creates innovative incentives for developers to construct new affordable housing units. The Housing Vermont Program shows how the state of Vermont has increased its supply of affordable housing by creating a unique mechanism for investing in low-cost housing. The Massachusetts Housing Partnership illustrates yet another approach to developing and preserving affordable housing units.

While the debate over housing has primarily been aimed at the decrease of affordable housing units, attention has been increasingly focused toward the problem of discrimination in housing and the effects of disinvestment in minority neighborhoods. The Fair Housing Testing and Enforcement Program demonstrates how violations of fair housing laws can be detected and remedied at the local level while the Racial Integration Incentives Program provides insight into one community's approach to achieving its goal of racial integration.

Creating and Preserving Low-Cost Housing: The Single Room Occupancy Residential Hotel Program

Life has not been easy for Stella Goff, but now she is making a comeback. Born into a poor family, Ms. Goff had run away from home as a teenager, had lived in several foster homes, and had eventually moved to San Diego where she developed an addiction to cocaine. Goff has successfully overcome her drug addiction and is gainfully employed in a local clothing store. She credits her comeback to the friends she has made since she moved to San Diego nearly a decade ago. They encouraged her to seek help for her drug problem and helped her find work. But Ms. Goff concedes that things might not have worked out this way; for over a year, she lived on the streets. However, thanks to an innovative housing program in San Diego, she was given the stability of a permanent shelter which she believes was the key to her more recent successes. "When you're on the streets," says Ms. Goff, "you have nothing."

The crisis of homelessness was recognized as one of the world's most pressing social problems when the United Nations declared 1987 to be the International Year of Shelter. The United States is certainly not immune from this problem. Recent estimates put the number of homeless people in the United States in the neighborhood of 600,000.[37]

Nationally, three sequential housing types have been identified to solve the problem of homelessness: emergency shelters, transitional housing (short-term housing), and low-cost permanent housing. In most American cities, the lowest-cost, private form of rental housing is the single room occupancy (SRO) residential hotel. Often, the SRO is the shelter of last resort for people like Stella Goff, who would otherwise be forced to live on the streets. The SRO residents are typically low income, single people. The elderly, disabled, and the working poor constitute a majority of SRO residents.

Like most large American cities, the city of San Diego experienced a significant decline in the number of available SRO housing units during the latter part of the 1980s, especially in downtown areas. The impact of losing the lowest cost housing was an increase in the city's homeless population. By 1989, there were an estimated 5,000 homeless people in the downtown area of San Diego. In addition to the SROs that had already been closed due to uninhabitable conditions, many of the remaining SRO units in San Diego were not safe and were also slated to be closed.

In response to the declining number of affordable SRO rental units, the city of San Diego initiated the innovative SRO Residential Hotel Program to preserve and rehabilitate old SROs and construct new subsidized SROs for very low income individuals. The program creates new incentives to encourage private market development of new SROs which are affordable for low income households without the need of any subsidy. The program also creates a new type of housing unit dubbed "the living unit" which is considered safer and more marketable than a typical SRO.

The SRO Residential Hotel Program

While many American cities had adopted SRO preservation ordinances to prevent the destruction of low income housing, and while rehabilitation of SROs was encouraged in Los Angeles and New York, San Diego was the first city to address the problem of a dwindling supply of SROs through new construction. This approach, in addition to the invention of the economically efficient living units, put San Diego in the vanguard of those communities providing new housing options to low income people.

The SRO Residential Hotel Program is most aptly described as a collection of initiatives designed to expand housing opportunities available to low income people. Some of these initiatives are aimed at changing codes and standards that impede the construction or rehabilitation of SROs. Other initiatives are focused on identifying and providing incentives that encourage the private sector to construct low income housing without construction, operating, or rental subsidies. (Such incentives often require the modification of zoning requirements and building standards. A task force representing developers, architects, building inspectors, fire department officials, and zoning officials has found a number of ways to modify the building codes and lower construction costs while maintaining structural quality and safety.) To the extent possible, the San Diego program also attempts to rehabilitate existing SROs into decent, safe, and sanitary housing resources. Finally, an evaluation mechanism is in place to monitor activities in the areas of construction, preservation, rehabilitation, and the impact that the program has on the number of homeless individuals in the area.

San Diego's Residential Hotel Program is particularly innovative because it encourages low income housing to be built by the private market without the aid of government subsidies. The 1991 budget for the SRO Residential Hotel Program was about $5.84 million. Most of these funds came from federal HODAG funds for new construction as well as revenues earned from the lease and sale of city properties. An important feature of this program is that private developers invested over $25 million in new construction during the first three years of operations. Compared with the $2.9 million in public financing over the same period, the ratio of 8.6 to 1 was considered by many to be an impressive return on public investment.

The results of the SRO Residential Hotel Program speak for themselves. By late 1991, over 2,000 new SRO units were completed or were under construction. About one-quarter of the old SROs had been repaired or renovated, and a special preservation ordinance has halted the destruction of old SROs (over 1,200 were lost in the last decade). All of these units are affordable to low income people without the need of any public subsidy. These results are especially noteworthy considering that they occurred in a city where housing costs are considered among the least affordable in the nation. A major achievement of the SRO Residential Hotel Program is that new, low income housing is being built by the private sector without the aid of any subsidies.

Target Population

Typically, residents of SROs tend to be single, low income individuals. The majority of SRO housing tenants are elderly men and women living on social security or other pensions and young single men and women working in low-paying service jobs. Often, residents have been referred to the SRO by a church or homeless shelter.

Since about one-third of San Diego's population is made up of single person households, and since over 40 percent of the total population are considered to be of low or very low income levels, homelessness and the need for
SROs is pervasive. The need for affordable housing is made even more clear
when one considers the fact that at the time the SRO Residential Hotel Program began, only about 4.6 percent of all housing units in San Diego were
affordable to low income individuals and those on government assistance.

Implementing the SRO Residential Hotel Program

The impetus for the SRO Residential Hotel Program came from a task
force on the homeless created in 1983 by Mayor Roger Hedgecock. The task
force was a regional consortium of public agencies, charitable foundations,
religious organizations, and community leaders.

At that time, the problem of homelessness was just beginning to gain national attention. The goal of the task force was to determine the magnitude
of the homeless problem in San Diego and give the City Council some basic
recommendation as to how to deal with the problem. A year later, the task
force presented its findings to the City Council in a report called "Downtown
Homeless." Since the report was one of the first of its kind, it gained widespread attention. The report estimated that there were about 3,000 homeless
people in downtown San Diego and an additional 3,000 in the surrounding
areas. *Newsweek* magazine did a follow-up report in which it linked the loss
of old SROs to an increase in the homeless population. By late 1984, the issue of
homelessness had made its way to the center ring in the local policy arena.

The Public Services and Safety (PSS) Committee of the City Council requested that the San Diego Housing Commission conduct an extensive survey
of existing SROs within the city's downtown area and provide detailed recommendations for their preservation as affordable housing. In late 1985, the
Housing Commission presented its findings. The commission documented a
loss of SROs during the previous 10 years at an astounding rate of over 100 per
year and recommended that the Council consider the adoption of a one-year
moratorium on the demolition of or conversion of SROs.

By mid–1986, the local Planning Department had prepared an SRO
emergency preservation ordinance to protect SROs from immediate destruction until plans could be made to renovate them. The City Council adopted
the ordinance and further directed the Planning Department to develop a
comprehensive work program which would coordinate various governmental
agencies to address issues of SRO preservation, rehabilitation, and construction. It was the final draft of this working plan that became the basis for San
Diego's SRO Residential Hotel Program.

A major obstacle in the development of the SRO Residential Hotel Program resulted from city codes and standards that did not contain appropriate

provisions for SROs. New and innovative code equivalency standards had to be negotiated and established.

In addition to the obstacle presented by the inadequate building codes and standards, proponents of the SRO Residential Hotel Program had to overcome a firestorm of protest from neighborhood groups who believed that SRO catered to certain undesirable clients and real estate developers who wanted to convert dilapidated SROs into more expensive forms of housing. The Housing Commission successfully minimized opposition to the SRO program by sponsoring walking tours through SROs for the media and prominent public officials. The media proved to be extremely important in developing a base of public support for the program.

In 1987, after several months of evaluating the building codes and altering them through the adoption of the SRO Preservation and Relocation Assistance Ordinances to make preservation and renovation of SROs easier, the Council went about creating incentives for the private market to construct new SROs. The result was the invention of the "housing unit," a single family unit which incorporates slightly smaller units with shared bath and kitchen facilities. By the end of 1988, private developers completed the first new SRO hotel in San Diego in 75 years. By mid-1990, the number of new units had climbed to over 2,500 as a result of this innovative housing program.

The Future of the SRO Residential Housing Program

Since the city of San Diego adopted the SRO Preservation and Relocation Assistance Ordinances in 1987, the rapid loss of SRO development has slowed as a result of continuous development. Importantly, the program has gained national recognition and has been considered in other areas of the country. The concept of the living unit would clearly be appropriate in most major cities and also in resort areas where low cost housing is at a premium. Although the preservation and rehabilitation components of the program would apply to older cities where SROs are already a part of the existing housing supply, the new construction innovations created by this program could be adopted wherever that enabling legislation is passed.

The SRO program is immediately transferable to other jurisdictions. The American Planning Association, the Housing and Urban Development (HUD) regional office in San Diego, and the California Building Industry Association have all publicly recognized the nationwide potential of this innovative housing program. Elements of the program have been adopted in a number of jurisdictions, including Orange County, Santa Monica, San Francisco, and New York.

Within California, legislation sponsored by San Diego has been passed which legalized the new housing unit format at the state level. *California Builder* magazine recently reported, "The city of San Diego has developed a new type of housing expected to sweep the state of California in the 1990s."

Although the program was originally intended to provide low cost, permanent housing for the homeless population, the new living unit is now considered suitable housing for the military, students, the elderly, and other low wage, single workers. Two main challenges remain in San Diego. First, there is a need to educate the entire community in an effort to minimize opposition to new SROs. Second is the creation of additional nonprofit housing corporations which can develop new SROs at rates even more affordable than those provided by for-profit developers.

Key Lessons from the SRO Residential Hotel Program

Officials of the SRO Residential Hotel Program believe that the success of their program stems from their ability to quickly reduce opposition to what was initially a controversial program. Opposition was reduced through tours and information sessions with public officials and neighborhood leaders. Additionally, program officials made it clear that it was necessary to change codes and building standards that stood in the way of preserving and constructing new SRO hotels. Finally, officials believe that a critical element of the program's success was the willingness of members of the task force to work together to achieve a viable solution to San Diego's housing problem.

REDUCE OPPOSITION THROUGH DEMONSTRATIONS. The SRO Residential Hotel Program demonstrated the program to reduce opposition. Demonstrating the SRO program to local officials, neighborhood leaders, and members of the media by giving them tours of facilities already in place showed that SRO housing could be aesthetically pleasing, well-managed, and not a major burden to taxpayers. Taking care to include the media in these efforts was especially fruitful since they became major advocates of the program during legislative debates on codes and standards.

CHANGE CODES AND STANDARDS THAT IMPEDE PROGRESS. Officials of the SRO program point out that for the program to be viable, architects had to come up with a more economical living unit. To accomplish this, officials had to first change building codes and standards which prevented the construction of the units. Efforts to change codes, laws, standards, or ordinances required a well-planned legislative strategy.

Enlisting the assistance of a professional lobbyist is probably a necessary first step in changing relevant codes. Winning the support of the media is probably a close second. At any rate, changing laws and codes takes time, energy, research, and persistent lobbying. At a very minimum, a keen awareness of the political process is necessary.

WILLINGNESS ON THE PART OF DIVERSE INTERESTS TO WORK TOGETHER. The SRO Residential Hotel Program provides us with a slightly different take on the concept of strategic alliances. Whereas we previously discussed them in the context of government agencies forging a close working relationship to further each party's goals, here we talk about something more akin to a public/private partnership between government agencies and private organizations. In the case of the SRO Residential Hotel Program, a task force was formed which included representatives from all of the diverse interests that had a stake in housing: developers, architects, building inspectors, fire department officials, and zoning officials. These varied interests worked together to discuss ways in which building codes could be modified to help house the homeless and ways in which construction costs could be reduced. Getting the input from all parties early in the process minimized the risk that there would be serious opposition in the future.

Encouraging Private Investment in Affordable Housing: The Housing Vermont Program

Many areas across the nation are facing a severe shortage of affordable rental housing. The shortage is expected to become more severe in the 1990s as lapsing federal use restrictions permit private owners of subsidized rental projects to convert their dwellings to expensive rental units or condominiums. The Tax Reform Act of 1986 further exacerbated the situation by drastically reducing incentives for new private sponsorship of affordable rental housing. As a result, many communities now find themselvs lacking both an adequate supply of affordable housing and a mechanism for ensuring affordability over the long run. Vermont is one state that has recognized the need for more affordable rental housing. Currently, it is estimated that Vermont needs an additional 20,000 units of affordable rental housing in order to meet the bloated demand. In an effort to address this growing problem, the Housing Vermont (HV) Program was established.

The Housing Vermont Program: Creating a Public Corporation

Housing Vermont (HV) is a statewide, nonprofit corporation which until recently was funded by the Vermont Housing Finance Agency (VHFA) to preserve and develop affordable rental housing. Since fiduciary responsibilities prohibited the VHFA from actively developing real estate, seed capital was provided instead to create the Housing Vermont Program. Today, the Housing

Vermont Program is self-supporting. Housing Vermont has already provided over 700 housing units that are virtually guaranteed to remain affordable for years to come. These units house approximately 1,550 residents.

The program was designed to spark innovative partnerships which use private funds to serve a public purpose. Specifically, the program offers private-sector organizations economic incentives to invest in affordable housing to fill the gap left by the loss of federal subsidies.

The primary goal of Housing Vermont is to acquire or construct 5,000 units of perpetually affordable housing by the end of 1995. It is estimated that these additional units of affordable housing will serve 50 percent of the potential client base by that time. Other objectives include maximizing private investment and spurring business involvement in the development of perpetually affordable housing. A long-term goal of the program is to expand into nonrental housing because it is believed that the Housing Vermont Program could make a significant impact in the permanent housing market.

An important characteristic of the program is that it promotes mixed income housing. Approximately 60 percent of the units acquired or produced by the program will be occupied by families which are below 60 percent of the area median income as defined by the Department of Housing and Urban Development (HUD).

The staff and board of directors of Housing Vermont attempt to identify communities with the greatest need for housing or in which there is an existing rental housing development at risk of being converted to more expensive housing. Once a development is acquired or constructed, the local nonprofit general partners (organized to manage the housing development) set tenant selection priorities, typically giving the highest priority to those most in need of housing who also have satisfactory references.

The completion of the first 700 units of perpetually affordable housing has demonstrated that the public good and private investment are not mutually exclusive. Not only do the partners receive a reasonable financial incentive to participate in the program, but a sizeable number of the housing units will eventually be owned by the tenants.

Perhaps as important as the actual development of these units is the credibility that Housing Vermont has engendered within Vermont. Housing Vermont has made the production and preservation of nonprofit, affordable housing acceptable among bankers, community officials, and housing advocates. This cooperative atmosphere will ultimately produce housing at a scale that will have a real impact on the housing situation in Vermont.

As of mid–1990, Housing Vermont had raised a total of $11.4 million in equity. On a per capita basis, this was an unprecedented private sector investment in affordable housing. In 1989, nearly $5 million was committed for the creation of 328 units of housing in three housing developments. These developments were mixed income, senior, and family housing. In addition,

$3.5 million was committed to three existing developments to acquire and rehabilitate 372 units that were at risk of being converted into more expensive rental housing. The combined development costs of these six projects represented over $43.5 million. During 1991, Housing Vermont constructed or acquired an additional 294 housing units with an equity investment of $3.4 million.

Considering the impressive amounts of equity generated by Housing Vermont, the program is surprisingly cost-effective. Housing Vermont's operating budget for the last calendar year was about $282,000. Most of these funds were used for administrative costs, including salaries for a full-time staff of seven. Funding sources include syndication fees (7.5 percent of gross equity), development fees, membership fees, partnership accounting fees from each project, interest earnings on investments, and project loans. No operating funds are received from state or local government other than through membership fees.

Although the program initially faced operating deficits, Housing Vermont now operates solidly in the black with surpluses held in a development fund. Currently, the program does not actively solicit donations, even though such contributions would be tax deductible. Housing Vermont will probably pursue donations in the coming years, but it will need to do so carefully so as not to compete with local nonprofit organizations.

The Investment Vehicle: Vermont Equity Fund

Since the main function of Housing Vermont is to purchase and construct housing, raising funds is obviously of critical importance. Although the program is now supported through fees collected from development and management fees, the funds that created the program were collected through an important adjunct to Housing Vermont called the Vermont Equity Fund. The Vermont Equity Fund is an investment vehicle designed to give corporate investors an opportunity to make relatively low-risk investments in housing.

As a general partner in the Vermont Equity Fund, Housing Vermont encourages private corporations to invest in affordable housing in exchange for low income housing tax credits. The Vermont Equity Fund has unique features which differentiate it from traditional real estate syndicates. In traditional syndicates, investors are entitled to receive the appreciated value of a property at the time the property is sold. Since permanent affordability is a major feature of the Housing Vermont Program, investors in the Vermont Equity Fund forgo these residual benefits. Instead, private investors get tax benefits. Local nonprofit organizations, including tenant organizations, may exercise favorable purchase options on Housing Vermont properties after 15 years. The Vermont Equity Fund exchanges investments from the private investors for 99 percent of the tax benefits generated by each project, as these tax benefits have no value for nonprofit organizations. Since tax benefits, not cash, are the primary benefit to investors, rents need to be raised only to cover increased operating costs. Many business organizations, especially banks, find such an investment to be extremely worthwhile. By syndicating the tax credits to corporate investors, Housing Vermont has been able to enhance their value by nearly twice the value of traditional syndication. This results in more equity available to housing developments, thus assuring greater affordability. The Vermont Equity Fund is the first investment vehicle of its kind supported by a state housing finance agency which is geared towards ensuring that housing will remain perpetually affordable.

In accepting the Housing Vermont bylaws for 501 (c)(3) purposes, the Internal Revenue Service has implicitly recognized that the creation of housing developments, like those created by Housing Vermont, are consistent with charitable purposes. As such, contributions are tax deductible.

Housing Vermont: A Unique Approach to Affordable Housing

The true innovations of the Housing Vermont Program stem from the fact that the driving force behind its creation was a statewide public entity, the Vermont Housing Finance Agency (VHFA). Originally, the VHFA explored the possibility of being an affordable housing developer in its own right. The agency's legal counsel, however, advised that a fiduciary conflict would result if the VHFA ventured into housing development and ownership. Consequently, Housing Vermont was established to function as statewide, nonprofit development corporation.

The Housing Vermont Program uses a variety of structural devices which differentiates it from other housing programs. A $2 million funding agreement between the VHFA and Housing Vermont allowed for the creation of an agency that functions at the operational level with the flexibility and independence of a private developer while allowing it to remain accountable to government bodies at the policy level.

Perhaps the most important policy innovation associated with the Housing Vermont Program is the concept of perpetual affordability. In its practical application, the term means that all available techniques are employed to assure that housing developments can sustain themselves indefinitely at rent levels that low income families can afford. In part, this relies on the ability of tenant organizations to purchase the developments at the end of the tax benefit period. It is also intended that the development will not be subject to exploitation for private profit beyond the tax benefits.

These objectives are met by keeping initial costs low, giving an option to purchase to a local organization that represents the tenants, and limiting the option price and future rent increases through the use of a special agreement called a Housing Subsidy Covenant. This covenant is a technical statute which, in effect, allows but does not attempt to impose perpetual affordability.

In addition to creating a new statute which authorizes the novel Housing Subsidy Covenant, other legal initiatives were pursued to further the goals of the Housing Vermont Program. For example, VHFA spearheaded a new statute authorizing banks to make equity investments in housing projects deemed to be qualified by VHFA. Designations are awarded on a case by case basis, and tend to be located in areas determined to be at-risk.

Another feature of the Housing Vermont Program is its unique partnerships with local nonprofit organizations. Since Housing Vermont operates on a statewide basis, it undertakes particular projects in partnership with organizations in at-risk communities. Housing Vermont provides the expertise and access to equity markets that ad hoc local groups often lack, while the nonprofit organizations make sure that there is a local stake in each development and that the development process is sensitive to tenant and community concerns. The local non-profit organization often serves as a management training ground for the ultimate takeover of the housing development by the tenants.

Governance of the Housing Vermont Program

Housing Vermont is governed by the 11 members of the Housing Vermont Board of Directors. The organization's bylaws stipulate that at least three of the directors must represent non-profit organizations which promote low income housing. Housing Vermont has always sought to maintain a mix of public and private sector representation on the board. The inclusion of private sector representatives has given Housing Vermont enormous credibility within the private sector as well as giving its methods of operating a more pragmatic, businesslike approach.

A majority of the directors are elected by sustaining members who pay much higher annual dues than regular members. Sustaining members, along with regular members, elect four of the directors and the governor may appoint one director. The board of directors is responsible for approving all Housing Vermont projects.

In return for funding received from the VHFA, Housing Vermont agrees to allow VHFA to approve the annual operating budget and allows it to reserve a number of other rights. While VHFA cannot mandate specific projects for Housing Vermont, an agreement between the two organizations specifies the general qualifications which each project must meet.

For the most part, Housing Vermont's organization is structured vertically, like most private sector organizations. The president, who is elected by the board, is responsible for hiring and supervising the staff and overseeing operation of the corporation. A vice president for development supervises the project manager and a development assistant. These individuals are responsible for overseeing the actual housing development projects and ensuring that there is enough funding to meet the financial goals of the program. A financial officer keeps the books and oversees the financial reporting of each housing project. Housing Vermont does not directly manage any projects after they are completed, but it does monitor each completed project for tax and fiscal compliance.

History of the Housing Vermont Program

The Vermont Housing Finance Agency created Housing Vermont on the basis of two existing charitable foundations. The Local Initiatives Support Corporation (LISC), a Ford Foundation spin-off, had successfully implemented something similar to the Vermont Equity Fund in Chicago. The Enterprise Foundation had also created a similar fund in Cincinnati, and concurrent with the creation of Housing Vermont, was advising the Maine State Housing Authority on the creation of a statewide, nonprofit organization for Maine.

After an evaluation of these programs, the Housing Vermont Program was designed with the intent of making it more comprehensive. For example, Housing Vermont is a statewide organization and is much more cost-effective insofar as a much higher percentage of the syndication proceeds are invested directly into the developments. Furthermore, the Housing Vermont financing structure assures that the units will remain affordable for the economic life of the development.

Before the Housing Vermont Program could become fully operational, sufficient funds had to be secured to cover start-up and operating costs. Housing Vermont advocates immediately realized that broad credibility, both within the public and private sectors, would be necessary to attract capital. Legitimacy was partially achieved as the result of a strong relationship with VHFA which already had a proven, 15-year track record in the state. A strong board of directors, representing both public and private interests, also contributed to Housing Vermont's credibility. The mixed interests of the directors gave the program an entrepreneurial orientation and acceptance within the public sector. Additionally, staff members were recruited who shared the general vision of the need to produce and preserve affordable housing but with the bottom line always in mind.

The initial seed capital provided by VHFA was almost immediately followed by successes in securing private investments. Debt financing for Housing Vermont projects has come from many sources including tax-exempt VHFA bonds and deferred loans from other state entities such as the Vermont Housing and Conservation Trust Fund.

Critical to the program's perpetual affordability was finding local, socially motivated investors willing to invest at relatively low rates of return with no residual benefit when the properties are sold. This obstacle was partially overcome by changing Vermont state laws which prevented banks from making equity investments in affordable housing. The banks themselves were instrumental in changing the relevant laws.

Since local non-profit housing developers were initially threatened by the prospect of a large, statewide entity entering the competition for scare resources, Housing Vermont actively pursued joint ventures to turn this potential conflict into fruitful cooperation. Concerns expressed in the local non-profit community regarding competition have been alleviated through clear development agreements between Housing Vermont and its partners which state the rights, responsibilities, compensation, decision-making process, budgets, and schedules for each project. Housing Vermont has made a policy decision to work closely with local non-profit partners whenever possible.

As the Housing Vermont Program has matured over the past two years, program administrators have faced several persistent obstacles which have prevented the program from reaching its full potential. In some areas of the state, community resistance to affordable housing continues to block Housing Vermont projects. Much of this resistance is due to a lack of understanding about the type of housing the program constructs and the residents who would inhabit it. In response, Housing Vermont is considering the creation of a separate entity which would provide consulting services to towns where the elected leadership has identified the need for affordable housing. The consulting service would help officials overcome public resistance as well as provide technical support during the construction of housing.

In addition to sporadic community resistance to affordable housing, serious financial obstacles also pose a threat to Housing Vermont's construction efforts. In particular, the lack of federal funds for housing and the uncertain future of the federal tax policy may make it more difficult to raise funds. Continuing innovation in financing techniques and the creation of public/ private partnerships will be needed to overcome the financial impediments to the creation and preservation of affordable housing.

Finally, an obstacle to success is created by the gentrification of rural Vermont. Significant disparity in housing prices between Vermont and southern New England has caused a wave of land speculation which has driven up the price of land significantly. Obviously, higher land prices make developing affordable rental housing much more difficult than it might be otherwise.

The Future of Housing Vermont

The need to serve the housing needs of low-income residents will not change until more federal resources are made available. In the meantime, state and local governments will need to provide substantial amounts of affordable housing. Given the status of the federal budget, it is likely that the burden of providing affordable housing will remain at the state and local level for years to come. Given this reality, the administrators of Housing Vermont plan to continue to focus their efforts towards meeting the housing needs of the working poor.

Planning and regulatory restraint on development is likely to increase in coming years. Housing Vermont will need to adapt to these changes, particularly in the areas of land conservation and environmental management. Such adaptations might include improved on-site sewage disposal, increased energy efficiency, and the use of select building materials. If Housing Vermont does not provide technical assistance to towns directly, it will need to find alternative ways to help communities plan for housing.

Mobile home parks and manufactured housing may become the only economically feasible alternatives open to affordable, owner-occupied housing. Therefore, Housing Vermont has already begun to explore possible developments in these areas.

Since the problem of affordable housing shortages is not endemic to Vermont, it is likely that other counties and states will develop programs similar to Housing Vermont. The basic legal structure, including organizational documents, the funding agreement, the Housing Subsidy Covenant, and the IRS-approved 501 (c)(3) application can be transplanted in its entirety to any of the 47 states which have housing finance agencies. It can also be duplicated in any substantial municipal jurisdiction which has a reasonably sophisticated housing development agency with the capacity to issue tax-exempt bonds.

Key Lessons from the Housing Vermont Program

In many respects, the Housing Vermont Program is quite similar to the SRO Residential Hotel Program. Both hinge on private sector investment in public housing through unique investment vehicles. Also, officials in both programs stress the necessity of changing laws and codes in order for the programs to be effective.

UNIQUE INVESTMENT VEHICLES. The initial fundraising for the Housing Vermont Program was done through an investment vehicle designed to give corporate investors an opportunity to make relatively low-risk investments in housing. The vehicle, called the Vermont Equity Fund, allows corporations to invest in affordable housing in exchange for low income housing tax credits. The Vermont Equity Fund was specifically designed to guarantee that housing developed under the Housing Vermont program would remain permanently affordable. To do this, investors do not receive the appreciated value of the property which would acrue until the time the property is sold (as is usually the case with real estate syndications). Instead, investors get tax benefits.

CHANGING LAWS AND CODES. Like the SRO Residential Hotel Program, the Housing Vermont Program would not have been able to accomplish its goals had certain laws preventing banks and other institutions from investing in low-cost housing not first been changed. Officials underscore the importance of identifying laws, codes, and ordinances which stand in the way of a program's goals, and then enlisting the support of legislators (and other public officials) to change them.

A State Helps Communities Create Affordable Housing: The Massachusetts Housing Partnership

Affordable housing became a major issue in many areas of the country during the mid–1980s. A decreasing rate of private household production combined with unprecedented increases in rents and housing prices made it difficult for low income working families to find permanent homes.

The lack of adequate housing opportunities for low and moderate income people was particularly troubling in the northeast where housing construction had been declining since the 1970s. In the Boston area, the median price of single family homes doubled between 1983 and 1986. Rents increased as well. As a result, the governor and Massachusetts Legislature decided to make affordable housing a major policy objective.

In January 1985, Governor Michael Dukakis announced plans for the formation of the Massachusetts Housing Partnership. Today, the partnership addresses the affordable housing crisis by encouraging increased housing development and preserving the existing stock of affordable housing.

The Massachusetts Housing Partnership

The principles and assumptions behind the Massachusetts Housing Partnership (MHP) are straightforward. First, the state's housing needs must be addressed by increasing the amount of affordable housing and by preserving that which already exists. Second, the success of this effort depends upon the creation of new partnerships between private housing developers and local government. Finally, the state's housing policies and development resources must be redesigned to empower local public officials and to facilitate and support local housing partnerships.

The MHP has consolidated resources from other agencies and has served as a clearinghouse for more than $500 million in loans, grants, and technical assistance funds to support local affordable housing initiatives across the state. The low and moderate income households affected by the program include the homeless, those at risk of displacement from affordable housing, and low income families that cannot afford market rents. The needs of potential first time home buyers who are unable to compete in the private market and those who cannot afford housing in areas with the greatest employment opportunities are also addressed by the program.

A primary objective of MHP is to motivate cities and towns to work with the private and nonprofit sectors to develop affordable housing and to provide technical and financial assistance to facilitate such initiatives. Often, this requires state housing and development agencies to find new ways of doing business that are more responsive to local needs. In particular, MHP crosses agency lines to make all state housing, planning, and community development programs responsive to the concerns of local housing partnerships.

The program achieves its purposes through several means. Technical assistance is provided to public and private development agencies by an eight member staff operating out of six regional offices. These staff members address their clients through frequent conferences and through publications developed by the partnership.

The Housing Partnership also provides direct financial assistance to clients through a homeownership production and challenge grant program. These funds are awarded to agencies that construct affordable housing. The Homeownership Opportunity Program (HOP) is a $40 million program to stimulate joint initiatives between communities and developers. HOP units sell for average prices of $75,000 or less and have low mortgage financing in conjunction with the Massachusetts Housing Finance Agency. Challenge grants of up to $50,000 each are provided from a $3 million fund which supports innovative approaches to meeting local housing needs.

Indirect financial assistance is also provided through other state agencies which administer planning and development funds to municipalities, nonprofit organizations, and private developers. The Municipal Advance Program (MAP) provides grants of up to $30,000 for predevelopment costs associated with affordable housing development. Such grants would cover the costs of feasibility analyses, site evaluations, developer kits, and negotiation costs. Grants from this $2 million program are made only to cities and towns with local housing partnerships. Front-end loans and technical assistance to nonprofits are provided from a $3.5 million MHP revolving loan program administered by the state's Community Economic Development Assistance Corporation.

The target population of MHP consists primarily of low and moderate income households. These are households, which are defined for purposes of state housing programs as earning between 50 and 80 percent of median income, respectively. Local housing partnerships are encouraged to formulate responses to a wide range of community housing needs which may, in some cases, go beyond the income eligibility limits of state housing programs.

The Massachusetts Housing Partnership and its local housing partnership affiliates do not actively own, operate, or develop housing. Instead, they act through intermediaries such as private developers, nonprofit organizations, local housing partnerships, and municipal governments. Direct contact with housing consumers is limited to providing general information on housing availability and putting consumers in direct contact with local organizations. All housing developed with partnership financial assistance must include an affirmative action goal and adhere to a fair marketing plan. Preference is also given to local residents in all MHP housing developments. Local housing initiatives sponsored by MHP are underway in roughly one-third of Massachusetts cities and towns, accounting for about two-thirds of the state's total population.

Organization of the Massachusetts Housing Partnership

The Massachusetts Housing Partnership operates on the premise that state housing policy should be developed and evaluated by those who are directly involved in the production and preservation of affordable housing. It is coordinated by a 30 member board appointed by the governor. (The governor also serves as an *ex officio* member.) The MHP board includes the chairperson of the committees on house and senate housing and urban development, eight housing developers (including four non-profits), two bank presidents, a mayor, a city manager, a realtor, a union executive, a legal services attorney, and advocates for the homeless, among others. New appointments are made on a regular basis to broaden the representation.

The MHP Board has six standing committees which frequently solicit involvement of nonboard members to represent key constituencies during the policy making process. Doing so allows the board to identify possible areas of disagreement and generate possible solutions. For example, the Housing Production Committee added a town manager, three city and town planning directors, and a small town's executive secretary to help design the Homeownership Opportunity Program. The input of these outsiders greatly enhanced the board's ability to create an effective and relatively conflict-free program. The At-Risk Committee routinely includes representatives of state human service agencies and advocate groups, such as the Alliance for the Mentally Ill

The principle of broad-based participation also extends to MHP operations. The MHP Challenge Grant Program relies heavily on an outside panel to allocate $1,000,000 in grants each year for housing innovations. The new MHP Committee on Standards and Evaluation annually reviews the performance of local housing partnerships based, in large part, on peer reviews by community representatives.

A large percentage of MHP's budget comes from the Massachusetts Housing Partnership Fund which was created by the legislature in 1985. The fund is managed by seven directors designated by the governor, including three representatives of the savings and cooperative bank industry, two members of the MHP board, the secretary of Communities and Development, and the secretary for Administration and Finance.

The MHP staff reports to a full-time director (who also holds the title of assistant secretary) and meets regularly with the secretary of Communities and Development. The MHP administers several of its program through contractual agreements with the Community Economic Development Assistance Corporation and the Massachusetts Housing Finance Agency.

Since MHP is regarded by state officials as a focal point for housing expertise, MHP makes recommendations on the allocation of state housing, land-use planning, and community development funds not directly within its budget.

The MHP budget is currently derived from three primary sources including the Massachusetts Housing Partnership Fund which derives its revenues from a state excise tax on bank withdrawals. It also receives direct financial support from the Massachusetts Housing Finance Agency and the legislature for the Homeownership Opportunity Program and for the general administrative expenses of the Executive Office of Communities and Development. While the partnership has enjoyed a budget of over $21 million in recent years, the severe fiscal crisis in Massachusetts may require the program to operate on substantially less in the future. Plans are already underway to replace the Homeownership Opportunity Program with a more limited program aimed at raising funds through the secondary mortgage market.

Achievements of the Housing Partnership

The MHP's most important achievement has been making affordable housing a mainstream political issue in the state's cities and towns. Chief elected officials (mayors and boards of selectmen) now take direct responsibility for an issue which was previously handled at the state level. This is evidenced by the substantial number of local housing partnerships formed as a result of the MHP program (nearly 200 by 1991). Further evidence is provided by the level of housing activity in suburban towns that had previously resisted affordable housing proposals and by the degree of cooperation between private developers and local officials seen in proposals submitted to MHP's homeownership program.

The favorable political climate and preference for local housing initiatives resulting from MHP's efforts has generated strong support in many areas. Local officials, legislators, organized labor, private and nonprofit developers, community organizations, and the press have all given their support to the Housing Partnership. This wide base of support has not only made local housing partnerships more common, but it has also led to the production and preservation of affordable housing. The partnership has created approximately 3,000 new, mixed-income housing units through its Homeownership Opportunity Program and preserved nearly 6,000 federally-subsidized, mixed-income housing units through redevelopment.

The greatest shortcoming of the program has been its inability to provide adequate information and technical assistance to all local housing partnerships. Limited staff makes it difficult to do so and imminent budget cuts make it unlikely that MHP will be able to expand these services in the near future. Nonetheless, the program has attempted to address this shortcoming by identifying a small number of communities that will receive extensive staff report. The MHP has also assigned consultants to assist several other communities identified through a needs survey. For communities which will not receive direct staff support, MHP has developed a self-help publication on forming and managing local housing partnerships. A workbook is planned to assist housing partnerships in assessing local housing needs. In the future, if funds permit, program officials would like to provide direct assistance to all communities that request it.

In addition to not being able to provide as much direct assistance as they would like, MHP administrators have identified other potential obstacles to success. One of the most significant has arisen from conflicts between private developers (especially those who are new to state housing programs) and local housing partnerships. In some cases, developers have tried to bypass the local political process and have argued that they will get permits and housing subsidies approved by the state despite local objections. The MHP has publicly backed the local partnership process in such conflicts and has denied state funds to several proposed mixed-income developments that were not negotiated in good faith with local officials.

A final obstacle has been the reluctance of some local housing partnerships to help provide housing for populations with special needs such as low income families, the homeless, and the mentally ill. The partnership has responded by promoting positive examples where local activists have created a base of political support for special needs housing. The partnership has also established financial incentives through a number of state grant programs for communities that do an exceptional job of providing housing for a range of housing needs and incomes.

Challenges for the Future

There are several challenges facing MHP in the next few years. In addition to surviving potentially devastating budget cutbacks, a major effort is needed to develop an effective vehicle for involving large business and institutional employers in efforts to develop and preserve affordable housing. Housing costs are frequently cited as a major impediment to future job growth in the state, yet the business community has historically stayed at arm's length from housing issues.

The partnership also needs to respond to the softening of the real estate market. It must redesign several market driven, mixed-income housing programs while emphasizing that significant unmet housing needs still exist.

The MHP continues to provide other states with a wealth of knowledge about the construction and preservation of affordable housing. In the future, the MHP staff will need to juggle increased requests for information from within the state with requests for information from other jurisdictions interested in starting programs similar to MHP.

The Housing Partnership is an initiative that can be easily transferred and adapted to other states. The primary obstacles to affordable housing development nationally are local land-use control and a lack of local political support for individual projects. The grass roots approach of MHP is directly responsive to these obstacles. Other states have recognized the potential of the MHP program and have requested assistance in forming similar programs. The partnership was featured at a national conference sponsored by the Council of State Community Affairs Agencies in conjunction with 22 national organizations. Connecticut and New York are developing affordable housing programs which are largely based on the MHP model. In time, other states are expected to follow.

Key Lessons from the Massachusetts Housing Partnership

There are three main lessons to be learned from the Massachusetts Housing Partnership. First, state officials indicate that there are clear advantages to utilizing resources at the community level when administering state programs. Second, given limited financial and managerial resources, it is imperative that program managers identify and prioritize areas of critical need and allocate limited resources accordingly. Finally, the Massachusetts Housing Partnership demonstrates a common way in which economic incentives can be used to encourage participation in a program.

UTILIZE RESOURCES AT THE COMMUNITY LEVEL. When administering a state program, it is often beneficial to utilize resources at the community level for four reasons. First, if local agencies and organizations (such as housing agencies) are already in place at the local level, it is probably more cost-effective to use them rather than setting up parallel agencies. Second, since agencies already in place at the community level are more familiar with the local environment, they are probably in a better position to understand the needs of the community. Third, use of community organizations to administer a state-sponsored program allows for hands-on management of the program. If problems develop, it is convenient to have people based in the community who can address them quickly. Finally, use of community resources gives a stake in the management of the program to those who are likely to implement the program, in this case, local officials, local developers, and community-based housing agencies.

PRIORITIZE NEEDS AND ALLOCATE RESOURCES ACCORDINGLY. Most programs operate under strict financial limitations. The Massachusetts Housing Partnership is no exception. It has come under increasing budget pressures as state officials have struggled to correct the state's financial crisis. As such, even though the program has as its goal helping all communities, it makes sense to identify those areas where need for a program is most critical. The Massachusetts Housing Partnership has been successful in identifying areas of the state where affordable housing is most in need, and it has focused more resources (mostly consulting services) toward those areas. The return on investment in such areas is greater than in areas where demand for the service is not as great.

ECONOMIC INCENTIVES, REVISITED. The Massachusetts Housing Partnership uses grants to encourage communities and local housing agencies to participate in the program. The Housing Partnership provides direct financial assistance to clients through a Homeownership Challenge Grant program. Other funds are also provided through state agencies which administer planning and development funds to municipalities, nonprofit organizations, and private developers. Program officials believe that these financial incentives have been key to the success of the program.

Ensuring Equal Opportunity in Housing: The Fair Housing Testing and Enforcement Program

Innovative housing programs can effect change in a wide variety of areas, including constructing and maintaining affordable housing, providing for the homeless, and stimulating racial integration. However, no single aspect of housing policy generates more debate than the issue of fair housing. Although the concept of fair housing is rigorously defined by federal and state laws, in practice, it basically means that people should have equal access to housing opportunities. In other words, two people who approach a realtor who are similar in every respect, except race (or sex, etc.), *should* be able to view the same housing units. Indeed, they may *choose* not to view the same units, but they should not be excluded from doing so because of the color of their skin, their sex, or a physical disability.

But what sounds simple on paper is much more complicated in practice. As well meaning public officials strive to provide fair access to the housing markets for everyone, they find that they must confront thorny social issues, including racism, sexism, and sexual preference. It is no wonder that fair housing is often given disproportionately less attention by public officials than other housing issues.

Those jurisdictions that have the courage to support fair housing initiatives often find themselves amid fire storms of protest, particularly from real estate interests that disapprove of the methods used to enforce fair housing laws. On the other hand, many real estate interests that support the principle of fair housing are strong advocates of fair housing enforcement programs.

One of the earliest non-federal attempts to enforce fair housing laws was the Systemic Fair Housing Testing and Enforcement Program, sponsored by the Massachusetts Commission Against Discrimination (MCAD). Founded in 1983, MCAD's program has not only provided redress for specific incidents of proven housing discrimination, but it has also increased the public's awareness of the problem and has given real estate agencies incentive to consider the consequences of their sales and rental practices.

Fair Housing Laws: The Basis for MCAD's Program

Since the beginning of the modern civil rights movement in the 1960s, a major concern of minorities and housing advocates has been equal treatment in the housing market. Since that time, fair housing laws have changed dramatically. In particular, new classes of protected categories have been added. These include disabled people, children, and, in some states homosexuals. Enforcement provisions have been greatly strengthened. At the federal level, the Department of Housing and Urban Development (HUD) has gained extensive enforcement authority, including awards of unlimited compensatory damages and civil penalties ranging from $10,000 to $50,000. At the state level, MCAD has gone from having a maximum damage limit of $2,000 to being able to award the same type of relief as that provided under federal law.

Under the provisions of the Federal Fair Housing Act (Title VIII), HUD is required to defer the processing of Title VIII complaints to state and local agencies that are certified as being substantially equivalent to HUD. In most parts of the United States, the enforcement of the Federal Fair Housing Act is carried out by state and local agencies. Accordingly, MCAD's Systemic Fair Housing Testing and Enforcement Program is designed to enforce both federal and state fair housing laws.

The Systemic Fair Housing Testing and Enforcement Program

Massachusetts policymakers were forced to act when they discovered that large-scale, institutionalized housing discrimination against minorities, women, and families with children was a significant problem in the state. Officials found that discrimination in housing had a direct link to the problem of homelessness. Thus, fair housing law testing and enforcement became central to the state's housing policy.

The Systemic Fair Housing Testing and Enforcement Program uncovered a discouraging 70 percent to 80 percent rates of discrimination against blacks and Hispanics in both the sales and rental markets. The program also uncovered evidence that discrimination against female-headed households is equally pervasive. The major goals of the Testing and Enforcement Program are to reduce the level of systemic housing discrimination and expand equal housing choices for minorities and women. The program also seeks to eliminate housing discrimination as a factor that impedes the ability of homeless families to secure permanent housing. Finally, the program increases awareness of fair housing laws.

In general, administrators of the Testing and Enforcement Program believe that few doors of housing opportunity are overtly closed to minority applicants. In contrast to the blatant discrimination of the past, most of the documented discrimination that occurs today is practiced without obvious racial reference. In many cases, the perpetrator might not even be aware that he or she has committed actions that might be construed as discriminatory under fair housing laws. It is difficult to detect these subtle types of discrimination for the purposes of fair housing law enforcement.

The MCAD program uses a technique called fair housing testing to uncover hidden forms of discrimination. Fair housing testing is an especially effective technique in areas where access to rental and sales markets is primarily controlled by real estate brokers. The policies and practices of these middle men can have far-reaching discriminatory impact. Such practices include steering minority applicants away from certain areas and discriminatory advertising. By concentrating on real estate agencies in selected grographic areas, the MCAD program has a widespread impact on eliminating these discriminatory practices.

The Systemic Fair Housing Testing and Enforcement Program, as its name suggests, is a two-part program. The first part of the program uses fair housing testing to investigate housing providers for compliance with fair housing laws. Matched sets of individuals (e.g. testers who are given similar credentials and references but who are of a different race or sex) pose as homeseekers. If MCAD suspects that minority testers are being discriminated against further investigations are conducted.

The second part of the program concentrates on the enforcement of fair housing laws. Housing discrimination complaints are brought against those agencies found to discriminate through the testing process. The settlement of these complaints has generated community-based responses to address the underlying problems of discrimination.

The MCAD has completed five major testing programs in different areas of the state. These programs have investigated real estate offices for discrimination against blacks, Hispanics, families with children, and female-headed households with rental subsidies. Complaints were eventually filed against 70 percent of all agencies investigated.

A major aspect of the enforcement program is to educate the community at large. In part, this is accomplished through widespread media interest in the program. Media interest was originally sparked by the testing programs, but the published results of each program was what really generated widespread interest in the program.

This publicity, by increasing public awareness and understanding of the fair housing laws, has also helped to eliminate discriminatory practices. As a result of the publicity, homeseekers have learned about their rights and about the commission's powers. Real estate offices, threatened by the possibility of testing in their areas, have changed their practices. The immediate effect of the publicity has been to give the state the highest rate of complaints processed in the nation. In many respects, the media attention has become a major, if unexpected, positive outcome.

Another key element of the enforcement program is to obtain innovative settlements that will serve to reduce discrimination in the future. For example, settlements have included the formation of a community-wide charitable trust, funded by real estate offices, to conduct fair housing activities. Settlements also created a staff position at a nonprofit agency to monitor the housing activities of realty firms and to assist the firms in meeting affirmative commitments to house minority families, families with children, and homeless families with rental subsidies. Innovative settlements of this kind ensure that discriminatory practices will be less likely to occur in the future.

The Systemic Fair Housing Testing and Enforcement Program is innovative among fair housing programs in several respects. First, the program was the first of its kind to conduct fair housing testing programs under the auspices of a state civil rights enforcement agency (MCAD). Previously, such testing programs were conducted exclusively by private agencies. Second, the program has developed unique ways to uncover fair housing violations, including testing for sex-based discrimination against female-headed households with rental subsidies. In essence, these innovations result from refined means of conducting matched pair interviews at real estate offices. Finally, the program is the first in the nation to examine the link between housing discrimination and homelessness. In particular, the program has found widespread discrimination against homeless people who receive rental subsidies and is attempting to remedy the situation.

Prior to the establishment of this program, fair housing violations were handled solely on a case-by-case basis, relying on individuals to file fair housing complaints which would subsequently be investigated. The system was unable to address many serious fair housing violations because, in many cases, people were not aware that they were being treated unlawfully. Even if individuals were aware that they were being discriminated against, many were reluctant to file complaints. Furthermore, the old system had no capacity to investigate broad-based patterns of discrimination.

The entire program reports to the commissioners of the Massachusetts Commission Against Discrimination. The commissioners are appointed by the governor and serve for three years. Additionally, the agency must frequently update both HUD and the state's Department of Public Welfare (DPW), since both agencies contribute to the program's $175,000 budget: HUD contributes 66 percent and DPW contributes the balance.

Precedence for the Testing Program

Some may view the concept of random fair housing testing as placing an unusual or unfair burden on real estate firms. Indeed, the most vociferous critics of the program have been agencies targeted by the testing programs. They have likened the process to a kangaroo court and have labeled it entrapment. Nonetheless, the basic concept of fair housing testing is not new. The precedent for such testing occurred during the civil rights movement of the 1960s.

More recently, HUD sponsored a nationwide testing study in 1977. The Housing Market Practice Survey was used to document the extent of housing discrimination in America. In the wake of the HUD study, many private housing agencies conducted their own testing studies. As testing methodology improved, state and local fair housing enforcement agencies were known to use testing on a sporadic basis in response to individual complaints of discrimination. It is only recently, however, that testing has emerged as a tool of these governmental agencies in the investigation of systemic practices.

Results of the Testing and Enforcement Program

Although reaching specific settlements against real estate concerns found to be employing discriminatory practices is an important element of the MCAD program, its emphasis is on preventing discrimination. Consequently, the best way to view the program's achievements is in terms of how the program has affected discrimination and how effective the program has been in testing and uncovering information on realty practices.

According to officials of the Massachusetts Commission Against Discrimination, media coverage of the program's findings is one of its major achievements. Media coverage is viewed as critically important by administrators because it makes both housing seekers and housing providers aware of the anti-discrimination laws.

The MCAD has held press conferences to present the results of each of its completed studies. These press conferences received extensive coverage on television and in local and regional newspapers. Shortly after a number of new reports on housing discrimination appeared in local newspapers, MCAD started to conduct tests in two predominantly white suburbs of Boston that had a history of denying equal access to minorities. Contrary to expectations, these tests revealed that the real estate agents in both communities were treating white and black homeseekers in a like manner. At least in the short run, the increased media attention appeared to have altered the behavior of the real estate community.

In addition to the media coverage, another aspect of the program's success is related to the type of settlements reached. This is important because it is necessary to provide redress for the problems uncovered. The MCAD's most recent settlements have been tailored toward the specifics of individual cases and provide for the creation of ongoing community mechanisms to oversee compliance.

Finally, the program's effectiveness in testing and uncovering information on realty practices has been an important accomplishment. Effective testing is essential to the integrity of the entire project. Information gathered by the tests must be accurate and unbiased. Furthermore, it is helpful for MCAD and other agencies to have an accurate assessment of the extensiveness of housing discrimination. Consequently, the program has maintained rigorously consistent standards throughout each testing program, resulting in verifiable conclusions.

Future of the MCAD Program

Legislative initiatives which seek to increase the scope of fair housing laws will require programs like the Systemic Fair Housing Testing and Enforcement Program to broaden the scope of their activities. For examples, MCAD plans to develop testing programs to investigate discrimination against persons with physical disabilities. Such a testing program would be the first of its kind.

The MCAD also plans to concentrate on negotiating more effective settlements of systemic complaints. Legislation passed in 1991 will authorize MCAD to assess penalties of up to $10,000 for the first offense, $25,000 for the second, and up to $50,000 for the third offense. It is anticipated that these legislative changes will have a major positive effect on MCAD's ability to negotiate satisfactory settlements of the testing-based complaints.

The MCAD plans to continue to educate other jurisdictions about the effectiveness of their testing and enforcement program because MCAD's program address problems that are nationwide in scope. The tools and methods developed by MCAD can be utilized by other state and local civil rights enforcement agencies.

In fact, several agencies have already modeled their fair housing law enforcement programs on MCAD's, including the civil rights agencies in Maine, New Hampshire, and Rhode Island. Boston's fair housing agency has also developed a program based on the MCAD model. Some of these agencies have adapted the MCAD methodology for conducting research into discrimination against low income, female-headed households.

The MCAD also hopes to increase its interaction with private housing agencies. In the past, MCAD has offered technical assistance to private agencies, including the Boston Bar Association's Lawyer's Committee for Civil Rights Under Law and Western Massachusetts Legal Services.

Key Lessons from the Fair Housing Testing and Enforcement Program

According to those who administer it, the key element of the Fair Housing Testing and Enforcement Program's success is its focus on problem prevention. Officials believe that broadly focusing on problem prevention may be a more effective means of attacking a problem than just concentrating on enforcement and other remedial efforts. Furthermore, officials stress the value of the media in preventing problems.

FOCUS ON PROBLEM PREVENTION. By focusing on problem prevention rather than focusing solely on enforcement, the Fair Housing Testing and Enforcement Program is able to eliminate many cases of discrimination before they happen. While enforcement is a necessary part of any fair housing program (as there has to be some disincentive to potential discriminators), increasing awareness of fair housing laws has the advantage of reaching realtors who might not otherwise be aware that their practices are discriminatory. To the extent that realtors are made aware of fair housing laws, and to the extent that they correct their own discriminatory practices, the Fair Housing Testing and Enforcement Program avoids costly legal battles, and potential tenants avoid the trauma of being victims of discrimination.

This unique program also teaches some important lessons about the use of testing. All tests used in conjunction with any enforcement program must be accurate, unbiased, and verifiable. It is, therefore, wise to share testing methodology with an experienced researcher before using it in the field.

The enforcement mechanism of the Fair Housing Testing and Enforcement Program is also unique. Not only does the threat of a fine keep potential discriminators in line, but the fines collected from guilty parties are used to strengthen the program.

STRATEGIC USE OF THE MEDIA. The media is used in a deliberate manner to increase awareness of the goals and results of the Fair Housing Testing and Enforcement Program. Officials invite members of the press to sessions during which the program's achievements are highlighted. While this strategy works to the extent that the program receives favorable coverage and realtors (and potential tenants) are made more aware of fair housing issues, unfavorable coverage can damage a program's credibility and jeopardize its financial support.

If the media is to be used deliberately, it is wise to have a well planned media strategy. Anticipate questions, prepare media kits that explain the program, and enlist the help of individuals who can give testimony in support of the program's achievements.

Breaking Down Barriers with Economic Incentives: The Racial Integration Incentives Program

One of the most troublesome issues facing communities today is the issue of racial integration in housing. Many communities that were at one time shared by members of different races have become largely segregated. Disinvestment has plagued minority neighborhoods, leaving behind substandard schools and housing. The sad result is that the quality of life in the community is greatly reduced for all of those who remain, and creates a strong incentive for those who can afford to leave. Eventually, the community loses its tax base, its human resources, and its pride.

What makes the issue so perplexing is that elected officials have long shied away from issues of racial integration because of its inherent racial overtones. It is doubtful that many politicians would risk any suggestion of forced integration, particularly in an atmosphere of heightened racial tensions. Nonetheless, some communities are forging ahead with voluntary integration programs. These programs are highly controversial and some, including the program described here, have been challenged in federal court. Regardless, the program has enjoyed great success in achieving the goals of the communities involved and is deserving of notice.

In response to an increase in segregation in housing, the neighboring cities of Shaker Heights and Cleveland Heights, Ohio, developed an unprecedented program to maintain the current levels of racial integration throughout their jurisdictions and maintain property values. The Racial Integration Incentives Program relies on voluntary, rather than mandatory, integration.

Homesellers, both black and white, in the Cleveland area found that demand for their homes and the projected return on their home investment declined substantially as racial segregation increased during the past two decades. This problem was exacerbated in many areas where there was a declining population and no shortage of housing.

Citizens with children in public schools became concerned that the quality of education would suffer as schools increasingly became one-race institutions. Real estate brokers and property owners felt the pinch as the demand for housing decreased in certain areas, especially demand from prospective white homeseekers.

The Racial Integration Incentives Program

The Racial Integration Incentives Program, although sponsored by Shaker Heights and Cleveland Heights, was designed to stem the tide of racial segregation throughout the eastern suburbs of Cuyahoga County, Ohio. The program relies on affirmative marketing techniques, homeseeker counseling, and financial incentives to attract homeseekers to areas where their race is underrepresented. Particular emphasis is given to attracting white families to southwestern Shaker Heights and selected areas of Cleveland Heights (which are predominantly black) and black families to six other suburbs throughout the county.

The principal activity of the Racial Integration Incentives Program is to attract prospective homebuyers and renters into areas considered in danger of becoming segregated. Special attention is paid to those with children who would attend public schools. In addition to making available financial incentives such as low-cost loans, other activities include marketing and employer outreach. The program also sponsors neighborhood and school tours; shows homes for sale and apartments for rent in cooperation with real estate agencies; and offers access to landlords and representatives of neighborhood organizations.

The primary vehicles for promoting racial integration are three public/private partnerships which finance the incentive program. The partnerships are the Fund for the Future of Shaker Heights (FUND), The Heights Fund (H-FUND), and the East Suburban Housing Service (ESCOC). All three of these efforts are funded by grants from Cleveland area philanthropic foundations. Both FUND and H-FUND are further funded by matching monies from local donors and ESCOC receives additional funds from dues paid by the municipalities and school districts which comprise its membership.

As the most recent of a series of efforts to maintain integrated living patterns which Shaker Heights has enjoyed for nearly 30 years, FUND addresses the threat of resegregation of neighborhoods by offering financial incentives to homeseekers making prointegrative moves. The H-FUND, a replication of FUND, addressed similar problems in Cleveland Heights, a city which became integrated ten years later than Shaker Heights and which shows greater risks of resegregation. The ESCOC, a consortium of three cities and two school districts (Shaker Heights, Cleveland Heights, University Heights, the Shaker Heights City School District, and the Cleveland Heights/University Heights City School District) was formed in 1984 to produce an open housing market with integrated residential and educational settings in suburbs which were almost exclusively white. Together, FUND, H-FUND, and ESCOC form an interjurisdictional, public/private effort to maintain racial diversity in one of the most racially segregated areas in the United States. The three funds have the potential to directly affect the racial balance in nine separate municipalities and five school districts.

The various elements of the Racial Integration Incentives Program were intended specifically to address that stage of integration in which Shaker Heights and Cleveland Heights found themselves at the end of the 1980s. Specifically, they found themselves entering an era of resegregation, particularly in the school systems.

The three funds differ substantially from privately financed efforts to desegregate or maintain integration in that they are amply funded, public/private partnerships that work across jurisdictional boundaries. Indeed, this was the first cross-jurisdictional governmental agency in the nation to join cities and school districts in an effort to achieve the common goal of peaceful racial integration.

The three funds are governed and financially managed by city-appointed boards rather than volunteers. All three initiatives have the direct support of elected officials (including mayors, council members, and school board members) who serve on their governing boards and are intimately involved in their day to day operations. They are sufficiently funded by both private and public monies to have a real impact, and they are welcomed by the real estate industry which prefers market-oriented interventions to litigation as a means of ending dual housing markets.

The primary goal of FUND, H-FUND, and ESCOC is to further the stated goal of fair housing by replacing ghettos (both black and white) with balanced and integrated residential and educational patterns. If the housing market in the Cleveland area was race blind and home purchases were based solely on income no area would have fewer than 11 percent or more than 27 percent black population. The funds are designed to counteract existing segregated housing and school patterns making the eastern suburbs more reflective of the county population as a whole. A secondary goal is to increase and maintain the property values of those residents already living in the affected areas by increasing the demand for their property.

Assessing the Results of the Racial Integration Program

The most direct achievement of the Racial Integration Program has been the extent to which foundations, corporations, and individuals have invested in the funds. Philanthropic support is evidenced by the renewed contributions of a number of foundations and corporations. The ESCOC's member jurisdictions have continued to support the program through their dues and representation on the ESCOC Board.

During its first two years of operation, the program completed around 50 loans which brought nearly the same number of white school children into the Shaker Heights School District. Since that time, the program has nearly doubled the rate at which it extends new loans to both black and white families participating in the program.

Before the formation of ESCOC in 1984, housing services in the Hillcrest area documented only nine prointegrative moves into the area. Since 1985, ESCOC has worked with nearly 3,000 prospects. Over 200 of these prospects have made prointegrative rentals or purchases, clearly underscoring the effectiveness of the program. FUND and H-FUND have met with similar successes.

A second, but equally important, achievement has been the increased awareness among community leaders, real estate organizations, and citizens of the local communities about the importance and consequencs of racial integration. Participation in meetings to introduce the integration program has enabled people to discuss housing and school race patterns in a sensitive, race-conscious manner.

Governance of the Racial Integration Incentive Program

Supervision of the program is left to appointed committees representing both private and public interests. The FUND program is governed by a fifteen member Board of Trustees, appointed by the mayor of Shaker Heights with the approval of the City Council. Trustees include the mayor, the director of the Community Services Department, a city council member, a school board member, and 11 citizen members.

The H-FUND is directed and governed by a board of 48 trustees, two-thirds of whom are appointed by the Cleveland Heights City Council. The other one-third of the trustees are appointed by the council of the adjoining city of University Heights. (Cleveland Heights and University Heights share a school district.) The board is responsible for policy, fund-raising, and distribution of funds. A Cleveland Heights staff member processes loan applications. Funds are administered by the City Finance Department.

The ESCOC is overseen by council and school board representatives from each of the member jurisdictions. The presidency of ESCOC rotates in order to foster a democratic spirit among members. The housing service staff consists of a full-time director, two full-time coordinators, two part-time housing representatives, and two part-time clerks. Loan applications are processed by the housing service coordinator and approved by member representatives to the ESCOC Loan Review Committee. The city of Shaker Heights has traditionally served as the fiscal agent for ESCOC. Auxiliary services such as those which provide demographic data and discrimination complaint services are subcontracted through other organizations. Combined, the three funds have an operating income in excess of $1,000,000.

History of the Racial Integration Incentives Program

Programs offering financial incentives for prointegration moves have been in effect in the Shaker Heights area since the early 1960s. Most of these early programs resulted from efforts made by neighborhood associations and through the Shaker Heights Communities Development Foundation, a philanthropic organization primarily concerned with local community development.

The volunteers who ran these early neighborhood integration programs provided the impetus for what would later become FUND, H-FUND, and ESCOC. By 1967, the city of Shaker Heights, in combination with the local school district, created and funded the Shaker Heights Housing Office to assist homebuyers and renters with prointegrative moves. In early 1983, Shaker Heights incorporated the Housing Office into the new Community Services Department.

Conceived by Mayor Stephen J. Alfred and the Shaker Heights City Council in 1985, FUND differs from its neighborhood-based predecessors in that it is sufficiently funded to make a significant impact on housing and school race patterns. Furthermore, FUND's operations are the direct responsibility of city government rather than neighborhood volunteers.

The ESCOC, founded in 1984, was created in response to the potential resegregation of neighborhoods and schools and the perceived unwillingness of real estate professionals to encourage minority customers to pursue nontraditional moves. The primary initiators of ESCOC were the city councils and school boards of the member jurisdictions, the directors and staff members of the Shaker Heights Community Services Department, and the Cleveland Heights Housing Service.

Created in late 1987, H-FUND was modeled after FUND. It was created by the city councils of Cleveland Heights and University Heights, which share a common school district. The Heights Fund was conceived as a means of replicating FUND's successes in Cleveland Heights.

Despite their original reluctance to take an active role in desegregation, the strongest early supporters of FUND, H-FUND, and ESCOC were local real estate professionals. They saw the importance of maintaining a strong demand for housing and appreciated the aspects of the Racial Integration Incentives Program that made it a market-oriented, rather than mandatory program. As the shrinking population in the Cleveland area caused a decline in overall demand for housing, buyers and sellers of housing began to support the program since they had a clear financial stake in their housing investment.

The program received a significant boost when the major local news organizations gave it strong editorial support. Obviously, local government and school district officials had likewise shown personal interest in this unique and successful initiative.

A major challenge to the success of Racial Integration Incentives Program was the acceptance on the part of many people that segregation and resegregation were a natural state of affairs. Much of this challenge was overcome by the fact that the program has always been voluntary and based on market incentives rather than forced integration.

Nonetheless, many citizens of all races had long been encouraged to avoid open, public discourse on race. This self-censorship was, and continues to be, caused by confusing race-consciousness with racism. Public discourse on integration has been challenging to pro-integration advocates because its discussion often elevates race-based anxieties. According to program officials, there is often a reluctance to accept integration as a positive value. The resistance on the part of some citizens combined with the laissez-faire attitude of many public officials and the cutbacks in federal funding have created a significant obstacle, but not one which is insurmountable. Stressing the positive educational and financial outcomes which result from housing integration has been very successful in overcoming the initial resistance.

The Future of the Integration Program

As obstacles to integration in housing are overcome by program administrators, the Racial Integration Incentives Program will continue to provide financial incentives for families to move into areas where their race is under-represented. Increased funding through grants, including a major grant awarded to the city of Shaker Heights by the Ford Foundation, will enable administrators to improve the program in the future. In particular, the Racial Integration Incentives Program has implemented several new projects aimed at furthering the cause of racial balance. Improved financial incentives aimed at renters have increased integration in rental housing. Financial incentives are now being offered to realtors who encourage pro-integrative moves. Finally, $25,000 has been set aside by the Racial Integration Incentives Program for educational and instructional program. Plans for the future include the establishment of a national consulting program which would help other communities establish similar integration programs.

The Racial Integration Incentives Program is transferable to other jurisdictions just as predecessor programs in Shaker Heights were transferable to FUND, H-FUND, and ESCOC. According to people connected with the Shaker Heights operation, the challenge is to generate the will among citizens to overcome resistance to integration. They also believe that affirmative programs are needed by many communities which are already integrated to prevent them from becoming resegregated.

Programs such as the Racial Integration Incentives Program are especially relevant to communities which believe in the positive social and financial reasons for integration, but find mandatory, court-ordered or quota-based integration requirements unacceptable. Many such communities would likely see the benefit in such an innovative program that achieves integration through market mechanisms and volunteerism rather than on nonvoluntary means.

Key Lessons from the Racial Integration Incentives Program

Although the lessons taught by the Racial Integration Incentives Program have been introduced in previous sections, they are important enough to be underscored once again. The main lessons are that both economic incentives and customer-orientation are powerful means of encouraging people to participate in a program.

ECONOMIC INCENTIVES. Although for some people, demonstrating the benefits of living in particular areas may be incentive enough for them to purchase a home in the area, officials of the Shaker Heights program believe that providing financial incentives has increased participation in the program. Homebuyers who participate in the Racial Integration Incentives Program are offered financial incentives in the form of low-cost loans which make it easier for them to purchase a home in areas where their race is underrepresented. Funds for the loans are raised through three public/private partnerships set up for that purpose. In all three of the partnerships, funds are raised through matching funds and membership dues.

Officials of the Racial Integration Incentives Program believe that understanding market forces, especially the relationship between the supply and demand for housing, and developing appropriate incentives to encourage racial integration is the most appropriate way to promote desegration. "People are more supportive of voluntary measures and are more likely to take advantage of economic incentives," says one official. "There's not the same level of resentment that you might find with other means such as court orders. It also makes a difference if neighborhoods integrate on their own rather than being held together by other means."

CUSTOMER-ORIENTATION. The Racial Integration Incentives Program is customer oriented in that it makes it as easy as possible for potential clients to understand the full value of participating in the program. In addition to offering guided tours of neighborhoods, program officials help clients evaluate schools and employment opportunities in the vicinity. Providing clients with these services not only makes them feel more comfortable about participating in the program, but it also recognizes that people purchase more than a home when they sign the sales agreement. They also purchase a neighborhood, a school district, and local employment opportunities.

Chapter 6

Economic Development

If a free society cannot help the many who are poor,
it cannot save the few who are rich.
—John F. Kennedy.

Decaying infrastructures, corporate flight, and the resulting decline in corporate tax revenues have exacerbated the unemployment and poverty rates in many communities. Reversing these trends of increasing urban blight and regional unemployment has thus become a top priority of state and local governments across the nation.

In the recent past, economic development strategies relied heavily on recruiting manufacturing firms by enticing them with tax breaks or other benefits. These programs, often packaged in the form of enterprise zones, have met with limited success. In some cases, plants left one community to take advantage of incentives in another. In other cases, enterprise zones failed to attract enough new jobs to justify the costly incentives. On a national basis, fewer new manufacturing plants are being built, and the average size of those that are being built is getting smaller.[38] Increased foreign competition and a shift away from manufacturing toward service industries have left many areas in a state of economic disarray.

Today, rather than focusing exclusively on recruiting new businesses, many communities are fighting the tide of economic decay by developing innovative and effective programs that bolster local industry which is already in place. They are helping local businesses increase market opportunities overseas, and they are providing residents with the skills they need to obtain meaningful employment in a rapidly changing economy.

This chapter presents only a handfull of the many noteworthy programs that are now being sponsored by state and local governments across the nation. Nonetheless, they are representative of the wide variety of initiatives that are capturing the imagination of policy entrepreneurs everywhere. The Garment Industry Development Corporation provides an elightening example of how government, management, and labor can forge a partnership to reinvigorate

151

a declining industry. The XPORT Port Authority Trading Company shows how government can help local businesses increase exports to foreign markets. The success of the Export Service Center illustrates the important role that government can also play in helping small businesses find new markets for their products overseas. The Attleboro Area Center for Training demonstrates how one community is effectively using human services development as a catalyst for urban renewal. Finally, the Employee Ownership Program offers communities a means of combating the increased numbers of plant closures and layoffs that have resulted from increased merger activity and intensified cost-cutting efforts.

Re-invigorating a Declining Industry: The Garment Industry Development Corporation

One of the most significant changes in postwar America has been the transformation in many urban areas from a manufacturing-based economy to one which is service-based. Since 1982, 91 percent of the new jobs have been in services, and 73 percent of all private-sector employees now work in service businesses.[39] As this change has taken place, many manufacturing industries, particularly those based in urban areas, have found it increasingly difficult to survive. Higher domestic production costs and fierce foreign competition have taken a toll on a wide variety of industries ranging from high technology products to more basic industries such as steel, coal, and textiles.

Although the trend is apparent throughout the United States, it was New York City that led the nation in the change from a manufacturing to a service-oriented economy. New York's financial, insurance, and real estate businesses expanded as manufacturing industries contracted to a mere fraction of their peak sizes. Increased demand for office space and the escalating rents that followed dealt a devastating blow to the city's manufacturing industries, particularly the once-thriving garment industry which had been in steady decline since the 1950s.

During the boom years following World War II, many apparel companies left New York for other locations that offered inexpensive land for new factories as well as a ready source of cheap, non-unionized labor. This exodus eventually dispersed the garment industry around the world. Many of the garment companies that remained in New York found that they could not compete with large-scale manufacturers overseas for mass production markets because overseas manufacturers enjoyed significant cost advantages in the acquisition of land and labor. In addition, foreign competitors often used more advanced (and less expensive) production technologies than American companies.

Local firms, shut out of mass markets, were forced to rely on the quick-turn-around demand created by wholesalers and retailers of New York City's fashion center. As leases expired and rents tripled and quadrupled, even this segment of the market was threatened with extinction.

Despite these problems, the apparel industry remained New York City's largest manufacturing industry, employing over 130,000 workers in 1980. Yet, increased pressures and the possibility that the garment industry would leave New York entirely created serious problems for the three different parties that had a stake in the garment industry: the local government, the garment industry labor union, and garment industry trade associations. For the city of New York, the loss of the industry would mean declining tax revenues and increased need for social services for those unable to re-enter the labor force. For the International Ladies Garment Workers Union (ILGWU), the union that represents organized garment workers, the loss of the garment industry would mean a loss of jobs for its members and elimination of many union locals. For the local trade associations it would mean bankruptcy or relocation for its members and obliteration of these organizations. All three stakeholders recognized the importance of stabilizing and strengthening the industry, and all three recognized that to do so they would have to work together to find a solution.

In 1984, a nonprofit corporation called the Garment Industry Development Corporation (the GIDC) was created by the New York City Office of Business Development to develop programs on behalf of city government, the ILGWU, and the trade associations. These programs would address areas in which the three players would need to change their policies to the mutual benefit of all. Each player had representation on the GIDC Board of Directors and all three contributed funds to the organization's upkeep. The New York City Office of Business Development contributes about 52 percent of GIDC's $48,000 budget, with industry and other city departments accounting for the remainder.

The GIDC is different from traditional industry organizations because it does not exclusively represent business owners or act as advocates or lobbyists. Rather, it is a comprehensive, industry-specific service organization which draws its support from city government, management, and labor. Although government programs are available to manufacturers that offer assistance in the areas of real estate management, training, and technology assistance, few are tailored to specific industries like the GIDC.

By drawing upon its member's connections to the many levels of the city's private, public, and academic sectors, the GIDC has been able to integrate into its operations some of New York's finest teachers, consultants, and facilities. Since its inception the GIDC has become a recognized leader in New York's effort to strengthen its garment industry.

The creation of the GIDC forced the city, the union, and management to examine each other's policies and to develop a better understanding of the issues involved and reach a common agenda. Through the GIDC, the parties have identified a number of problems facing the industry. In particular, they have focused on rising real estate prices, a shortage of skilled labor, and a failure to adopt the latest technologies as critical issues facing garment industry in New York.

Bringing together disparate parties that had often been at odds with each other was, by no means, an easy task. Each party did not immediately accept the other's assessment of the problems or possible solutions. This is not surprising, given the potentially conflicting goals of each stakeholder. For example, the city was hesitant to alter the direction of the real estate market because it represented increased tax revenue and a booming service economy. The union was reluctant to confront the shortage of skilled labor because increasing the supply would weaken the ILGWU's position at the bargaining table. Management was hesitant to invest in new technologies because of their fear that, should market forces further hinder the ability of companies to get contracts, there would not be sufficient income to cover debt service for badly needed new equipment. Each party, however, knew that if these problems were not addressed the industry would suffer. The mutual goal of long-term stability of the apparel industry motivated each party to make compromises, resulting in one of the most innovative economic development programs in America.

Meeting the Needs of a Changing Environment: The GIDC

The formation of the GIDC was one of several recommendations contained in a 1983 study of the New York City garment industry. Since much of the industry was located in the Chinatown area of New York, the report focused on that area. The study, which was financed by a local affiliate of the ILGWU and the New York Skirt and Sportswear Association, described the explosive growth which the Chinatown segment of the industry experienced between 1960 and 1980. The report also underscored the critical interdependence between the garment center manufacturers in mid–Manhattan and the Chinatown contractors, as well as the growing threat to the industry created by rapidly rising real estate prices in Chinatown.

Having documented the critical role played by Chinatown firms in the survival of the entire citywide industry, the study was presented by several trade associations to the New York City deputy mayor for economic finance and economic development. With the support of the deputy mayor, the city, management, and labor were able to reach agreement for each party to provide funding for the project and participate in its leadership.

The traditional antagonism between labor and management was seen by many as a potential stumbling block to any partnership effort. Opposition to the GIDC concept was overcome, however, by the persuasive arguments of the initiative's early supporters within each group that emphasized the common interests in strengthening the industry and the possibility of obtaining greater public assistance.

Activities of the Garment Industry Development Corporation

The goal of the Garment Industry Development Corporation is to design and implement strategies that increase the productivity and profitability of New York's garment firms while increasing and improving employment in the apparel industry. The GIDC provides the garment industry with a wide range of services including employee training, technology assessments, research, and information about real estate management.

Training includes hands-on courses designed to upgrade the skills of both management and labor. This training familiarizes workers with the latest techniques in garment manufacturing and makes them more competitive. The GIDC also offers a training program for displaced garment workers. This program gives garment workers additional skills they may need to find a new job in the industry. Technology assessment conducted by the GIDC helps companies understand where they are lagging behind domestic and foreign competitors in technological advancement. The goal of the technology assessment program is to ensure that New York's garment industry remains at the cutting-edge in terms of technology used in the manufacturing process.

The GIDC has conducted and participated in research designed to inform public policy makers about the current status of the industry. The GIDC's studies have also evaluated different ways of organizing the industry so that it can reduce costs and remain competitive. For example, GIDC's studies have examined strategies to develop industry clusters outside of the high rent central business districts. Studies have also evaluated the feasibility of building a high technology production center and a human resources training center. The GIDC is currently identifying market opportunities for New York garment manufacturers and examining the potential impact of improved child care services on employee productivity.

The GIDC offers members advice and information about real estate in an effort to overcome many of the rent problems that have forced companies to relocate. Companies are given advice on rent negotiations and are helped with relocation within New York City if necessary.

Beneficiaries of the GIDC Program

The GIDC currently limits its clients to women's and children's apparel manufacturers and contractors (and their employees) located in New York City.

Each of these manufacturers must have also signed collective bargaining agreements with the ILGWU. These are roughly 270 manufacturers and 600 contractors in this group. The typical manufacturer tends to be a fairly small business and includes design, sample making, showroom, sales, and shipping operations. These manufacturers usually employ between 10 and 20 people. Contractors tend to be somewhat larger, employing between 40 and 50 workers, most of whom are sewing machine operators.

There are 45,000 employee members of the ILGWU who are eligible for GIDC's programs. They are overwhelmingly minorities, primarily female immigrants from Asia and Latin America and virtually all have low incomes. The average salary of a sewing machine operator, for example, is about $8,000 per year.

Organization of the Garment Industry Development Corporation

Although the GIDC is an independent, non-profit corporation, the New York City Office of Business Development exercises control over the corporation through its participation on the Board of Directors. Likewise, labor and management also play an important role in guiding the GIDC through participation on the board. The Board of Directors is divided into three classes of five members each, all with equal voting power. The primary function of the board is to provide policy guidance and approve major management decisions. As such, the Board is not a rubber stamp mechanism; rather it takes a hands-on approach to management.

A number of companion contracts stipulate the terms by which the GIDC is to receive funds and in-kind support from the city, the ILGWU, and the trade associations. For example, the contracts include provisions requiring the GIDC to provide bimonthly activity reports and to seek approval of the Office of Business Development, the ILGWU, and management for any subcontracts in excess of $1,000. In addition, the Office of Business Development conducts financial audits twice each year. The GIDC must also fulfill the reporting requirements of its many financial supporters and sponsors. As the burden of this task has increased, the GIDC has seen its administrative systems evolve from scraps of paper in a shoe box to a well-organized, computerized accounting and tracking system.

The president of the GIDC must present bimonthly activity reports and an annual report to the Board of Directors. The report must account for program finances, evaluate and reassess missions and goals, and present numerical indicators of progress.

In addition to these formal requirements, the GIDC staff work closely with the Office of Business Development, the ILGWU, and the associations to implement GIDC's actual services. Recruitment for GIDC's training programs is conducted jointly with the union and associations through a number of means including newsletters, flyers, special mailings, and announcements at industry gatherings. Clearly, every effort is made to include as many people as possible in the training programs.

Depending on the service, the GIDC may enter contractual relationships with other government agencies to implement specific services. For example, the GIDC approached the New York City Department of Employment (DOE) with a proposal for a program to retain dislocated workers. This proposal was consistent with the board's desire to upgrade the skills of sewing machine operators who are typically among the first to be laid off during difficult times. The proposal was accepted, resulting in a contract between the GIDC and DOE. The contract award provides DOE with funds for a specific training program and includes a separate set of reporting requirements. The GIDC has established similar relationships with the Port Authority of New York and New Jersey and the New York State Industrial Cooperation Council to provide funding for GIDC's study of changes in apparel marketing and technology.

The GIDC benefits from a unique relationship with the state university system. In particular, the GIDC has close ties to the Fashion Institute of Technology (FIT). Not only is the president of FIT a member of the GIDC's Board of Directors, but FIT also assists the GIDC in program development and implementation, often providing faculty and space for GIDC programs. Moreover, FIT often applies (on behalf of the GIDC) for the New York state vocational training funds which are reserved for educational institutions. While FIT receives the funds, the GIDC plays a critical role in recruiting program participants, administering the program, and satisfying the grant's reporting requirements. Thus the GIDC's relationship with the state educational system provides both expertise and funds to the program.

Evaluating the GIDC: Contributions to the Garment Industry

A 1987 study of the human resource needs of the garment industry, sponsored by the GIDC, concluded that the industry was threatened by a growing shortage of skilled labor and that the industry lacked adequate mechanisms to recruit and train workers. This study inspired the GIDC to make training a central part of its agenda. A significant obstacle to the effective delivery of training, however, was the absence of a modern training facility. As a result, the city of New York set aside $110,000 to create the GIDC Training Center and purchase state-of-the-art training equipment. At the same time, the GIDC conducted a needs assessment survey to determine what skills should be taught. The plan articulated industry needs, defined the types of training needed, and inventoried the equipment currently used by the industry.

Although the Garment Industry Development Corporation has made substantial headway in a number of key areas, administrators believe that the single most important accomplishment has been the establishment of the GIDC Training Center. Up to 250 students per year participate in a wide variety of programs at the center, including sewing skills, samplemaking, and use of advanced machinery in the production of garments. Many of the specialized training programs that take place there are conducted in cooperation with the Fashion Institute of Technology.

The training programs at the center broaden participants' skills, making the industry more competitive and making the workers' jobs more secure. Between 1984 and mid-1991, the GIDC had provided training to over 350 managers and laborers. The placement rate for GIDC's Dislocated Workers Program is 85 percent, an exceptionally high rate of achievement for any job training program. Training programs are constantly evaluated and improved to meet the needs of workers and the industry. Each training program includes a midpoint and final evaluation to determine if it is meeting the immediate needs of participants and to improve the program for future participants.

The training center will also enable the GIDC to cut its training costs and increase its services. Prior to the creation of the center, the GIDC was forced to rent training equipment at rapidly increasing rates. Purchasing the equipment allows the GIDC to dramatically cut costs.

Although the establishment of the training center has been the most tangible accomplishment of the GIDC, the organization has been credited with substantial achievements in other areas. For example, the GIDC sponsors research which monitors and assesses the needs of New York City's garment industry. The GIDC's goals of strengthening the industry, improving the productivity and profitability of the firms, and raising the standard of living of garment workers rely on the industry's ability to respond to changes in the competitive environment. Accordingly, the GIDC studies have focused on garment industry real estate issues, training needs, technology assessments, market research, and garment worker child care needs.

In addition to serving as a training mechanism and a source of critical information, the GIDC has also provided valuable technical assistance to apparel companies. Between 1984 and early 1991, the GIDC provided technical assistance to over 100 firms. Since the GIDC is able to serve as a sort of clearinghouse for technical information, the entire industry benefits from the technical services provided by the GIDC. Firms are increasingly viewing the GIDC as a source of information on the latest technological advances in garment production.

A continuing area of difficulty for the program is the impatience on the part of the industry with government process and the pace of program development. This is not a problem unique to the GIDC. Using government funds introduces requirements for competitive bidding, background investigations, and contract documentation which are not necessarily relevant to private industry. There is also a certain tension between the government's need to plan and describe GIDC's services in concrete, quantifiable terms which can be embodied in a contract. While this tension may never be completely resolved, it has been reduced by communication fostered by the GIDC. The industry now has a greater appreciation for the limits of government and the need to follow specific procedures.

Government, on the other hand, has allowed the GIDC greater flexibility in its contracting than it otherwise might permit through the control it exercises over the GIDC Board of Directors. In addition, GIDC's continued involvement in the government process has increased its capacity to move items through the process more quickly. In fact, one of the strengths of the GIDC model is its ability to quickly identify problems and opportunities which may not have existed early in the contract period and to develop responsive programs on relatively short notice.

Future Plans for the GIDC

The most important issues facing the GIDC in the 1990s will be changes in demographics, technology, and markets. Demographic changes will decrease the number of workers entering the labor force. Furthermore, changing attitudes have discouraged young people from pursuing vocational education at the high school level. These two trends threaten to deplete the region's skilled work force. Changes in immigration law make this source of labor even less certain. Complicating matters further is the fact that recent immigrants tend to be less skilled and the industry lacks the training mechanism to upgrade entry level workers to replace the loss of the most highly skilled laborers. To counter this trend, the GIDC plans to expand its training efforts, paying particular attention to upgrading skills. In addition, the GIDC is exploring ways to encourage those outside the work force to enter the industry.

The GIDC has made two seminal efforts to attract new sources of labor to the industry. Neither effort, however, has yet reached fruition. The first is aimed at recruiting and training welfare recipients. A pilot program offering specialized training to welfare recipients resulted in 12 graduates, but they proved to be difficult to place, and none of the program's graduates remained employed for more than one week. The GIDC is reassessing this effort and plans to devise new strategies for accessing the welfare population. A second effort to attract new blood to the industry resulted in a study of how improved child care programs might improve the quality of life for garment workers and attract more labor. The results of the study have not yet been assessed.

In addition to dealing with increasingly scare labor, the GIDC will also have to contend with changing technology during the next several years. The anchor keeping the apparel industry in New York is the fashion center with its agglomeration of designers, wholesalers, and retailers serving the largest consumer market in the country. To keep up with high fashion's demand for fast turnaround production, the garment industry will need to keep pace with new technologies. These include the advances made in computer-aided design and other computer applications to garment production. The GIDC is conducting a comprehensive study of changes in apparel marketing and technologies.

The GIDC also plans to build upon its technology assessment services by providing full-scale technology enhancement programs in the future. The GIDC would like to offer engineering assistance, promote the joint ownership of equipment (to reduce fixed costs), and encourage pilot programs to demonstrate the advantages of advanced flexible manufacturing systems.

Finally, the GIDC will continue to explore new market opportunities for local manufacturers. Some believe that enhanced promotion of the local production industry will increase the number of contracts manufacturers receive from wholesalers and retailers. The GIDC market and technology study will investigate this possibility.

Applying the GIDC Concept to Different Areas and Industries

Although the Garment Industry Development Corporation was designed with New York's garment industry in mind, the overall framework of the program is applicable to many urban areas that have witnessed declines in manufacturing employment in the face of foreign competition. Furthermore, the concept of the GIDC partnership is transferable to virtually any industry.

The GIDC concept is particularly appropriate for older cities which have seen the growth in the service sectors drive real estate prices in their central business districts beyond the reach of manufacturers. The policymakers have directed much of their effort toward developing innovative ways for government to assist industry. Nonetheless, these efforts often fail because the government is in the unenviable position of having to sell a package of preconceived, generic services to companies. Companies view this assistance as too general and unresponsive to their particular needs. Rarely do these programs involve organized labor. Thus, they are insensitive to the population which this activity is intended to benefit. Efforts such as the GIDC which bring government, management, and labor together as equal partners are critical to addressing the problems created by the deindustrialization of urban America.

Key Lessons from the Garment Industry Development Corporation

The above discussion of the Garment Industry Development Corporation provides as a useful opportunity to underscore several key lessons developed in earlier chapters. First, it is wise to solicit the input of the key party's that will be affected by a new program. In this case, frequent and close contact between the city government, labor unions, and trade associations ensured that potential conflicts would be addressed sooner rather than later. A related lesson is that partnerships can be very beneficial to a program, especially when the partnership is between local governments and private industry. In the case of GIDC, the formal partnership between government, labor, and management has allowed the program to benefit from each party's ties to resources, both financial and otherwise. Finally, the GIDC stresses the value of developing programs which are holistic in nature. The program is able to combat the complex problem of industry decay on a variety of fronts through consulting, technical assistance, research, and training programs.

LIMITED DEGREE OF AUTONOMY. The GIDC also sheds light on autonomy, another attribute that can contribute to the success of a government-sponsored initiative. Since members of the public ultimately hold government officials responsible for how their tax dollars are spent it would be unwise to sponsor programs which are run without at least a modicum of government oversight. Yet, a case can be made for allowing some programs like GIDC to operate with a degree of autonomy. Allowing programs to operate as semi-autonomous organizations gives them the elbow room they need to retain an entrepreneurial culture. In also enables them to take advantage of their nongovernment ties to private resources while at the same time retaining access to the resources of their sponsoring-agency. In the case of the GIDC, the organization is operated as an independent non-profit corporation. It enjoys ties to both labor and management resources, but retains access to those provided through the New York City Office of Business Development. Furthermore, its distance from the city bureaucracy allows it to pursue its economic development goals with a single-minded determination that might not be possible if the program were administered within a large agency by officials who had other competing responsibilities.

A Broad Approach to Increasing Exports: XPORT Port Authority Trading Company

In recent years, the net export figure has received widespread attention. Although exports have made up an increasingly large component of Gross National Product (GNP) in recent years, less than 100 large corporations account for more than half of all U.S exports. Although the U.S. trade deficit has declined, it has been as high as $100 billion. The net export figure receives so much attention because exports are very important to the overall condition of the economy. Exports provide jobs, increase corporate profits, build the tax base, and improve the overall competitive position of America in the international marketplace. Moreover, exporting accounts for a large portion of the domestic work force. Nearly one out of every nine manufacturing jobs and one out of sixteen of all jobs in the United States are created by exporting.

Nonetheless, many exporting opportunities remain untapped because small and medium-sized companies are often intimidated by the prospect of entering the complicated and risky international marketplace. Public officials in New York and New Jersey recognized the lost potential created by the virtual absence of small and medium-sized companies from the export business. They acted to take advantage of regulatory changes which would permit state and local governments to form trading companies and entitle them to use the resources of the nation's major financier of international trade, the Export-Import Bank of the United States (Eximbank). The result was the formation of the XPORT Port Authority Trading Company (XPORT).

XPORT: *Government Helping Business*

Government sponsored export programs, including the XPORT Port Authority Trading Company, represent a refreshing government approach to working with the business community. The stereotypical view of government standing in the way of free enterprise by over-regulating the marketplace is cast aside as these new trading companies help private companies break through potential barriers to trade by providing technical assistance and access to government resources.

To help smaller companies begin sales overseas, XPORT offers businesses a full range of services, including marketing research, advertising and promotion, and developing pricing strategies. In addition, XPORT helps companies with distributor contracting, shipping, documentation, and export finance. In many cases, XPORT is in a position to help businesses gain admittance to overseas trade shows. The provision of all of these services is done in a manner that is both friendly and cost-effective. Best of all, the program is generic in nature and could be easily adopted in other jurisdictions.

Since XPORT began operations in 1982, it has introduced 130 small and medium-sized companies to the global marketplace and generated over $150 million in export sales for small businesses. It was presented the U.S. Department of Commerce "E" Award for Excellence by the president of the United States. The award was presented in recognition of the program's contributions to the increase of U.S. trade abroad.

In addition, the program has been recognized for its achievements by the Ford Foundation. The states of Washington and Alaska have passed legislation enacting trade programs based on the success of the XPORT Port Authority Trading Company.

XPORT: A Unique Approach to a Familiar Issue

The need to stimulate overseas sales of domestic products has long been recognized. Consequently, most state and some local governments have developed export promotion programs to address the trade deficit and the loss of manufacturing jobs. While many of these programs are quite effective, most are not. Many programs encourage companies to travel overseas and attend trade shows and provide assistance with industry networking, but they stop short of seeing that business is generated as a result of their efforts. Potential leads on overseas clients are often not properly handled, and the efforts are wasted. The XPORT program, on the other hand, offers businesses direct assistance in *all* phases of exporting, from making the initial contacts to shipping the products.

In most cases, government plays a limited role in developing exports. Instead, small and medium-sized businesses rely on well-paid private export trading companies. These trading companies are unwilling to incur the initial developmental costs required to manage smaller company exports. They are also concerned about exclusion from subsequent transaction once a relationship has been developed with overseas buyers. In contrast, XPORT provides tailored market research (including foreign government testing and certification information), assists in acquiring export licensing, and provides export financing and insurance. In many cases, XPORT advises companies on payment terms and is able to manage the shipping of products overseas once the terms are settled. Companies that use XPORT services are not required to pay for services rendered up-front. Instead, they pay a predetermined commission after the client has been paid. The provision of all of these services has given the small business community reason to reconsider the role of government in stimulating exports.

An "Export Marketing Agreement" solidifies XPORT's client relationship by committing the two parties to promote export sales for a period of three years. The company is graduated from the program at the end of that period. It is assumed that the company will have become proficient in managing its own export operations by the end of the contract period.

Goals of the XPORT Port Authority Trading Company

The primary goal of the XPORT program is to create new jobs for the region's skilled and unskilled workers by introducing small businesses to new, previously untapped markets. As domestic consumer spending has slowed during the last year, it has become even more important for companies to find new customers for their products in order to prevent employee layoffs.

The second goal of the XPORT program is to increase ship and airplane traffic through the New York and New Jersey port region. This goal stems from the fact that the XPORT program is administered by the New York and New Jersey Port Authority. The Port Authority wishes to increase traffic in exports in particular because exports represent a disproportionately low percentage of all port and airport traffic in terms of value and tonnage.

The third goal of the program is to provide export services to companies that the private sector has neglected because of the developmental costs involved. Many of the services provided to XPORT clients consist of planning, negotiating, and assisting with licenses well in advance of any payment from overseas customers. As mentioned previously, the private sector has so far been unwilling to assume the relatively high degree of risk associated with small-business exports.

The final goal of XPORT is to serve as a laboratory of ideas. The aim is to serve as a prototype for future federal, state, and local government efforts aimed at providing export assistance to small and medium-sized companies.

Who Uses XPORT Services?

The many services of XPORT are available to any manufacturer in New York or New Jersey that needs help exporting products to any market overseas. Most of its clients have sales of less than $5 million. Of the 70 XPORT clients in 1991, only about 10 percent have sales in excess of this amount.

Unfortunately, increased interest among companies to find markets overseas has caused a surge in demand for export services like XPORT. The program has been able to serve only about one-third of the 900 firms that have applied for enrollment. Although XPORT is constantly trying to increase its scale, it is only able to represent 70 clients at any given time. Staff constraints and the wide range of services provided to each client make this restriction necessary. Thus, XPORT has to select a limited number of clients from the pool of applicants.

The program selects its clients based on several criteria. The most important of these is the export potential of the client's product. Export potential is assessed by judging the quality of the product, accounting for foreign market restrictions and regulations, and evaluating the price competitiveness of the product, including shipping costs. Another important factor is the client's commitment to exporting their product. This is exhibited by the company's willingness to modify the product to meet the requirements of particular foreign markets. Other indicators of commitment include travel to the market, the production of quality foreign promotions and export literature, and a positive attitude about the importance of an export market.

Once firms are enlisted in the program, they are assigned to one of six product groups: biomedical products; communications and process control equipment; consumer products (including food, cosmetics and apparel); industrial and laboratory instrumentation; specialty chemicals; and forestry products. Categorizing firms by product group enables XPORT officials to provide focused attention tailored to the needs of each client.

Oversight of the XPORT Port Authority Trading Company

Although XPORT is administered by the colossal New York and New Jersey Port Authority, it operates with a great deal of autonomy, giving the program a single-minded focus and an entrepreneurial atmosphere. Of course, it relies on its affiliation with its parent agency to give clients access to other agencies including banks and insurance institutions.

The XPORT program is directly managed by a general manager who reports to the director of the Port Authority's Department of World Trade and Economic Development. The director, in turn, reports to the executive director of the Port Authority. It is further divided into operating units according to product categories.

The program's operating budget of about $1.8 million comes from the Port Authority's budget. The Port Authority is a self-supporting governmental agency which receives no tax revenues. About one-third of XPORT's total budget comes from the commissions it charges to client companies. It is believed that XPORT is cost-effective in that it creates jobs, increases the tax base, and increases the flow of traffic through Port Authority facilities.

The XPORT program was recently selected to be a designated branch office of the Eximbank, operating under a cooperative agreement whereby XPORT screens applicants for bank loans and guarantees, and it then assists companies in assembling the application. In addition, under contract to Eximbank, the Foreign Credit Insurance Association offers foreign political and commercial risk protection insurance through XPORT to regional companies. Program officials are also directly responsible for administering a $1.75 million fund provided by the New York Job Development Authority which makes low interest export financing available to small companies.

Roots of XPORT: The Export Trading Company Act

Congress passed the Export Trading Company (ETC) Act of 1982 in response to a rapidly growing trade deficit, a rising dollar, and heightened public pressure to increase the amount of federal resources dedicated to international trade development. The act encourages more effective utilization of export trade services by giving firms incentive to band together to make exporting easier and more profitable without violating U.S. antitrust laws. The ETC Act enables banks, associations, individuals, and others to create and invest in export trading companies. In this manner, the ETC Act bridges the gap between banking and trade which is often cited as one barrier to the ability of U.S. companies to compete with manufacturers overseas. The act also encourages state and local governments to form trading companies and allows them to gain access to the resources of Eximbank.

The executive director of the Port Authority recognized that the act offered government an enormous opportunity to help small businesses become more competitive. These businesses needed more than just the information that was being offered by the Port Authority. They also needed a full-service program that would provide a total range of export services. As such, XPORT was not intended to duplicate services already in existence. Instead, it was designed to put them all together in a comprehensive manner that would be easier for small companies to take advantage of.

The mere establishment of the XPORT program was nowhere near sufficient to guarantee its success. Indeed, many small companies were initially reluctant to take advantage of XPORT's services. They were, for the most part, satisfied with the potential of the large domestic market and were not willing to make the long-term investments necessary to develop an overseas market. Officials believed that in large measure, this reluctance to invest in overseas expansion was due to the American educational system which does not sufficiently emphasize the importance of the global market. Moreover, many small businesses tend to be oriented toward the short-term. This reluctance to participate in the XPORT program required administrators to serve in an educational role, as well as in an administrative role, in an effort to increase the perception among small businesses that XPORT's offers of assistance were sincere and potentially effective.

Another major obstacle faced by XPORT officials is the persistent shortage of federal assistance to domestic manufacturers compared with foreign manufacturers. For example, the Japanese government spent over $14 million on export promotion in 1988. During the same period, the U.S. government spent only $4 million.

XPORT: A Local Innovation with National Potential

Although XPORT was developed specifically with the needs New York and New Jersey in mind, the concept could be of great value nationwide. In broad terms, the XPORT concept addresses two national problems: the trade deficit with all of its implications for the U.S. economy and the shrinking participation of small businesses in the domestic and global economy.

The XPORT program plans to continue to address the trade deficit and the problems of small businesses by redefining an export transaction to include all forms of participation in international business by small- and medium-sized firms. The federal government must recognize the changing face of the U.S. economy and must train its work force to capitalize on its strengths in order to keep pace with the changing global economy and to maintain its competitiveness.

The program has strongly advocated the use of government-sponsored trading companies in other jurisdictions. Officials have worked with economic development officials in Florida, Michigan, Alaska, and other locations to assist them in the development of similar export programs. The XPORT approach to export development is easily transferable to other areas because the essential model of the trading company is relatively simple. At present, the U.S. Department of Commerce and most state governments are collectively spending millions of dollars each year taking representatives of small companies overseas to attend trade shows and to introduce them to foreign buyers. These organizations could spend the same amount of money and become full-service export companies. In fact, they could probably use the same employees if they provided training in sales and export management.

Key Lessons from the XPORT Port Authority Trading Company

Like the Garment Industry Development Corporation, the XPORT Port Authority Trading Company provides clients with a wide range of services. These services include virtually every phase of exporting, making the program more accessible and more useful for clients. Moreover, the program also enjoys a degree of autonomy from its parent agency. Finally, the XPORT Port Authority Trading Company is partially supported by fees collected from those who benefit from the service, thus defraying some of the costs.

BUNDLING EXISTING SERVICES. Although many of the services offered by XPORT were created from scratch, several services were previously offered in the area. A unique aspect of XPORT is that it was designed to enhance those services already in place, rather than duplicating them, by putting them together in a comprehensive manner. As such, small businesses find it easier to take advantage of the wide variety of programs encompassed within the XPORT framework.

A Focused Approach to Export Development: The Export Service Center

While innovative economic development programs can effectively serve the export needs of many communities, other jurisdictions may prefer a less expensive, more focused export development program. It is appropriate to outline a simple, yet highly successful, alternative. The Export Service Center of the Oregon Department of Agriculture offers one such alternative.

The Export Service Center initiative differs from XPORT in four major ways. First, the Export Service Center narrowly focuses on food products, specifically processed foods such as wine, meat, juice, and gourmet products. A second difference is that the Export Service Center serves client companies that are specifically interested in exporting to the Japanese market. Thus, the Export Service Center takes advantage of Oregon's geographic advantage in Pacific Rim trade. The third characteristic that differentiates the Export Service Center from the XPORT program is that it considers the Japanese market to be a client of the program. In fact, program officials regard the program as a customs lab for the Japanese market. The fourth and final difference is that the Export Service Center solicits client businesses from around the U.S., rather than just focusing on the needs of locally-based food processors. (However, a majority of clients are located in Oregon.) Increasing the scope of the client base increases the revenue opportunities for this self-supporting program.

Understanding the Export Service Center

The purpose of the Export Service Center is to make it easier for U.S. firms to export processed food to Japan. In the past, domestic firms have been reluctant to invest the required up-front funds to export food products to Japan because of the risk that products might be refused by customs officials *after* the products had already been shipped to Japan. The Japanese have particularly strenuous quality standards for foreign food imports, making long-term relationships with Japanese importers a virtual necessity. The Export Service Center offers its clients a well-established (and well-connected) entrée into the Japanese market, while offering the Japanese government a trusted, American-based affiliate. A major advantage of using the Export Service Center is that it is the only program in the nation that has the approval of the Japanese Ministry of Health and Welfare to precertify processed food products going to Japan. Since products are already assured of meeting the stiff Japanese import standards, the risk that goods might be refused at the point of entry into Japan is eliminated. Consequently, a major barrier to trade is overcome by using the Export Service Center.

Although the efforts of this initiative are narrowly focused on processed foods manufacturers, the services available to clients are reasonably comprehensive. The Export Service Center is unique in that it provides all of the information needed by a manufacturer or processor to evaluate and precertify a high value processed food product for export to Japan. The program uses a hands-on, technical approach to meeting the needs of customers.

Clients of the Export Service Center are offered consultation on import procedures, product evaluation, and label review to ensure that products comply with Japanese import specifications. The Export Service Center also offers clients assistance with quality assurance testing, along with quota and tariff information. The center often undertakes special projects that make it easier to export specific products, depending on the particular needs of clients. Staff in the center also evaluate food ingredients and conduct relevant analytical tests to identify any restricted food additives, preservatives, or pesticide residue that are in violation of Japanese import restrictions.

In a sense, the center duplicates many of the same tests that would ordinarily be conducted on the dock in Japan. The center effectively serves as a customs lab for the Japanese government. Yet, conducting these tests on this side of the Pacific eliminates the need for time consuming dockside testing in Japan, minimizes the chances that the product will be rejected in Japan, and thus reduces the overall risk to American exporters.

Although the services provided to food processors are comprehensive, the program is surprisingly inexpensive to operate. The budget for the current fiscal year is only $160,000 most of which goes toward salaries for analytical and support personnel. The program is entirely supported by charges made for analytical and consultation services. No tax dollars are used in the administration of this self-supporting program.

Program officials say that the single most important achievement of the Export Service Center has been its positive impact on Oregon's economy. Many current clients of the program have experienced increased sales as a result of their exports to Japan. This has created jobs, strengthened the tax base, and has improved the competitive position of these companies. As the program grows and more clients are retained from out of state, benefits will accrue to areas around the nation.

Current Business Clients of the Export Service Center

The clients targeted by the Export Service Center are domestic food manufacturers and trading companies that export food products to Asia. The program currently serves more than 200 food processors, many of which were referred to the program by the Foreign Agricultural Services, an export-oriented branch of the U.S. Department of Agriculture. Other clients are referred by companies who have used the center's services in the past. In total, the Export Service Center has assisted over 400 clients.

To reach more of the potential client base, the center is developing a public relations program to advertise its services. Most of this advertising will be aimed at trade and government publications. A presentation folder has already been created that includes a brochure and a fact sheet.

Organization of the Export Service Center

Consistent with its overall simplicity, the Export Service Center enjoys a relative degree of autonomy from its parent agency. There are no government departments, boards, or committees, outside of the Oregon Department of Agriculture, involved in policy decisions or administration of the Export Service Center.

Although center officials maintain open channels of communication with other governmental agencies, especially the Foreign Agricultural Service and the agricultural trade officers in the U.S. embassy in Japan, the contacts are strictly informal. These informal contacts enable officials to keep abreast of the latest information regarding trade in Japan without bogging them down with formal reporting requirements.

This is not to suggest that the Export Services Center is a free-wheeling, laissez-faire operation. Rather, the program manages its communication channels to keep open the necessary flows of communication without taking on unnecessary burdens. All formal administration and policy setting for the center is internal, originating with the director of the Department of Agriculture and the assistant directors. The director of the Export Service Center reports only to the assistant directors.

Origination of an Innovation: A Convergence of Events

Perhaps the most interesting aspect of the Export Service Center, from an historical point of view, is how the idea was generated in the first place. According to program officials, it came about in a "funny way," as the result of "serendipity, timing, opportunity, determination and patience."

The seed of the idea was formed nearly 10 years ago when three "seemingly unrelated" factors came together. A young employee of the Oregon Department of Agriculture, who just happened to be a member of the Association of Official Analytical Chemists, visited Japan to see a former exchange student he had befriended several years earlier. Coincidentally, the association was interested in getting authority from the Japanese government to "certify federal U.S. labs to perform the tests Japan requires on products exported to their country." The planned visit to Japan provided the perfect opportunity for the young chemist to meet some officials of the Japanese Ministry of Health and Welfare and check out the prospects for accreditation of U.S. labs. The trip to Japan provided him with valuable contacts in the Japanese government and gave him a cursory knowledge of Japanese culture. Unknowingly, he was laying the foundation for what would later become the Export Service Center.

Shortly thereafter, budget and antitrust considerations led the chemists' association to drop their plans for an accreditation program. The Oregon Department of Agriculture, however, remained interested. In 1982, serious negotiations began with the Japanese government to allow the Department of Agriculture to act as a precertification service. The effort proved to be monumental. For example, the ministry required the Department of Agriculture to fill out a 300 page application. Three years later, after completing the application and visiting Japan several times, the department received the accreditation it sought.

The negotiation process proved to be a major, although apparently surpassable, obstacle. The Japanese government prefers to deal with federal governments, not state or local governments. Persuading the Japanese to accept state entities or individual laboratories required great perseverance and patience. The lack of a U.S. federal program to accredit general food-testing laboratories made obtaining approval of the Oregon state laboratory a special challenge.

The approval eventually bestowed on the Export Service Center meant that the department's laboratory staff could perform analyses on processed food products that were being exported to Japan, and that these tests would be accepted by the government, eliminating the need for dockside testing in Japan.

The program got off to a relatively modest and inauspicious start in 1985. It originally provided only analytical services (testing) to its handful of clients. During its first two years, the program grew slowly. Then, in 1987, the value of the yen skyrocketed compared with the U.S. dollar. This meant that Japanese consumers could buy almost twice as many American goods for the same price as one Japanese good. Interest in exporting goods to Japan surged and the Export Service Center saw its client list increase fourfold in less than three years.

Along with the increase in clients came an increase in services. Up until 1987, the center did analytical testing only. After 1987, the center offered a wide range of services, including consultation, product evaluation, and label review. Today, the center is a full service export center.

Export Service Center: Anticipating the Future

It is expected that exports to Japan will increase significantly in the future as trade talks between the United States and Japan continue. Oregon's exports to Japan are on the rise, in part because of the Export Service Center. Exports of meat products from Oregon to Japan have quadrupled, exports of processed fruit and berries rose nearly 60 percent, and grass seed exports jumped 50 percent. Similar figures hold for the United States as a whole.

Although the Export Service Center is specifically aimed at the Japanese market, Oregon Department of Agriculture officials are working with the Korean, Mexican, and Taiwanese governments to develop similar programs for firms that export to those countries. A long-term goal for the Export Service Center is to expand to the point where it can serve as a source of technical information and analytical testing for U.S. firms that export food to countries outside of the Pacific Rim countries, including the European Community.

Export Service Center officials are confident that their export model is replicable in other jurisdictions and have fielded numerous requests for information. Implementing such a program, however, should not be taken lightly. It requires an enormous investment in time and resources to gain the approval of the Japanese government. Officials stress that anything less than a first class effort would lead to errors and irrevocably damage the program. It could even harm trade relations with Japan if the Japanese government felt for any reason that it could not rely on overseas preapproval testing centers.

Key Lessons from the Export Service Center

The Export Service Center provides a workable alternative to the XPORT Port Authority Trading Company. Although its services are comprehensive, they are more narrowly targeted toward processed food exports to Japan. The program is, therefore, slightly less complicated to manage and considerably less expensive. Indeed, the Export Service Center costs taxpayers nothing – all expenses are paid by clients using the service.

Like the XPORT Port Authority Trading Company, the Export Service Center operates with a degree of autonomy from its parent agency (the Oregon Department of Agriculture). This autonomy gives the center a little more elbow room to chart its own course and allows officials to focus on increasing exports.

In addition, the Export Service Center relies on a public relations program to publicize its services. In order to reach the most appropriate audience for its services (at the lowest possible cost), the center limits its advertising efforts to trade and government publications. In addition, the center has developed a brochure and fact sheet which can be sent to prospective clients.

Integrating Human Development and Economic Development: The Attleboro Area Center for Training

Although urban decay is primarily a problem associated with large metropolitan areas, smaller cities and towns are increasingly finding it necessary to undertake urban development programs. These relatively small jurisdictions are facing many of the same problems as their larger counterparts, including infrastructure decay, corporate flight, decreased tax revenues, and increased levels of unemployment and poverty.

Solutions to the problem of urban blight frequently come in the form of increased expenditures on infrastructure maintenance (roadways, malls, waterfront parks, etc.). While such tangible improvements are important to the rebirth of any community, cities cannot neglect the importance of maintaining human services which make residents more employable and less susceptible to poverty.

Attleboro, Massachusetts (population 34,196), has begun to reverse urban decay and promote economic development by focusing its efforts on providing job training and related services to local residents. The philosophy behind this unique approach is that maintaining human services will allow the residents themselves to serve as the catalyst for urban development. Providing residents with job skills will help them achieve vocational success, reduce welfare rolls, and possibly attract new businesses to the area.

The Center for Training

Although the Attleboro vicinity has long prided itself on its ability to support human services, federal and state funding cutbacks in the early 1980s, combined with a local cap on property taxes, provided a serious challenge to this tradition. Without funding, the city found it difficult to combat the interrelated problems of providing support to those in need, promoting economic development, and reversing urban decay. City officials spent long hours considering innovative ways to provide a sufficient level of human services, even in the wake of severe financial restrictions. In 1982, a group of business leaders, concerned citizens, and public officials created the Attleboro Area Center for Training (ACT).

One of the most unique aspects of the ACT program is its effective use of municipal facilities. Program officials identify and then lease surplus municipal buildings on a long-term basis for only one dollar per year. The buildings are then renovated by using funds solicited from local businesses, foundations, private citizens, and federal and state agencies. In this manner, the ACT is able to provide affordable and stable office space to human service agencies displaced by rising real estate prices. At the same time, the program improves and preserves capital assets for the city. The center collects a reasonable rent from its tenant agencies (60 to 70 percent of current market rates) which is used to develop and implement vocational training and educational programs that complement the economic development activities of local agencies and business groups.

The ACT determines which service programs to implement by identifying training and educational needs that are not being met by any existing program. After the need is identified, center officials go about the task of soliciting funds from local sources to support the program. The ACT often finds qualified local human service agencies that are able or willing to run the new program. If such an agency is located, its help is often enlisted in the search for funds. If no qualified local agency is able to operate the new program, then a search is conducted outside of the immediate area for any agency that is able to successfully run it.

The ACT develops its training and vocational programs to meet the needs of local businesses and the most economically disadvantaged residents of the Attleboro community. The program has helped find employment for disadvantaged residents, including the disabled, welfare recipients, illiterates, minorities, ex-offenders, and the unemployed. During the past five years, the programs initiated by the ACT have assisted a majority of the people served by publicly funded training programs in the Attleboro vicinity.

The ACT leases space to a wide variety of local human service agencies, among them Head Start, St. Vincent dePaul Society, Young Children's Community Center, Comprehensive Social Services of Attleboro, Worldwide Educational Services, Displaced Homemaker Program, and others. These organizations collectively serve over 5,500 individuals each year. Most of these agencies requested assistance from the ACT because they were unable to secure affordable, long-term leases in other privately-owned facilities.

How the ACT Differs from Other Economic Development Programs

Officials who are responsible for administering the ACT program cite four ways in which the Attleboro Area Center for Training program differs from other urban renewal programs. First, the program operates as a nonprofit organization that will eventually become entirely self-supporting through the development of income producing ventures. A majority of the program's $95,000 budget is derived from earned income. This is in marked contrast with most non-profit organizations which typically rely exclusively on public funds and charitable contributions for financial support.

The program has raised funds to convert part of a vacant school building into a day care center for local families. It is hoped that the center will generate revenues by serving a mixed-income population. The center is consistent with the ACT's desire to diversify its source of funds by developing revenue producing programs. Other revenue programs being implemented by the ACT include a career resource center which offers high quality career counseling and vocational testing services.

Second, Attleboro is the only municipality in the region that leases surplus property to a non-profit corporation which then renovates the property, pays the operating expenses (including maintenance and repair), and uses it to serve the needs of the community. Thus, the city retains ownership of the premises without having to pay operating expenses. Other communities mothball unused facilities or sell them to private developers, often incurring additional expenses and losing access to affordable facilities. Renovation of municipal facilities is made possible by funds raised by a major capital campaign designed for that purpose. The campaign raised over $200,000 which was used to renovate the vacant school building. A new heating system was installed, windows were replaced, corridors were repainted, and other renovations were completed, as well. The ACT plans to renovate additional surplus property in the future and offer broader training and educational programs.

Third, the center develops training and educational programs and then turns them over to qualified agencies which actually run them. As such, the city does not compete directly with existing local agencies, but instead assists them in bringing much needed services to the community. Turning over the programs to other organizations allows the city to avoid the overhead costs associated with administering the programs. The organizations, in turn, benefit from the ACT's expertise in planning and funding programs.

Finally, program administrators believe that its approach to human services benefits the entire community, not just the economically disadvantaged. Since it serves as a catalyst for urban and economic development, the entire community stands to gain from the program. Indeed, a major element of the program is the integration of human capital development with the economic development activities of local service agencies and business groups.

The ACT: A Simple, Autonomous Organization

An important goal of the ACT founders was to keep the organizational structure as simple as possible. Doing so has made channels of authority clear and internal communication easy. Formally incorporated in 1982, the ACT operates as an independent, non-profit corporation under the guidance of a board of directors. The board comprises community leaders, business executives, and elected officials, including the current mayor of Attleboro. The board does not just provide program administrators with a rubber stamp approval for ACT projects. On the contrary, the board plays an active role in keeping down operating costs and raising new funds for the program.

The day to day responsibilities of the program rest with the executive director. The executive director is the only full-time staff member of the program and is responsible for keeping the board up to date on program activities. He or she must justify the program's performance to the board on a regular basis. The ACT relies on temporary staff as needed and subcontracts for professional services such as legal, accounting, and clerical assistance.

Accomplishments of the Attleboro Area Center for Training

The ACT has placed over 950 people in jobs with over 250 nearby businesses since its inception in 1983. This has been accomplished within the constraints of a balanced operating budget. This last point is important, as the balanced budget helps the ACT avoid increasing the rent it charges tenants for the renovated ACT facility.

This record of achievement has helped the program to earn strong public support for its efforts. In 1987, the Attleboro Municipal Council and the mayor voted to renew the ACT's lease for the legal maximum of ten years and to appropriate $53,000 for the purpose of improving its main facility. Additionally, the title to another city building was transferred to a partnership, including the ACT and the local housing authority, for the purpose of developing low cost housing and a day care center.

The ACT as a Role Model

Without question, the ACT's approach to urban economic development could be duplicated in other jurisdictions. As mentioned previously, urban decay is common to communities large and small, and both could benefit from increased human services. In particular, municipalities that suffer from limited human services budgets but have unused or underutilized facilities could easily develop programs like the ACT. As the program demonstrates, excess facilities can be leased out to provide non-profit agencies with affordable space. In addition to providing space for worthwhile organizations, this unique initiative provides city governments with an alternative to boarding up or selling unused facilities.

Key Lessons from the Attleboro
Area Center for Training Program

Officials of the ACT credit the success of the program to its cost-effectiveness and its simple organizational structure. The program's unique approach to cost-effectiveness provides a major source of public support for the program since the ACT enjoys measurable results and is attempting to become self-supporting. The simple structure makes the program easier to manage.

UNIQUE APPROACH TO COST-EFFECTIVENESS. The Attleboro Area Center for Training uses a combination of approaches to ensure cost-effectiveness. First, the program is attempting to become fully self-supporting. As such, the program would not create any additional burden for taxpayers and tax resources could be used to meet other needs. Second, the program allows the city to lease unused facilities to non-profit corporations which renovate them and pay their operating expenses. The city is spared both the costs of mothballing facilities and paying operating expenses for facilities that are not being used. Furthermore, the city is able to retain the ownership of buildings which it might need in the future. Finally, the ACT program achieves cost-effectiveness by developing human service programs and turning them over to other agencies. This allows the city to create programs that will benefit the local residents but enables it to avoid overhead costs associated with operating such programs.

SIMPLE ORGANIZATIONAL STRUCTURE. Although the limited funds initially available to the ACT program left it with no alternative, the simple organizational structure used by ACT has several advantages, according to program officials. First, officials say that the simple, linear reporting relationships make lines of authority clear. Everyone knows who is supposed to report to whom. Second, the clear lines of authority make communication within the organization easy. Although such a structure benefits a small organization like the ACT, more complex organizations probably could not get by with nearly so simple a structure. The lesson of simplicity of structure, however, should be kept in mind regardless of the size of a given organization.

An Alternative to Closing the Local Factory: The Employee Ownership Program

The decade of the 1980s will be remembered by economic development experts as one of the most tumultuous in recent history. In addition to a major recession during the early part of the decade, it was during this time that a wave of corporate mergers and divestitures swept the nation. In an effort to increase profitability and to fend off unwanted hostile takeovers, many corporations focused their efforts on streamlining operations. In many cases, this led to plant closures and lost jobs for thousands of workers.

Although many believe that this surge in cost control efforts and merger mania improved the competitive position of many corporations, some of the communities in which these companies operated were arguably hurt. In particular, many small towns that relied on a limited number of companies for a majority of their employment and tax dollars found themselves in dire straits when their factories were closed in the name of corporate profitability.

Recognizing the serious economic implications of factory closures for communities, the U.S. Congress passed numerous pieces of legislation intended to remedy the problem. Most conspicuous among these pieces of legislation were bills encouraging employee ownership of businesses for the purpose of stabilizing firms, improving productivity, and increasing the distribution of capital in society.

Understanding Employee Ownership

In its most simple form, employee ownership allows the employees of a company to purchase the assets of the company from the current shareholders. In many cases, the employees retain an investment bank to raise funds sufficient to purchase the company. The employees then become the actual owners of the company. Although employees have bought entire corporations, most employee ownership deals result in the purchase of only part of a company, frequently just a single factory.

Employees, the company they work for, and the community in which the company is located may all benefit from an employee ownership arrangement. In many cases, employees have purchased local mills that have been slated for closure. In doing so, the employees keep their jobs, the company does not have to incur the costs associated with closing the plant and laying off employees, and the town maintains its corporate tax base.

Despite its apparent benefits, the employee ownership tool created by Congress was largely unused by economic development officials in many states until the late 1980s due to a general lack of education about its potential uses and benefits. Additionally, setting up employee ownership programs is technically complex, leading some officials to shy away from using them.

Economic development officials and business professionals in the state of Washington became interested in using the employee ownership technique in the aftermath of lumber mill closures in several communities. Lumber towns were especially susceptible to losing their primary source of jobs in the wake of extreme consolidation in the plywood industry during the latter part of the decade. State officials believed that employee ownership could provide an appropriate solution to this vexing problem.

In 1985, the Washington State Legislature passed a bill requesting that the Department of Community Development create a plan to "encourage and assist" the formation of Employee Stock Ownership Plans (ESOPs). This request came shortly after the state had become directly involved in the highly publicized employee buyout of Anacortes Plywood. The following year, the department proposed the establishment of an educational program that would help businesses adopt ESOPs. In 1987, legislation was adopted that encouraged employee ownership of Washington businesses. The Employee Ownership Program received funding in 1987 and commenced operations immediately.

The Washington State Employee Ownership Program

The purpose of the Washington State Employee Ownership Program is to assist in stabilizing and improving businesses within the state by educating economic development officials, business owners, and employees in the use of federal tax provisions favoring employee ownership. Founded in 1987, the program provides technical assistance to businesses considering employee ownership and offers extensive private resource referrals. Businesses are thus able to utilize the resources provided by the private sector to the fullest extent possible while at the same time gaining access to the relevant public sector economic development resources.

The staff of the Employee Ownership Program is also developing a support network of employee-owned firms. The purpose of this network is to foster communication between managers and employees of employee-owned businesses and to allow for the joint purchase of goods and services. Of course, this network also serves as an important source of information for other companies considering the implementation of employee ownership.

The program operates by helping local economic development officials recognize potential employee ownership opportunities and identify successorship options for retiring business owners. The program seeks to educate local officials about the benefits of employee ownership as well as the options available to interested companies. Most of the assistance provided by the program is hands-on, usually conducted in the form of workshops and site visits. This format effectively allows for the handling of requests for information, referrals, and technical assistance.

The Washington Employee Ownership Program is different from other economic development initiatives because the state takes direct steps to promote the use of federal tax code provisions and provides state employees to coordinate the state's response to employee ownership cases. Although other states have also encouraged the use of employee ownership programs, Washington is the only one to have done so directly. Instead, other states have approached the issue through the use of stand-alone programs (New York), funding of non-profit organizations (Oregon), or funding through a university.

Those familiar with economic development programs will recognize the use of employee ownership programs as a unique means of fostering economic growth. In the past, local governments were inclined to seek outside buyers for companies in danger of being closed or moved. Many believe that employee ownership programs are preferable in both cases because the local community maintains control of the company. The more the community relies on the successful operation of the company, the more important it is to maintain control at the local level.

Since the Washington program is relatively new and its resources are limited (its budget is $106,000 from state general funds), administrators have chosen to focus their efforts on businesses that are in danger of closing, being divested, or are owned by individuals nearing retirement. Many companies that face the difficult problem of successorship after the owner of the company retires will find the option of employee ownership comforting.

The program's enabling statute requires that transactions assisted by the state must initially result in at least 30 percent employee ownership with future plans for majority employee ownership. A final requirement is that businesses assisted by the Employee Ownership Program must be involved in manufacturing or must be substantial employers in their area.

It should be noted that there are several means by which employees can retain control of a company. Becoming employee-owners through the use of

Employee Ownership Stock Plans (ESOPs) is but one option. In addition, cooperative and profit-sharing plans can accomplish nearly the same results as outright ownership by employees.

Employee Ownership Program Administration

The Employee Ownership Program is one of five major programs overseen by the Revitalization Strategies Unit of the Community Preservation and Development Division of the Washington State Department of Community Development. The Community Preservation and Development Division manages the economic development programs initiated by the Department of Community Development. The division has 48 staff members and four units, one of which is the Revitalization Strategies Unit. In addition to managing the Employee Ownership Program, the Revitalization Strategies Unit is also responsible for managing programs focusing on downtown and community revitalization, rural revitalization, and timber community assistance.

The Employee Ownership Program has only two full-time employees. They are responsible for the management and direction of the program, the provision of technical services and information to interested businesses and employee representatives, and arranging workshops on employee ownership. In performing these many tasks, the staff members assigned to the Employee Ownership Program are assisted by support staff from the Revitalization Strategies Unit and an advisory panel.

The advisory panel is comprised of 12 private individuals who offer their perspectives, expertise, and linkage to economic development councils, legal and banking firms, universities and labor unions. The director of the Department of Community Development appoints the members of the advisory panel. The panel members actively participate in setting program direction, developing workplans and brochures, reviewing presentations, hiring and evaluating the staff, and assisting with cases when it is appropriate to do so. Given the diverse composition of the advisory panel's members, it is easy to see how the advisory panel plays a key role in providing both private and public sector referrals to Employee Ownership Program participants.

Accomplishments of the Employee Ownership Program

Program officials cite the case of the Omak Wood Products buyout as an example of one of the greatest accomplishments of the Employee Ownership Program. Omak was one of the largest employers in one of Washington's poorest and most remote counties. When county officials notified the Employee Ownership Program that the company was going to be sold or closed, program officials quickly developed a plan for employees to purchase the company. Consultants were enlisted, taxes were calculated, and industrial insurance rates charged by the state were renegotiated to make the buyout more favorable to employees. The transaction was of significant size, involving 635 employees, and required the Employee Ownership Program staff to work closely with officials from a small community, a Wall Street investment banking firm, and a multi-national corporate seller. In addition, the program provided job training opportunities for employees. The transaction spawned widespread, supportive publicity for employee ownership in Washington and nationwide.

Program officials believe that the Omak buyout provides an apt example of how a community can benefit from employee ownership. First, the lumber mill, a major and profitable community employer, was returned to the control of the local community. Second, the profits from the mill continue to circulate within the local area as a result of work force ownership.

There have also been other interesting, unanticipated benefits from the buyout. Community pride has reportedly been boosted by the return of the mill to local control, and there has been over a million dollars in productivity improvements since the plant was turned over to local control.

In 1990, the Employee Ownership Program assisted nearly 60 businesses with employee ownership issues, resulting in over 1,100 new employee business owners. Firms assisted by the program have been diverse. Clients included a truck distributorship, a blueprint company, a grocery store chain, two weekly newspapers, and three lumber mills.

Since the program is relatively new, obstacles to success remain. The major obstacle is limited funds. Although the program can continue to operate at its current level, expansion of services will be difficult until more funds are raised. Administrators are currently seeking funds from outside sources, including charitable foundations.

Another obstacle is the perception that employees are buyers of last resort for businesses. The implication is that some of the businesses referred to the program were marginal businesses that no one else could assist. This perception is gradually changing as an increasing number of companies are bought out by employees that are financially solid but need assistance in ownership transition or need to increase incentives for productivity.

The Future of the Program

The next few years will create interesting economic development problems for officials in the state of Washington. Metropolitan counties have experienced rapid growth in recent years while rural areas have languished. Differences in prosperity will require the Employee Ownership Program to deliver services through locally-based programs in order to meet the special needs of each community.

Firms will increasingly be looking for ways to increase productivity and retain employees in order to compete in a rapidly changing and increasingly global marketplace. Since the environment in which firms operate is expected to change, it makes sense for the program to be prepared to adapt to the changing needs of businesses. Administrators of the Employee Ownership Program believe that the best way to prepare for the changing environment is to train local economic development agencies to recognize and assist employee ownership cases in their communities. Enabling local agencies in this manner will help expand the scope of the program and allow for maximum flexibility in meeting local needs.

The continued development of a network of employee-owned firms in the state will also increase the scope of the program by making it easier to deliver organizational development and management services to participating firms in a cost-effective manner. In addition to developing the network, program officials plan to concentrate more resources on developing business start-ups in economically depressed parts of the state.

Key Lessons from the Employee Ownership Program

According to program officials, information is the key to the Employee Ownership Program. Consequently, they stress that getting information to the relevant players (corporations, employees, and local economic development officials) is the main thrust of the program. A number of public awareness tools are used by the program to dissseminate information about employee ownership.

PUBLIC AWARENESS TOOLS. The Employee Ownership Program uses many public awareness tools, including workshops, tours, site visits, and information sessions. Officials make every effort to include local development officials in these efforts since a major goal of the program is to empower local governments to manage their own employee ownership efforts. Program officials make themselves available to local governments to handle requests for information, referrals, and technical assistance.

Chapter 7

Lessons for Better
Program Management

This chapter summarizes the attributes that program managers identified as central to the success of their programs. For ease of presentation, these attributes have been grouped into six broad categories: prerequisites for success, program content, program management, program organization, program clients, and program funding.

1. Prerequisites for Success

A few prior conditions must exist in order for most innovative public sector programs to succeed. There must be a clearly identified need for the program and it must have community support.

Clearly Identified Need

The most basic element of success for any public program is that there is demand for the service. The demand must be clearly identifiable, measurable, and verifiable by others. In addition, the demand must be met more effectively by the new program or at a lower cost than existing programs. Often, successful innovations do both.

Identifying and measuring demand for a particular service is important because estimates of the need for a service will be required by those who might be approached to support the program. Supporters typically include local government officials, potential employees, financial supporters (especially taxpayers), and residents of the community.

Quantifying demand often requires thorough research. Not only does current *local* demand for the program need to be assessed, but future demand should be estimated in order to determine the scale of the program. Marketing surveys are often helpful in determining the scope of the program and determining what services should be provided.

183

Many of the programs detailed in this book were developed only after exhaustive surveys clearly established that there was sufficient demand for them. For example, the Massachusetts Housing Partnership was created only after the potential client base was estimated. Similarly, the Medical Care for Children Project identified a potential client base of 19,000 indigent children who were not currently receiving adequate medical care. A majority of the 26 programs profiled made use of such surveys. Such hard estimates make it easier for program sponsors to justify the program to the community.

The second prerequisite for success that is closely predicated upon establishing demand for a program is obtaining community support for the program.

Community Support

Public support is not coincidental. While demonstrating a clear need for a program helps to build public support, it is not sufficient. Many program officials indicate that a deliberate and well planned approach is often necessary to obtain the public support a program needs to succeed. There are many ways to build such support, and the means used are often determined by the needs of the local community. For example, Seattle relies on an extensive public education program to explain the benefits of its recycling program. Officials of the I.Q. Water Program obtained support for their water conservation efforts by demonstrating that it was less costly than any reasonable alternative. Finally, educators in New York City cemented public support for their alternative high school program by obtaining constant input from those who were directly affected by the program, including tenant residents, tenant managers, students, and educators.

In addition to establishing demand for a program and building community support, two other factors can contribute to success: the existence of a primary mover and the willingness to challenge the status quo.

Primary Mover

Although community support is required once a program has begun operations, many of the innovations described in this book would not have made it out of the starting gate without someone demonstrating a major commitment to the program's development. I call these people primary movers. They are individuals who spend months, often years, relentlessly building support and funding for a program. The programs profiled are full of such individuals Sarah McWhite, who tirelessly pushed for the establishment of alternative schools in public housing projects; George McLean, who set up a nonprofit organization to collect funds on behalf of schools; and Dr. John Jones, who spearheaded the drive toward extended school hours in his local school system. Although these individuals and others are uncommon in their devotion to their programs, in many respects they are not much different from you or me.

Willingness to Challenge the Status Quo

One of the most important factors for success, in many cases, is a willingness on the part of program officials to challenge the status quo. Over many years, public and private sector institutions tend to develop rigid operating procedures. These organizations are often reluctant to change such procedures, perhaps for no other reason than they are used to doing things in a particular way.

Any changes made to an institution will usually result in a reallocation of that institution's internal distribution of power. Consequently, well-entrenched players within an organization are skeptical about what change might bring. Teachers in the local schools are hesitant to accept programs that force them to cede power in their classrooms, doctors at community health centers are reluctant to give up their authority over the management of health care programs, and labor unions at local factories are hesitant to accept economic development programs that might weaken their position at collective bargaining sessions. Programs that seek to render significant changes to important local institutions must, therefore, overcome the challenges that will be posed by their internal bureaucracies.

A number of generic strategies for overcoming the status quo emerge from the programs which I evaluated. Many programs conduct replicable and verifiable studies that prove the superiority of the new program over current practices. For example, golf course managers were originally reluctant to buy treated water supplied by the I.Q. Water Program to irrigate their courses because they had become accustomed to using drinking water. Program officials eventually gained the support of golf course managers by demonstrating that the treated water was a more reliable means of irrigation in times of drought. Public health officials were also reluctant to accept treated water as an alternative because they were concerned about the possibility of contaminating ground water sources with unsatisfactorily treated water. Program officials were able to convince the local health department that the treated water was safe by enlisting the skills of a *neutral* research organization.

Similarly, county commissioners in another part of Florida were reluctant to approve recycling materials from a local landfill via the Landfill Reclamation Project because of environmental concerns. Program officials conducted an extensive, verifiable study that demonstrated that the recycling process was safe, practical, and cost-effective. This study was critical to overcoming concern among public officials.

A second strategy used to challenge the status quo is to solicit the input and participation of entrenched players in the development of new programs. Allowing those who have a direct stake in the current way of doing things to contribute to the development of the new program gives them an ownership stake in the program and a stake in its success. An added benefit is that the early participation of directly affected parties ensures that potential objections to the new program are identified and addressed sooner rather than later.

Many of the programs discussed in this book recognize the importance of obtaining input from affected parties. The Extended School Program, for example, is partially administered by a committee that has administrators, teachers, parents, school board members, and union representatives as members. The committee is responsible, in part, for addressing concerns that individual stakeholders may have about extending school hours beyond the traditional six and one-half hour school day. The Garment Industry Development Corporation is a partnership between the local government, labor, and industry organizations—groups which had been at odds in the past.

A third strategy for overcoming resistance to new programs is to publicly recognize and reward entrenched players for their participation in the new program. Rewards can come in any number of forms, ranging from enthusiastic public praise to financial support. Volunteer mentors who meet with at-risk students outside of school are given praise by program officials for their contributions to the Community Mentors Partnership Program. Many housing programs offer tax exemptions and other benefits to real estate developers that participate in the rehabilitation and construction of low-cost housing.

A fourth strategy for challenging the status quo is to seek revisions of laws and codes that prevent the establishment of new programs. Officials of the Housing Vermont Program had to change local laws which prohibited banks from investing in low-cost housing before the program could be established. Likewise, sponsors of San Diego's SRO Residential Hotel Program had to lobby for changes in local building codes in order to refurbish outdated residences. Clearly, this strategy relies on strong ties to legislators who are in a position to change laws and ordinances. It is often worthwhile for program officials to enlist the support of state legislators and local public officials who can assist their program in this manner, provided that the officials are reliable and have an understanding of the type of program being considered.

A final strategy for challenging the status quo is to develop a communications strategy. It can be either a publicity campaign that increases awareness of the program and its benefits, or it can be a public education campaign that sheds light on the problem and suggests how participation in the program will help alleviate the problem. The Parents as Teachers Program relies heavily on a publicity campaign that increases awareness of parents' role as their child's first teacher and how the program can help parents become more effective in this role. The City of Seattle Recycling Program, on the other hand, relies on more of a public education campaign. Their approach not only increases awareness of the recycling program, but more generally teaches residents about the need for recycling and increased attention to environmental issues.

Tangentially related to the issue of communications is the issue of media exposure. Favorable media exposure is also an effective means of challenging the status quo. In many cases, programs rely on free media exposure to trumpet the benefits they offer. Favorable publicity not only increases awareness of the program, but it serves to bolster public enthusiasm. The SRO Residential Hotel Program received widespread public support in the wake of numerous positive newspaper and television accounts of the program's achievements. Some organizations use media attention as a strategic management tool. The Fair Housing Testing and Enforcement Program reports that widespread publicity about the organization and fair housing laws has resulted in a decreased number of bias complaints against realtors. As such, media attention can further the goals of many programs that require the public to be well informed.

Negative media exposure can seriously harm a program's prospects for success. The Racial Integration Incentives Program was recently challenged as being racially divisive on the front page of the *Wall Street Journal*. This kind of publicity can only serve the interests of opponents to the program. Not all positive media attention, however, is necessarily desirable. Many program officials complain that positive stories in the media have created such strong demand for some services that they have been overwhelmed by clients. In many cases, clients have been turned away, leading to negative feelings toward the program. The Community Mentors Partnership Program, for example, has many more applicants than they can accommodate as a result of constant favorable media exposure.

2. Program Content

The second broad area that we have examined is the content of the program. Although the specific content of any given program will have to be tailored to the particular needs of the community, the success of the programs in the preceding chapters suggests that there are broad considerations that innovators should keep in mind with respect to program content. Specifically, programs should address the underlying causes of problems, not just the symptoms. Addressing either on its own is insufficient. Program innovators should also be oriented toward preventing problems as well as remedying those that have already occurred.

Officials of the Environmental Compliance Service found that a root cause of pollution in many communities is a lack of understanding among small businesses about how environmental codes apply to them and how they can most effectively comply with them. The program informs business owners of codes that apply to them and offers technical assistance in complying with the codes. In this manner, the program addresses the underlying causes of pollution rather than just focusing on pollution code enforcement. The program also attempts to prevent pollution from occurring rather than just cleaning it up. The program also backs up its educational and technical assistance efforts with a coordinated enforcement effort.

Similarly, the Parents as Teachers program recognizes that early childhood development is critical to later academic success. The program focuses on early childhood development rather than remedial education for older children. In this respect, the program is preventative in nature because it tries to alleviate conditions that facilitate poor academic performance rather than just remedying it after the fact.

The Massachusetts Commission Against Discrimination approaches discrimination in housing from a preventative posture by addressing the major underlying causes of discrimination. The program includes public awareness campaigns that increase the public's knowledge of discrimination and warns realtors that discrimination will not be tolerated. In many cases, realtors are not even aware that they are in violation of fair housing laws. The preventative nature of the program allows realtors to assess their sales techniques privately. Again, the program backs its preventative efforts with fines for those realtors that fail to comply with the laws.

Finally, in addition to addressing the underlying causes of problems and focusing on preventative measures, many programs benefit from taking a coordinated service approach to solving problems. That is, many of the innovators we have observed achieve success by making program content broad enough to encompass all of the major problems faced by clients. This attribute for success recognizes that many societal problems are complex and need to be addressed on a number of fronts. For example, it is widely recognized that many factors outside of the classroom contribute to poor academic performance. These other factors include poor health, family problems, and economic problems. Project Hope provides an excellent illustration of an educational program that addresses a wide variety of these problems that hinder educational performance. The program differs markedly from other educational reforms that are more narrowly focused on remedial education in the classroom.

The XPORT Port Authority Trading Company also provides its business clients with a wide range of export services. Rather than just helping clients make contact with distributors overseas, the program offers clients assistance with all phases of exporting. In this manner, the program is better able to ensure that all of the problems that prevent companies from exporting are addressed including lack of overseas contacts, lack of information about import restrictions, and lack of financing for exports.

A word of caution, however, is in order. A coordinated services approach is not always desirable and is more difficult to manage. If financial and human resources are limited, trying to tackle a problem from several fronts may dilute the overall effort. In such a case, an effective, more focused approach may be better than an ineffective, yet broad, campaign. Program managers should only fight a problem from several fronts to the extent that they are effective on each one. Furthermore, a multifaceted approach implies that managers need to spend more time coordinating various parts of the program.

3. Program Management

Even if a program meets the above prerequisites for success, addresses the root causes of a problem, and provides clients with an holistsic approach to solving their problems, the program's success is not guaranteed. The program must also be well managed. All of the programs in this book use sound management principles similar to those employed in the private sector.

In addition to conducting extensive research to identify and quantify the projected demand for a given program's service, most managers also rely on sophisticated strategic planning, forecasting, and market research techniques to guarantee the relevance of their services to their clients. These entrepreneurial public officials also sell their programs to their clients in much the same way that a manager in the private sector might sell a product to a consumer. These farsighted public officials are also making sure that sufficient resources are devoted toward program development so that their program is able to meet the needs of clients in the distant future.

What sets most of the programs apart from other public sector initiatives is that they have clearly articulated objectives and strategies for achieving those objectives. In many cases, the objectives are defined such that progress is easily measurable. In the most successful programs, it is the program managers who are responsible for identifying and articulating the objectives and strategy to those below them, who are responsible for operating the program on a daily basis. Since the community support is a critical component of any successful program, managers must also make certain that the public is aware of and supports the program's objectives.

Some ogranizations also find it useful to identify a broad mission for the program. Articulating the mission helps everyone in the organization understand, in a broad sense, what it is that the program is trying to accomplish. For example, the mission statement of the Community Mentors Partnership is "to empower at-risk students to attain success both personally and academically." This mission differs from the program's objectives, which are more specifically stated in terms of numbers, and the strategy, which is the means of achieving the objectives.

While the value of embracing these principles is obvious, the actual process of defining an organization's mission, objectives, and strategy is difficult.

Officials of many programs make clear the need to constantly evaluate program results and make changes to the program, as necessary. Constant evaluation of results and refinement of the program will help the organization remain effective in achieving its stated goals. The need to constantly evaluate the effectiveness of the program makes clear the need to select objectives that can be measured. Such measures provide a clear ruler by which managers can gauge performance.

4. Program Organization

The fourth broad area we will consider is determining how the program will be structured. Although there are any number of approaches to program structure, some means of organizing are more effective than others. A majority of the programs outlined in this book share seven broad organizational attributes: congruence between program structure, objectives, and strategy; congruence between personnel, objectives, and strategy; simplicity; strategic alliances; a degree of autonomy; reliance on volunteers; and an ability to accommodate rapid expansion. Let us look at each in turn.

Congruence Between Structure, Objectives, and Strategy

An important attribute that is shared by most innovative programs profiled is that the organizational structure of the programs is consistent with their objectives and strategies. For example, if a program wishes to improve the educational system by increasing the participation of parents and local businesses in the educational process, an organizational structure that promotes linkages between these two groups and the schools is most appropriate. The Public/Private Partnerships in Education program is one example.

The comprehensive nature of many of the programs outlined in this book makes the public/private partnership form of structure particularly appealing. In many cases, the government administers the program, and private institutions (or individuals) assist in funding or managing the program. In other cases, advisory committees composed of representatives of the various parties govern the program. Regardless of the specific form of partnership created, government officials are increasingly finding that public/private partnerships enable public sector programs to be run with tremendous efficiency. These linkages will become increasingly important in the current environment of heightened demand for government services on one hand, and increased fiscal pressures, on the other.

The choice to use a public/private partnership organization is driven by the answers to several questions. First, who needs to be part of the organization? In the case of the Alternative High Schools program, the expertise of both the housing and education authorities was needed, suggesting a close working relationship. Second, who has a stake in the implementation of the program? In the case of all of the educational programs in this book, parents, teachers, educators, and local government officials all had obvious stakes in the outcome of each program. Third, who pays for the program? The answer suggests a role for those who pay to start and maintain a program.

Although public/private partnerships clearly cede some formal power to groups and institutions other than government, they can achieve impressive results. Not only do they meet the needs of many programs that require structures that promote linkages between the public and private sector, they also improve communication between the parties involved. The school district in Tupelo, Mississippi, developed a public/private partnership which has fostered improved communication between parents, teachers, administrators, local businesses, local child development agencies, and potential financial contributors to the educational needs of the city. As such, the partnership has access to the information and financial resources it needs to realize its strategy of addressing the factors that interfere with academic performance within and outside of the classroom.

In addition to improving communication between various parties, public/private partnerships also ensure that all parties that are directly affected by a program are allowed to offer their input on a formal basis. Such formal input is important because it contributes to the feeling that interests in the community (other than government) are being represented in a consensus-oriented, decision-making process. As mentioned above, parties that are allowed to provide input are more likely to actively support it. For example, the Health Care Access Project depends on the willingness of health care providers to offer services at a discount to poor people. By making physicians a partner in the program through the use of a public/private partnership, officials have successfully addressed the concerns of physicians. Many physicians now actively support the program and contribute to its management. Similarly, San Diego's low-cost housing program works in close partnership with real estate developers to ensure that their needs are met so that they will participate in the redevelopment of affordable housing.

Congruence Between Personnel, Objectives, and Strategy

In addition to making sure that a given program's structure is consistent with its objectives and strategy, program officials typically make certain that the people employed to administer the program have workstyles, ambitions, and personalities which are compatible with the program's objectives and strategy. In many cases, personnel are carefully screened and selected to make sure that they possess the skills and disposition to be effective in carrying out the strategy and in meeting the objectives of the program. Once they are hired, appropriate training is rendered so that personnel have the skills and information they need to carry out the objectives of the organization.

An effective screening and selection process requires careful planning. Officials of many of the programs in this book indicate that they conduct some form of skills audit to determine what skills are needed for each of the positions in their programs. In the same manner, they determine what personality types are most consistent with the organization's objectives and strategy. Skilled recruiters armed with this information are better able to select individuals who are most capable of meeting the needs of the program.

In addition to developing a careful hiring process, officials should make sure that any incentives or rewards directly linked to performance foster behavior consistent with the strategy and goals of the program. Increased salary, promotions, or even public recognition can go a long way toward reinforcing desirable behavior. For example, the Community Mentors Partnership Program publicly recognizes the accomplishments of outstanding volunteer mentors. In a like manner, any incentives that work against the goals or strategy of the organization should be eliminated. For example, if a program values risk-taking, such initiatives should not be punished.

It should be noted that personnel must also be selected with the structure of the program in mind. If the program relies on contacts with other organizations through some form of partnership, only individuals who can work well in such a structure should be hired. Individualists would probably not do as well within such a structure as would team players.

Simplicity

A hallmark of many of the successful government programs we have examined is that they are surprisingly simple in terms of both design and approach. Simplicity of design means keeping the management structure as lean as possible while still achieving the goals of the organization. In the case of partnerships, it is particularly important to include only parties that have a direct stake in the outcome of the program in the inner decision-making circle. Including too many parties can make reaching a consensus difficult and diffuse the program's focus. This can cause confusion and unnecessary delays in implementing the program. Officials of the Attleboro Center for Training attribute much of its success to a simple organizational structure. Clear lines of communication and well-defined areas of responsibility for all employees makes managing the program relatively straightforward.

Simplicity has the added advantages of making programs easy to understand, manage, and explain to others. They are also easier to transfer to other locations than more complex projects.

Simplicity of approach means using the most simple method available to achieve the stated goals of the organization. A large city spends $250,000 each year testing for a variety of specific contaminants in its waterways to see if the water is too polluted for fish to survive. Meanwhile, the Environmental Compliance Service uses a much less expensive method (live fish in a container) to accomplish the same task. If the program's goal is to determine if the water is clean enough for fish to survive, the latter method can achieve the same results at a much lower cost.

Strategic Alliances

One of the most interesting attributes of these programs is that most of them rely heavily on nontraditional alliances between previously unrelated government agencies. Typically, the broad objectives of the programs impact problems that are within the jurisdiction of more than one agency. For example, the Alternative High Schools in Public Housing Program requires the input of both the New York City Board of Education, which administers the program, and the New York City Housing Authority, which provides and maintains the classrooms in the tenant buildings. This alliance is important for both agencies because the program solves a drop-out problem for the Board of Education and a vandalism problem for the Housing Authority. As such, the alliance is strategic because it furthers the objectives of both organizations.

A similar alliance has been formed between the Community Mentors Partnership Program and several local community colleges. At-risk students who participate in this educational program are invited to attend workshops and information sessions at the local community college. They are also invited to speak with professors and visit classes. This strategic alliance helps the partnership meet its objective of sending participants to college, and it helps local community colleges attract students from a select pool of highly motivated applicants.

Forming strategic alliances among agencies is not always easy. Alliances must be monitored with great vigilance to prevent them from deteriorating. This is particularly the case when two or more highly independent agencies are working together. For example, the Environmental Compliance Service in Buffalo, New York, is run by the Health Department. The program checks storm drains for pollution. The storm drains, however, are managed by the Water Department. Clearly, there is potential for conflict when one agency is in a position where it can accuse another of not doing its job. (In this case, however, the director of the Water Department has said that he appreciates the check on his agency's performance.) In addition, there has to be a legitimate basis for a partnership. Forcing two agencies to work together when there is no real value to doing so may destroy a workable program.

Degree of Autonomy

Many of the programs that successfully achieve their objectives enjoy a relative degree of autonomy. They enjoy the advantages of being associated with large, influential agencies, but thrive on being able to exercise considerable latitude in terms of daily operations. This creates a more entrepreneurial atmosphere within the ranks. Program managers are less likely to feel like their programs are lost in the bureaucracy. At the same time, programs are able to access the wide range of resources available to their parent agencies. For example the XPORT Port Authority Trading Company is operated as a semi-autonomous organization. Management decisions are made within XPORT, and customers work only with XPORT officials. The program, however, is able to link customers with other services available through the Port Authority.

A degree of autonomy may be particularly beneficial to those programs that operate at the grass roots level because people in the field usually are more familiar with the conditions and needs at the local level, and can tailor the program accordingly. The Extended School Program, for example, conducts all of its own staffing and administration at the local level and makes curriculum decisions at the individual school level. At the same time, it still maintains close ties with the school system administration. The program's authority to manage itself on a relatively autonomous basis has proven to be beneficial, since conditions vary substantially from one school to the next.

Reliance on Volunteers

Volunteers, by their very nature, tend to be highly motivated and dedicated to the program's objectives. The use of volunteers can be of strategic value to the extent that they reinforce grass roots support for a program. The City of Seattle Recycling Program, for example, uses volunteer block captains to enlist the support of their neighbors for the program. Enlisting volunteers who are already highly skilled at a given task can also help a program expand much more rapidly than if it had to hire and train its own employees. The Medical Care for Children Project, for example, enlists qualified physicians to help administer its program.

Using volunteers, however, requires more vigilance on the part of program managers. In most cases, the program staff will require a full-time volunteer coordinator who can oversee the volunteers. Volunteers must be carefully screened to guarantee that they have the skills necessary to render services on behalf of the program and to make certain that they can dedicate sufficient time to the program. They must also be properly trained to carry out their required functions in an informed and professional manner. Finally, volunteers must be well versed in the mission and objectives of the organization so that everyone is working toward the same ends.

Ability to Accommodate Rapid Expansion

Success provides serious challenges for program officials. In particular, many of the programs in this book have enjoyed such overwhelming demand for their services that they have had to cope with rapid expansion.

Since failure to expand carefully can have disastrous results, one of the key attributes for success is an ability to accommodate rapid expansion. Such an ability is not coincidental. It is built into the structure of a program. When planning for expansion, it is worthwhile to divide it into three categories: expansion of existing services, replication of services within the same jurisdiction, and expansion into new jurisdictions. The experience of the Parents as Teachers Program illustrates how all three kinds of expansion can be accommodated within the context of one program.

Shortly after it commenced operations, the Parents as Teachers Program received widespread publicity in wake of studies that suggested that the program was highly successful in providing children with a strong foundation for academic achievement. This publicity led to a surge in demand for the program. Unfortunately, the program did not have enough trained volunteers to accommodate all of those who sought to participate in the program, both in the immediate area and in surrounding jurisdictions. In order to expand the program locally, new volunteers would have to be trained. In an effort to do so on a regular basis, program officials set up training programs in conjunction with the state university system. Regional training centers and model Parents as Teachers sites were also set up to demonstrate the operation of the program to interested parties in other areas. These steps have enabled the program to adapt to rapid expansion by providing both a ready pool of available volunteers and models after which new sites can be shaped.

There are several generic strategies for dealing with rapid expansion. First, to make the program easier to replicate in other areas, officials should keep the organization as simple as possible and should standardize procedures. Of course, this means that officials will have to determine which procedures can be standardized. Administration, training programs, and appropriate modes for dealing with clients and others are easier to standardize than complex technical procedures. Nonetheless, making someone available as a consultant can help standardize even complicated procedures.

For example, the Medical Care for Children Project has not only developed a standardized curriculum, text, and video tape to help others replicate similar programs, but the program staff is also willing to provide training in the field. Since many of the procedures are written down, time can be saved compared with the amount of time it would take to rebuild a program from scratch. One caution—over-standardizing can make it difficult to adapt programs to local circumstances. This should be kept in mind when deciding which elements of a program should be standardized.

A third strategy for dealing with rapid expansion is to expand incrementally within projected budget resources. Careful expansion and allocation of resources will prevent financial and administrative resources from becoming too thinly stretched. Using resources such as facilities and labor that are already available in a given area will help conserve valuable administrative and financial resources. The Medical Care for Children Project, for example, expands into new areas where demand for child health services is greatest by enlisting the help of existing medical facilities and health care professionals rather than using their own clinics and health care providers.

5. Program Clients

Several programs are based on an almost fanatical attention to users of the programs. Most rely on some form of customer-orientation. Although they are mindful of the needs of taxpayers, legislators, and other powers, the focus of the programs centers on meeting the needs of direct service clients. The City of Seattle Recycling Program, for example, has an active customer relations function which answers questions, educates residents, and solicits suggestions about how the program can better serve its clients. The Environmental Compliance Service also goes to great lengths to be customer-oriented by holding regular workshops at convenient locations to assist local businesses in complying with environmental codes.

Most of the programs actively seek clients who would most benefit from the program rather than just waiting for clients to discover them. The Alternate High Schools In Public Housing Program counts on tenant associations, teachers, and the students themselves to identify and recruit students who could benefit from the program. The Extended Schools Program relies on referrals from teachers and principals.

In many cases, the programs go to great lengths to create public awareness of the services they provide in order to recruit clients who could benefit from the program. The Medical Care for Children Project prints public awareness brochures in several foreign languages to attract non–English speaking clients. Other programs use public service announcements on radio and television and some even recruit clients door-to-door. The Environmental Compliance Service sends out mail to likely clients. Obviously the down-side to recruiting clients and creating public awareness is that the program can be overwhelmed with demand. The astute official will have to carefully balance these competing forces by taking into account available resources.

An important part of the client philosophy of many innovative programs in state and local government is that clients choose to participate in the programs. In some cases, the client must go even further and pledge to make the most of the program. The Community Mentors Partnership requires both clients and volunteer mentors to agree to meet at least 10 times during a five month period. Those who breach this contract may be expelled from the program.

Another extremely important component of many of the successful programs is that they offer economic incentives that encourage clients to actively participate or to encourage desirable behavior. These incentives come in a variety of forms, including tax breaks, access to funds, financial rewards for appropriate behavior, and pricing structures that induce desirable behavior.

Tax exemptions are used by Vermont's housing program to encourage organizations or individuals to invest in a fund that supports the development of low-cost housing. In Massachusetts, state funds are awarded through the state's Housing Partnership Program to encourage developers and small communities to jointly develop low-cost housing. Similarly, the Racial Integration Incentives Program near Cleveland offers direct financial assistance to families who want to move into areas where their race is underrepresented. Financial rewards are used by the school system in Tupelo to encourage teachers to implement innovative classroom programs and techniques that enrich the educational system. Cash awards are also offered by the program to teachers who excel in college-level courses which directly increase their effectiveness in their own classrooms. Finally, a unique garbage collection pricing structure is used by the city of Seattle to encourage residents to recycle. In effect, residents are penalized by the pricing structure for throwing away refuse rather than having it recycled.

Important considerations when using economic incentives are to make certain that they are inducing the desired behavior, and are not creating adverse impacts in unforeseen ways. For example, housing programs that offer economic incentives to developers to concentrate on developing low income, owner-occupied housing may lead to a shortage of low income rental housing. Such potential negative repercussions should be identified before using a given incentive.

A final element that relates to the client-orientation of many programs is that they give recognition and rewards to program clients for their efforts. There are many ways in which this can be done. The Community Mentors Partnership Program offers awards, public recognition, and scholarships for outstanding participants. Outstanding program volunteers are also rewarded at a regular recognition ceremony attended by all participants.

6. Program Funding

The final area with which program managers should concern themselves is how their program will be funded. Officials will have to give this matter increased attention in the future because federal assistance may continue to decline and opposition to new taxes to pay for programs will likely continue to be strong. In many areas that are strapped for funds, new programs may have to by financed without tax dollars.

Creative financing, cost-effectiveness, and use of existing resources are three strategies that are being used by many state and local governments to fund programs and to stretch financial resources as far as possible. Each of these strategies is described in turn.

Creative Financing

In addition to depending on tax dollars and federal grants to finance innovative programs, state and local governments are increasingly relying on new sources of funding. Among the most popular means is raising funds through tax-exempt investment vehicles. These vehicles allow individuals and organizations to invest directly in programs in exchange for tax breaks. The Public/Private Partnership in Education Program has set up a subsidiary organization that collects funds on behalf of a local school district. Investors receive a tax exemption, and the school district receives $30,000 annually to support innovative educational initiatives. In a like manner, the Racial Integration Incentives Program has set up a tax exempt fund through which investors can help promote desegregation efforts. Finally, the Housing Vermont Program received much of its initial financing through the state-coordinated Vermont Housing Finance Agency.

Cost-Effectiveness

Perhaps the single most important attribute for success shared by virtually all of the programs in this book is cost-effectiveness. Cost-effectiveness can be derived from tackling problems through the most efficient use of resources possible. Other elements of cost-effectiveness include developing programs that provide only those services required to meet the needs of the community and developing programs that are self supporting.

The Extended School Program is a case in point. Extending the school day by providing educational programs before and after school adds 11,000 hours of school time each year, but the increased costs associated with providing this additional educational opportunity are minimal. The extended hours use the same teachers and facilities that are utilized during the regular school day.

The Medical Care for Children Project provides an excellent illustration of a program that saves money for the community in the long-run. Providing indigent children with access to basic medical services early in their life spares both the children and the community the increased health expenditures that might otherwise result later in life.

The Environmental Compliance Service is probably the most interesting example of a program that provides only those services necessary to meet its objectives. As mentioned earlier, the program relies on a simple test which uses live fish to determine water quality rather than much more expensive tests that provide unnecessary amounts of information.

Finally, the I.Q. Water Program provides an example of a program that pays for itself without the support of tax dollars. The program sells purified water to golf courses for a fee that covers the cost of providing the service. The XPORT Port Authority Trading Company also charges clients for its services in an effort to become self-supporting. Similarly, the Landfill Reclamation Project is able to sustain itself by selling landfill cover materials, a by-product of the mining process.

Use of Slack Resources

One way to make certain that a program is cost-effective is to use slack resources to the extent possible. Since the most significant operating costs incurred in the operation of many programs are those associated with personnel and facilities, many programs rely on existing labor resources and facilities to ensure cost-effectiveness.

The Extended School Program and the Medical Care for Children Project both make effective use of slack sources of labor to realize cost-efficiencies. The former program depends on teaching students at a local college to administer educational programs at a lower wage than tenured teachers. The latter program relies on private physicians who accept program patients in their own offices as their schedules permit rather than setting up specialized clinics.

The Alternate High Schools in Public Housing Program, the Attleboro Area Center for Training, and the SRO Residential Hotel Program all achieve cost-effectiveness by setting-up their programs in slack facilities. The Alternate High Schools operates its educational programs out of vacant New York City Housing Authority spaces. Although modifications of the facilities are required in order to meet safety codes, such alterations of existing facilities are much less expensive — and more convenient for clients — than would be new facilities. Similarly, the Attleboro Area Center for Training operates its job-training and educational programs in vacant city premises. The city of San Diego has found it cost-effective to renovate old residential hotels rather than incurring greater expenses building entirely new housing projects.

A Concluding Note

My main observation from my studies has been that despite public opinion which holds a contrary view, government *is* capable of tremendous innovation and effective management. I found it particularly interesting that the success of the programs outlined in this book is no accident. All of the programs were carefully planned. In all cases, success was achieved by addressing persistent problems with highly innovative approaches.

But there was more to the success of these programs than just planning or innovative thinking; content, design, and management structure were all central to the success of the programs. All of the programs focused on content for which there was a clearly identified need and at least some community support. The design of the programs took into account the objectives of the programs, their clients, and other factors such as cost-effectiveness and whether or not volunteers are used to administer the program. The management structure of the programs was also a determinant of success.

One of the most significant findings was that economic incentives are a powerful means of encouraging participation in a program and facilitating desired behavior. The City of Seattle Recycling Program was just one example.

Finally, many of the programs in this book offer various manifestations of cost-effectiveness and unique financing schemes as sources of financial resourcefulness in times of tight budgets.

Readers skeptical about the role of government should be heartened by the quality and success of the programs I have discussed in this book. Each offers an interesting new perspective on public sector management and suggests the possibility of significant gains in the areas of education, health care and drug abuse, environmental management, housing, and economic development. I hope that this book will serve as a vehicle for spreading the word about these innovative programs and the potentially important role that they could play in America's future.

Notes

1. Department of Education, *The Nation's Report Card* (Washington, D.C.: Education Department, 1990)

2. International Association for the Evaluation of Education Achievement, *Science Achievement in Seventeen Countries* (Oxford: Pergamon Press, 1988), 51–54.

3. National Assessment of Educational Progress, *Literacy: Profiles of America's Young Adults* (Princeton, NJ: Educational Testing Service, 1986), 15–16, 21.

4. National Assessment of Educational Progress, *The Writing Report Card* (Princeton, NJ: Educational Testing Service, 1986), 3.

5. Ibid., 46, 48–50, 78.

6. U.S. Department of Education, *Condition of Education,* 1988.

7. Harold Hodgkinson, *All One System,* Institute for Educational Leadership, Inc., 1985.

8. See Chapter 10 in James Q. Wilson, *Bureaucracy* (New York: Basic Books, 1989).

9. Estimate provided by Murfreesboro City Schools System.

10. James Q. Wilson, *Bureaucracy* (Basic Books: 1989) p. 366.

11. Edward M. Kennedy, *The Health Care Crisis: A Report to the American People* (Washington, D.C.: 1990), 1.

12. The Pepper Commission, "A Call for Action" (Washington D.C.: 1990), Executive Summary, p. 2.

13. Edward M. Kennedy, *The Health Care Crisis: A Report to the American People* (Washington, D.C.: 1990), 3.

14. The Pepper Commission, "A Call for Action" (Washington D.C.: 1990), Executive Summary, 2.

15. Ibid., 2.

16. Edward M. Kennedy *The Health Care Crisis: A Report to the American People* (Washington, D.C.: 1990), 5.

17. Ibid., 6.

18. Ibid., 10.

19. The Pepper Commission, "A Call for Action" (Washington D.C.: 1990), Executive Summary, 5.

20. Joe Davidson, "Cries for Help," *Wall Street Journal,* 4 September, 1990, 1.

21. Ibid., 1.

22. Ibid., 12.

23. Edward M. Kennedy, *The Health Care Crisis: A Report to the American People* (Washingotn, D.C.: 1990), 5.

24. Based on testimony before the Pepper Commission. The names have been changed.

25. Pepper Commission, Executive Summary, p. 5.

26. Mr. Young related this story in testimony before the Pepper Commission.

27. National Governors' Association, *Curbing Waste in a Throwaway World* (National Governors' Association, 1990), 6.

28. Ibid., 24.

29. Ibid., 6.

30. Office of Technology Assessment, *Catching Our Breath* (Office of Technology Assessment, 1988), 1.

31. National Association of Counties Achievement Award in recognition of innovative county-sponsored programs; Western District of New York Merit Award for outstanding service to the criminal justice system; New York State Department of Environmental Conservation Award for Community Hazardous Waste Reduction program.

32. Based on a 1988 study by Martha Burt of the Urban Institute.

33. William Apgar, Jr., Denise DiPasquale, Jean Cummings, Nancy McArdle, "The State of the Nation's Housing 1990," Joint Center for Housing Studies of Harvard University, 1990, p. 23.

34. See the National Housing Act of 1938.

35. Institute of Medicine, *Homelessness, Health, and Human Needs* (Washington, D.C.: National Academy Press, 1988), 25.

36. Ibid., 25.

37. Based on a 1988 study by Martha Burt of the Urban Institute.

38. Timothy Bartik, et. al. "Saturn and State Economic Development" in *Forum for Applied Research and Public Policy,* Spring 1987, p. 29.

39. Robert B. Reich, "The Real Economy," in *The Atlantic Monthly,* February 1991, p. 40.

Index